T0382873

Reform and the Structure of the Indian Economy

The Indian economy has traversed a rising growth trajectory since the turn of the 1970s, but economists have observed that growth has come mostly from the service sector. Can the service sector maintain such momentum when manufacturing fails to pick up steam in spite of all reforms aimed at this objective? *Reform and the Structure of the Indian Economy* studies pitfalls in value added accounting of sectoral growth in the context of liberalization of the Indian economy. Growth of gross value added in a sector can systematically deviate from that of final expenditure (and gross output) ascribable to the sector, while maintaining the broad national accounting identity between the respective aggregates. Uneven technical progress and the related trend in relative prices play an important trick. This book studies this point in depth, which will be of interest to students of the Indian economy. For an investigation along these lines, input–output transactions tables provide invaluable information. The book discusses at length tricky questions of handling and interpretation of data.

Madhusudan Datta, Professor of Economics at Kalyani University, India, taught macroeconomics and mathematics-for-economists at the undergraduate and postgraduate levels in several institutions across the country. His research spans the area of structural change in the economy, the tertiary sector, industrial productivity, and measurement of capital input.

Reform and the Structure of the Indian Economy

Output–Value Added Symbiosis

Madhusudan Datta

CAMBRIDGE
UNIVERSITY PRESS

University Printing House, Cambridge CB2 8BS, United Kingdom

One Liberty Plaza, 20th Floor, New York, NY 10006, USA

477 Williamstown Road, Port Melbourne, VIC 3207, Australia

314–321, 3rd Floor, Plot 3, Splendor Forum, Jasola District Centre, New Delhi – 110025, India

79 Anson Road, #06–04/06, Singapore 079906

Cambridge University Press is part of the University of Cambridge.

It furthers the University's mission by disseminating knowledge in the pursuit of education, learning and research at the highest international levels of excellence.

www.cambridge.org
Information on this title: www.cambridge.org/9781108496377

First published 2020

Printed in India by Nutech Print Services, New Delhi 110020

A catalogue record for this publication is available from the British Library

ISBN 978-1-108-49637-7 Hardback

To

Jhumur and Mumcy

Contents

Tables

Figures and Box

Figures

Box

Preface

The hallmark of a modern economy is technological change that continuously transforms the existing order. Measurement of economic variables in such a dynamic backdrop poses great challenge to the economic statistician. The nature of the product has been changing as has been the technique or the use of factors of production. That impacts prices of products, but not uniformly. The different sectors of the economy are interlaced but we have the concept of monetary value added by each sector. Value added is easy to measure, but does that quantity show the level of activity of a sector as reflected in its output? The question presumes that we know what real output is; apparently simple concepts with respect to a firm become quite tricky when applied to aggregates. Nevertheless, the question is important for understanding the changing structure of an economy, and that motivated the present study.

Economic growth is essentially a quantitative idea and growth comes hand in hand with changes in industrial structure. So, an analysis of structural change is inevitably data intensive. I have tried to be careful, taken care to go into the nature of data and its consistency with the overall national accounting framework. In a sense, the analysis in the book gives data precedence over prevailing ideas about the development of the Indian economy. Some simple frameworks have been devised to explain the observed trends; the findings, in large part, go against mainstream ideas. Further research will resolve any lingering doubts about my findings.

The basic results of the study have been published in several journals – *Applied Economics*, *Money and Finance*, *Structural Change and Economic Dynamics* (*SCED*) and *Journal of Asian Economics*. My teacher Mihir Rakshit read one of my core working papers and suggested a number of improvements that I have incorporated into the work. Improvements have also been suggested by some editors and anonymous referees of the above-mentioned journals and the Cambridge University Press. Soumyen Sikdar provided encouragement at different points in the course of my work. I am grateful to all of them.

The study started, without a conscious plan of a book, with a project and then carried forward by another project, both granted by the Indian Council of Social Science Research (ICSSR). Subsequently the ICSSR gave me a Senior Fellowship that helped to initiate writing the book. Obviously, I am in great debt to the Council. Sulagna Bhattacharya processed most of the data utilized in the book. I deeply appreciate her dedicated and efficient work. Chiranjib Neogi was my colleague in one of the projects and a coauthor of a paper in *SCED*. Also, he has always been a constant source of assistance and encouragement. Arijit Roy extended his cooperation and helped me logistically even without my asking. I am indebted to all of them.

I have incurred debts in various ways to many other persons from among whom I would like to mention specifically Debasish Mondal, Supriya Bhattacharya and Prasenjit Sarkhel for their interest in my work. That helped. And I cannot fail to mention the important support I received from the office staff of the Department of Economics of Kalyani University. I express my gratitude to all of them.

Finally, it is my pleasure to express deep appreciation of the work done by the Cambridge University Press. Anwesha Rana, Aniruddha De and others have made my publishing work a smooth, delightful and, also, learning experience. Great guys, my sincere thanks to them.

1

Introduction

The Take-off

No power on earth can stop an idea whose time has come.

—Manmohan Singh, quoting Victor Hugo, in his budget speech on 24 July 1991

The Historical Background

At Independence in 1947, India was a laggard by far, more than a hundred years, compared to the advanced countries of the time, led by the United States and the United Kingdom. The preindustrial level of per capita income of the developed countries was several times higher than that of the mid-twentieth-century underdeveloped countries, of which the classic examples were India and China.[1] These great old civilizations remained unaffected by the reverberations of economic and technological revolutions that started in the late eighteenth century in Europe – changes that define much of the content of modern economic development. Almost two centuries[2] of subjugation by an aggressive Western power distorted the country's internal organization, both economic and social. However, it did leave a heritage of having sown the seeds of a democratic political system, complete with an entrenched legal framework and a structure for modern education.[3] This brought India to the moment 'when the age ends, and when the soul of a nation, long suppressed, finds utterance'.[4] What was the state of the Indian countryside at that time? A picturesque description is given by a British civil servant E. H. H. Edye for the period between the two world wars: 'Bicycles appeared in every village, electric torches and cigarettes; it became a custom to drink tea, a thing unknown among the peasants before 1914. This was material progress' (Mason, 1985: 278). Three-fourths of the labour force was engaged in agriculture, but the country's social milieu had a fine upper crust of extremely well-educated Indians while the illiteracy level was 83 per cent.

At that time, India had a small but eminently capable and spirited group of entrepreneurs. However, central planning, in one way or the other, caught the fancy of many, including the new government of independent India, with its strong inclinations towards Fabian socialism. A few initial years post Independence were spent in bringing the house to order after the terrible events and all-round mess created by the partition of the country. The real development efforts started with the Second Five Year Plan. The spirit underlying the strategy had a link to the idea of *swadeshi*, which was the rallying cry of the Independence movement in the early decades of the twentieth century and, thus, ingrained in the national mindset. Though this dirigiste course is widely criticized these days, the direction seemed to be almost natural after the Great Depression and initial successes of Soviet industrialization based on a strategy of building heavy industries as well as machine and light industries under virtual autarky.

During the decades after India's Independence, the Soviet Union was able to achieve a high rate of growth of output and capital formation. Though there was much confusion about the precise figures, it was generally accepted even by the Western experts that actual rates of growth were much higher in the Soviet Union than in the United States. The Soviets were also spending with great enthusiasm on education and research. Some even feared that they might surpass the capitalist West in terms of productive power and scientific know-how. The power of planning under totalitarian control not only beckoned to the imagination of the newly emancipated country of India, but also rattled the Western world into thinking about the desirability of direct government investment through borrowing or taxation (Baumol, 1959) to stimulate economic growth and create employment.

The guiding principle of Western economic thought was to encourage private enterprise and in this scheme, government intervention in the economy was thought to be better when restricted to areas essential to national interest but not served, or capable of being served adequately by private enterprise. In addition, of course, the government ought to maintain regulatory alertness in areas like antitrust laws, collusion and, in general, the protection of investors and consumers to provide the right ambience for competitive free enterprise. The need to invest a higher proportion of national resources in education through government initiative has also been emphasized as complementary to the aim. But automatic functioning of a 'circular flow' economy has been undermined by business cycles, which came to be viewed as '… the inevitable by-product of growth and economic progress' (Hansen, 1941: 302). To ameliorate the stress created by business downswings and reinvigorate the role of private enterprise, intervention in the form of public expenditure came to be viewed as essential.

There developed a trust deficit for capitalism and much sympathy for the Marxian view summarized by Trotsky (1940: 11):

> After stimulating the progressive development of technique, competition gradually consumes not only the intermediary layer, but itself as well. Over the corpses and semi-corpses of small and middling capitalists emerge an ever decreasing number of ever more powerful capitalist overlords. Thus out of honest, democratic, progressive competition grows irrevocably harmful, parasitic, reactionary monopoly.

Even the Bombay Plan (1944) formulated by India's top industrialists[5] recommended wide control and direct participation by the state in industrial development, though, understandably, it wanted much greater freedom of private enterprise than was allowed by the industrial policies adopted in 1948 and thereafter. The business world sang praises for planning, with G. D. Birla, Bombay's powerful Federation of Indian Chambers of Commerce and Industry and even officials in the British administration being no exceptions (Engerman, 2017: 24). The nascent government of India was inexperienced and in considerable hurry to deliver. It inclined towards dirigisme. The Second Plan document prepared under the direct guidance of the legendary scientist turned statistician P. C. Mahalanobis became 'possibly one of the most important documents in the world at that time' (Das, 2000: 89).[6] Mahalanobis, with his penchant for securing the endorsement of leading economists, facilitated a stream of highly regarded visiting economists from all over the world to conduct a 'brain irrigation' of Indian economists. The contrarian voices[7] that seem so natural in hindsight were drowned in the flood of endorsements. The Indian capitalists, some of whom were ardent participants in the Independence movement, were allowed to work and even prosper but with restrained initiative.[8]

Facing the challenge

The Great Depression of the 1930s spurred economists to pursue the question of whether steady state growth is possible. Harrod's (1939) and Domar's (1946) answers were that it was unlikely, except sporadically in time and space. The effort to build models of growth to capture some fundamental relationships among determining factors, which may be viewed as valid for all market economies, has been enlightening in a broad way.[9] A richer model giving technology a more realistic representation than assuming constant capital–output ratio came with a more positive view of steady state growth (Solow, 1956) in the midst of the sustained growth of the capitalist world after the Second World War. Sustained investment is the mechanism through which an economy expands and employment is created; capitalists take up the task in their self interest, or out of their internal urges of animal spirit or insatiable greed, as Keynes or Marx would say. But for an underdeveloped country, where saving is low and the capitalist class is not sufficiently capable or trusted to take up the task of rapid industrial expansion, what should be the course? This is the question India faced at the turn of the 1940s with per capita availability of food declining from 18.6 ounce per day in the first quarter of the century to 14.4 ounce during 1940–44 (Ray, 2010) and net domestic saving rate well below five percent in the early 1950s (GOI, 2011: 2). The planned development of the public sector was widely viewed as the most appropriate option as there was great enthusiasm for rapid development. This stemmed from some trust in the ability of, and a high expectation from, the newly formed state to mobilize saving internally as well as to generate the goodwill of friendly countries to supply technology and saving.

The Mahalanobis (1955) strategy asserted that investment should be allocated predominantly to the capital goods sector, to make machines that make machines, and ultimately achieve faster growth in the consumer goods sector than what would otherwise be possible. The strategy could have been better tested had the private sector been given greater freedom and much needed encouragement to compete and grow in parallel, bring technology and conduct export. Further, had labour laws been less stringent to allow entrepreneurs to operate near shadow prices they could achieve some comparative advantage.[10] But, in reality, license and permit raj gradually established their stranglehold and made operations unnecessarily difficult for substantive private ventures. It was hoped that village and small industries would take care of several gaps in the consumer goods sector in the absence of serious competition. But the dirigiste policy did not take any direct initiative in the growth of the small scale sector; on the contrary, stringent labour laws actually put hindrances in its growth path. It is not exactly clear how their performance in this regard should be rated. From casual reading, unregistered manufacturing[11] accounted for 60 per cent of gross value added in the whole manufacturing sector in 1950–51, a number that came down to 50 per cent in 1979–80. The registered sector includes the public sector where capital formation went ahead at a rather fast pace while the private corporate sector lumbered along, struggling to overcome all the restrictions.[12] Later studies (for example, Sundaram, Ahsan and Mitra, 2013) have found a strong association between the growth rates of the formal and informal sectors of the Indian economy. The association supposedly comes from outsourcing by the formal sector, agglomeration and other effects.[13] Viewed from this perspective and the development experience of other countries, one might expect the growth of the small scale sector to be faster if the private medium and large sectors had grown faster (related issues have been discussed in Chapter 5).

An important aspect of the enthusiasm with heavy industry in India was the inevitable under-emphasis on agriculture. It took its toll during the second and the third plans in the form of a food crisis leading to imports and consequent pressure on external balance, further precipitating stricter import restrictions and a stress on import substitution. Over and above the problems on the agricultural front, two wars fought in 1962 and 1965 forced the abandonment of planning for three years. The subsequent green revolution brought some succour. Emphasis on the public sector continued into the next decade and early signs of change in thinking appeared only in the early 1980s. By this time the Indian basic and heavy industries made some notable progress and India started exporting some metal products, machines and tools.

Progress during 'Take-off'

India's real national income increased by more than 180 per cent between the beginning of the First Five Year Plan and the end of the Fifth. Over twenty-eight years (1951–79), the growth rates of gross domestic product (GDP) and gross value added (GVA) in registered manufacturing, the prime targets of planning, fluctuated to a large extent due to demand and supply side factors related to agriculture. These are dependence of agricultural production on the vagaries of weather where there exists a strong linkage between agriculture and industry, particularly in the early stages of development when agriculture accounts for a very large part of the GDP and agricultural raw materials constitute an important ingredient of industrial production (Rakshit, 2009: ch. 2). The compound annual growth rate of GDP over the period comes to 3.75 per cent (a little above what has been dubbed as the Hindu rate, 3.5 per cent, basically due to the good performance under the Fifth plan). This growth, even though supposed to be below the potential by far, has inevitably brought in its trail substantial change in the structure of production as well as quality of life and composition of consumption.

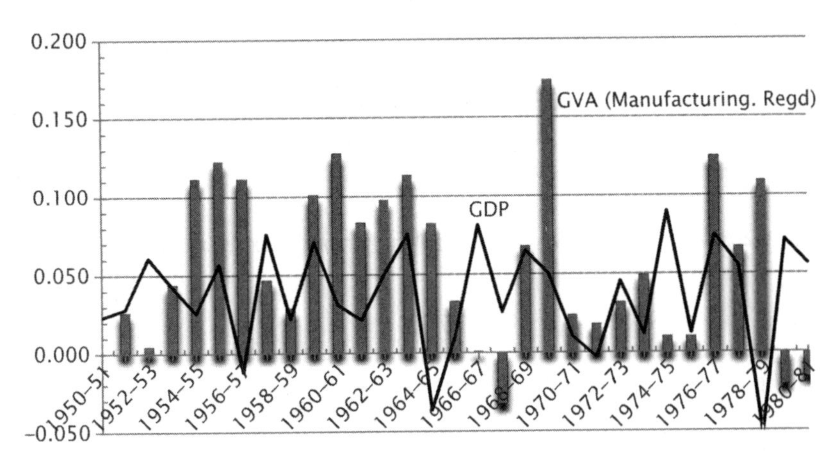

Figure 1.1 Annual Growth Rates (Constant 2004–05 Prices)

Source: Government of India (GOI) (2011).

Table 1.1 Average Annual Growth Rates (Based on Constant 2004–05 Prices)

Period	Real Gross Domestic Product	Real Gross Value Added Manufacturing (Registered)
First Plan	0.036	0.062
Second Plan	0.043	0.083
Third Plan	0.028	0.082
1966–69	0.039	0.012
Fourth Plan	0.034	0.059
Fifth Plan	0.049	0.064
1979–80	(–) 0.052	(–) 0.021

Source: GOI (2011).

Table 1.1 (and also Figure 1.1) shows that registered manufacturing grew much faster than GDP,[14] and Table 1.2 shows that the secondary (comprising of mining, manufacturing, construction and utilities) and the tertiary (or services) sectors grew faster than agriculture (and allied activities), the share of which in the GDP declined from 52 per cent in 1950–51 to 35 per cent in 1980–81. The lion's share of the GDP-share released by the agriculture sector has been taken by the secondary sector, which grew to almost one-fourth of the GDP. Aggregate net domestic savings as a proportion of GDP grew three-fold, to be close to 15 per cent. Indian exports as a proportion of the GDP were 7 per cent in 1950–51, but then fell way below 5 per cent in the 1960s. In spite of export pessimism, in the 1970s, export proportion started recovery; by the end of the decade, the export of metal products and all machinery, which was negligible in the 1950s, stood at 12 per cent of total exports, which crossed the 6 per cent mark. By the usual criteria of industry share in GDP after controlling for income, India was a super-performer among developing countries in terms of industry performance (Datta, Neogi, and Sinha, 2015).[15] But modesty of performance is shown by the fact that per capita national income increased over the last three decades by barely 40 per cent and literacy was still a meagre 44 per cent.

The economy completes the 'take-off' phase.[16]

Table 1.2 Shares of Major Sectors in GDP (at Factor Cost) at Current Prices

Sector	Agriculture and Allied Activities	Industry	Manufacturing*	Tertiary
1950–51	51.8	14.2	10.5	33.9
1960–61	42.6	19.3	13.7	38.2
1970–71	42.0	20.6	13.7	37.2
1980–81	35.5	24.5	16.2	39.8

Source: GOI (2011).

Note: *Manufacturing is a part of Industry.

Literature on the Challenge of Development

All the countries that have gotten out of poverty and the misery of underdevelopment have taken the path of industrialization that has its core in manufacturing. Manufacturing is the base that supports not only mining and construction but also major services like transport, distributive trade and finance. This is why manufacturing gets central attention in discussions on economic development. How does the transition from a traditional agricultural subsistence economy to a modern industrial economy take place? Small and cottage industries are, of course, of immense help. But modern industries must be of some scale which cannot but be large in view of generally prevailing increasing returns. The implication is that large scale investment is often a precondition for a profitable venture. But large scale investment in a poor country is constrained not only by the scarcity of capital, but also the lack of domestic demand and opportunity for export (Chenery and Syrquin, 1975). This means industries will be interconnected for survival both from the demand and the supply sides. One of the early expositions of interdependence among sectors and the consequent need for coordination came from Rosenstein-Rodan (1943). Nurkse (1952) quoted J. S. Mill to highlight the need for balanced growth, 'Every increase in production, if distributed without miscalculation among all kinds of produce in the proportion which private interest would dictate, creates, or rather constitutes, its own demand'. Structural imbalance and rigidities, with excess labour and scarce capital and foreign exchange in underdeveloped countries, pose special problems to the application of general economic principles to the field. Rao (1952) points to the ineffectiveness of the concept of the multiplier in this context. Chenery (1955) gives a very lucid exposition of interconnectedness of project prospects, or external economies, to argue for the case of joint development of projects and the inadequacy of the private sector in underdeveloped economies. Murphy, Shleifer, and Vishny (1989) provide a formalization of the insights gleaned from the literature on balanced growth and the big push. They show, when complementarities between industrializing sectors work through market size effects, a programme that promotes industrialization in a number of sectors simultaneously can boost income and welfare considerably even when any one sector taken separately may appear unprofitable. This is especially true for a country whose access to foreign markets is limited by high transportation costs or trade restrictions. The government may well play a role here.

Hirschman (1958) and others looked at the problem from a different angle. Since, by the nature of the problem balance has to be achieved, lack of balance acts as an incentive for investment, and to make investment possible, development and maintenance of social overhead capital is important. The doctrine presumes structural rigidities are not binding so that investment flows freely to restore balance. Hirschman proceeded further to discuss the interlinkages among sectors and develops the notion of the leading sector. We will discuss these ideas in the context of the Indian economy in Chapter 8. From an economy-wide perspective, a lucid and systematic discussion of the process of transition from a traditional labour-surplus agricultural economy to a modern industrial economy is given by the celebrated model of Arthur Lewis (1954). His idea has been further developed into a dual economy model with a demand driven industrial sector by Ranis and Fei (1961). These simplified expositions of the development process[17] were based on the utilization of surplus labour at subsistence wage through capital formation. Subsequent development of the literature focused on technological progress. P. M. Romer (1990) treated technological progress as endogenous, being the result of build-up of knowledge stock through investment in research. Another strain of the new growth theory focuses on productivity growth through development of human capital (D. Romer, 1996). The literature on this subject is now very large, but the common message hints at the importance of resources spent on education and research to explain cross-country differences in income.

Indian planners, however, did not depend on the path of industrialization utilizing surplus labour at subsistence wage. This option was practically scuttled as the private sector was put on leash and stringent labour laws were purposively made to protect labour's interest even though, arguably, the result was limiting the growth of employment. In this context, the Chinese experience is worthy of perusal. China also started with Soviet-style heavy industrialization but after almost three decades, started vigorously to experiment with township and village enterprises (TVEs). In two decades, employment in TVEs grew five times from 2.8 million in 1978.[18] The TVEs absorbed a significant part of surplus rural labour; Saich (2001) mentions that in Jiangshu and Shandong provinces 30 per cent of the rural workforce got employed thus. The TVEs evolved from the former commune and brigade enterprises and their ownership pattern changed to be mostly collective. Hence, wage determination was mutual, depending on the financial health of the enterprise.

Schumpeter (1947) writes that capitalism generates dynamism 'that incessantly revolutionizes the economic structure from within'. The Indian development strategy of building a protected public sector lost sight of the need for efficiency both within the enterprise and in industry as a whole through relentless improvement in productive techniques and organization of production. The phenomenal growth of the Soviet Union deflected attention from the progressive aspects of capitalism. India barred fresh private investment in 'commanding height' industries,[19] making these industries free from all possibilities of competition. The other industries were, more or less, open to the private sector subject to all regulations regarding import of machinery and raw materials and monopoly power as well as the employment of labour. As for education and research, we will argue in Chapter 5 that adequate attention was indeed paid to tertiary education though primary and secondary education remained relatively neglected, and this neglect has ultimately blunted the initial advances in tertiary education.

Liberalization and Globalization

Early signs of India waking up to the need to extricate itself from the noose of the import substitution mindset became visible as, in 1981, Indira Gandhi, in a modest but loud signal of change in ideological moorings, contracted a huge loan from the International Monetary Fund (IMF), which not only gave the government some respite from the foreign exchange crisis caused by shooting oil prices due to the Iran–Iraq War, but also allowed for some relaxation of constraints on import of more efficient machines than were hitherto available (Desai, 2009). Extremely complicated procedures and high tariff on the import of machinery weighed heavy on the head of a growing industry. Just how debilitating these restrictions were, is expressed in the following quotation from Baba Kalyani (2017: 304–05) of Bharat Forge, a firm that has grown into the largest integrated forging company of the world after liberalization took place.

> There was a growing realization that if we were to succeed in global markets, it was imperative to invest in modern equipment and technologies.... When we decided to import two forging press lines in 1990 from Germany, Bharat Forge's turnover was about Rs.100 crore, while the cost of the equipment was Rs.150 crore. There are always a few defining moments in a company's history. Today ... every second heavy truck [class 8 and above] manufactured in the US runs on a "Made by Bharat Forge, India" front axle beam; ... this would not have been possible if India had remained a closed and protected economy.

Worldwide, the technological revolution over the past decades has wreaked a disrupting impact on the economic structure. The revolution in information and communications technology, and improvements in transport have virtually shrunk the globe. As pointed out earlier, new growth economics emphasizes accumulation of knowledge and human capital along with physical capital accumulation and, moreover, knowledge is viewed to be free from the shackle of diminishing marginal productivity (P. M. Romer, 1990; Mankiw, Romer and Weil, 1992). This analysis comes handy in explaining perennial increase in productivity. Since knowledge is hard to be confined within boundaries, a backward country can expect to learn by opening up. India finally decided to jump into the fray. Success stories from China and the East Asian countries along with the domestic crisis on the external front provided the necessary motivation.

While the 1980s saw hesitant and halting steps towards market orientation, the comprehensive economic policy reform of 1991 marked the decisive divorce from the dirigiste mindset. On the industrial policy front, industrial licensing was practically abolished irrespective of the level of investment, except for a specified list reflecting special concerns. Foreign investment came to be viewed as an instrument promoting exports and technology transfer. Further, exclusivity for the public sector got substantially narrowed down, diluting the idea of 'commanding heights'. On the trade front, in the course of a decade and a half, tariff rates came down from nearly 80 per cent to close to 12 per cent. The import licensing system was dismantled within two years in respect of capital and intermediate goods. The reform also encompassed the financial sector autonomy, exchange rate convertibility as well as (slowly) small scale industries'[20] de-reservation. The most notable void remained for labour reform,[21] but the attitude of the law enforcement authorities changed, leading to drastic decline in strikes and lockouts (Maity, 2019; Bhattacharya, 2019).

China already joined the fray in her own way in 1978. The two largest less developed countries (LDCs) have caught up to some extent with developed countries and have emerged as beneficiaries. China has emerged as a manufacturing hub of the world while India has established itself as an exporter of information technology related services since the late 1990s. During the period of five years after India liberalized in 1991, the share of foreign direct investment in total investment in the Chinese economy was around 40 per cent (Yueh, 2013: 163), giving a boost to the growth of manufacturing. Contrast this mind-boggling statistic with the development in the service sector of the Indian economy: during the decade up to 2004–05, export of services as a proportion of services in the GDP increased from 5.3 to 14.1 per cent when the share of services in GDP increased from 44 to 52 per cent and GDP itself grew at an exponential rate of almost 6 per cent (Rakshit, 2007). A transformation of the above magnitude has been possible because the traditional backward economy has been able to convert a substantial part of its workforce to be capable of working as agents in a knowledge economy where the brain increasingly replaces brawn. How far is the spread of the knowledge economy directly instrumental in increasing the relative importance of the entire tertiary sector in India? It is not immediately clear as the information and communications technology-based services in India started growing almost from scratch. The major services like trade, transport and finance are intimately linked to manufacturing (discussed in detail in Chapters 5 to 7). Economic measurements are in terms of values, though we deflate them to make comparisons over time in real terms. A bug in the measurement is suggested by Baumol's analysis of the increasing cost of services (Baumol, 1967). Does the bug whittle away manufacturing's share in the Indian economy, which has not budged in spite of all efforts to boost it? It is with this question in mind that we discuss the evolution of the structure of the Indian economy in the present study.

Structural Change

Change in the productive structure at the aggregate level is generally spelt out in terms of a three-fold division of the economic activities: the primary, the secondary and the tertiary sectors, or alternatively, agriculture, industry and services. Colin Clark (1940) and Simon Kuznets (1957, 1971) are the pioneers in the study of economic structures of nations. Their observations were based on almost all the advanced countries and the major developing countries outside the socialist bloc over two centuries, starting in the mid-eighteenth century for some western European countries where data were available. The crux of their observation is that the relative share of agriculture in GDP declines almost invariably and rather steadily in the course of economic growth. The other two sectors, but more specifically industry, generally gain in relative share in the initial stages of development but the rising trend of industry's share loses momentum and ultimately stops and gets reversed at a relatively advanced stage of development; thereon, only the tertiary sector, constituting all sorts of services, moves up in terms of GDP-share at the cost of the other sectors. This is a clearly discernible and fairly general pattern that has been restated and analysed later by several scholars (Chenery and Taylor, 1968; Chenery, Robinson and Syrquin, 1987). These are stylized facts, not based on formal models; though scholars have sought to simulate the pattern using formal models (Echevarria,1997; Kongshamut, Rebelo and Xie, 2001).

Structural change in an economy is of fundamental interest to observers as it goes against the idea of a balance or symmetry in development and immediately kindles interest in the existence of a rule or order in the change. Change is inevitable as the impulse for change coming from technological progress and consumer's taste does not impact all activities the same way. Further, the structure of production interrelates with the potential rate of growth and the degree of ease with which the economy can operate under different contingent circumstances.[22] Indeed, there is no general theory of the path that the long run growth of a country would take.[23] The path depends on a lot of factors beyond the realm of conventional economic theory. These factors include resource endowment, the socio-political structure reflected in the nature of institutions, educational structure and the stock of productive knowledge, and a lot more (Hausmann et al., 2013). In the absence of a general theory, one seeks to find out the prevailing dominant pattern, or what we may call stylized facts and understand the underlying influences in the path traversed by countries that have achieved significant economic progress. So, it is only natural that we would try to evaluate the course of India's economic growth by the standard evident from the recent history of other countries. This is the subject matter of our study in Chapters 3 and 4.

As an economy grows, its different sectors do not grow at the same pace, just as, though for more complex reasons, consumption of different kinds do not grow at the same pace as income grows. In this sense, the economic growth of a nation is basically uneven (Ray, 2010) but not without a pattern even as diverse activities take place under diverse impulses and initiatives in geographically and socially diverse regions of the world. In view of this unwieldy diversity, the measurement of aggregate product is a great challenge. The challenge is both physical and, no less, conceptual (consider the concept of quantity of services or value added); because a lot of information needs to be collected and before that one must know precisely what sort of information is needed. Inevitably, the measures involve some degree of error though still useful if carefully handled. We have discussed the relevant issues in Chapters 2, 3 and 4.

Changes in relative prices is a common source of measurement blues for real economic magnitudes.[24] Sectoral GDP-shares reveal the sources of value added; but what often remains unappreciated is that value added does not truly stand for the level of activity of a sector. Modern workshops are not represented by the 'hammering man'. Clean and virtually unpeopled factory floors with machines, maybe intelligent machines, erected by some design – all being controlled from a point by some skilled operator looking at the computer screen, is fast becoming a common picture of a factory with the rapid changes in technology. This technical progress coupled with competition for market tend to take prices of products downward, and drive value added to sectors where skilled labour is needed in relatively large quantity or where labour service itself is the product, like in schools and hospitals. In such cases value added will cease to be a reliable indicator of quantity produced. Further, the product of an enterprise may not be visible to the consumer though it is crucial for her consumption. Thus the services of 'designers, IT specialists, accountants, logistics experts, marketing staff, customer-relations managers, cooks and cleaners, all of whom in various ways contribute to the factory'[25] are not aimed directly at the final users of products of factories. But, the growth of these services is directly related to the growth of factory production. Lots of products of enterprises are intermediate inputs unknown to final users. Thus, the level of activity of a sector may not be reflected in the final use (consumption or investment) ascribable to the sector. We must be careful about what we want to measure and what we actually measure. An apparently paradoxical development is that the trend of GDP-share of the manufacturing sector in India ceased to increase, more or less, as the economy's growth trajectory shifted upwards. Transition to the higher growth trajectory came along with rising exports of not only information technology related services but also of engineering goods, which require intensive use of manufactured inputs. This development inevitably brings a 'technical structure effect'. Overcoming this positive impact on manufacturing production, as we have argued in Chapters 5 and 6, there was an 'adjustment effect' causing value added to move away from manufacturing to services. This is precisely the case where measurement issues are of paramount importance; we must know where to look.

Adjustment of value added being a generic explanation, could be relevant for other LDCs too. It explains the undercutting of the growth of value added but does not explain why India should be an outlier when compared to other LDCs, as discussed in Chapter 4. What is relevant in this regard is that from the very beginning, the labour surplus and capital scarce country chose the path of skill-based planned industrialization while looking at private entrepreneurs askance. Policies towards private capital and stringent labour laws that survive have discouraged the segment of relatively low-skill large industry, unlike in the countries of East Asia or China. The failure to utilize the potential comparative advantage in low-skill manufacturing in spite of considerable success in skill-based manufacturing seems to explain why the relative share of manufacturing has apparently reached a peak early in the development process. However, as Chapter 5 shows, this does not mean that the growth of manufacturing (output) lagged behind services either quantitatively or qualitatively.

The composite service sector includes a number of services drawing their logic of existence in different degrees from the material goods sector (the primary and secondary sectors). From this point of view, trade and transport as well as finance and business services should be distinguished from other services like public administration, education, health and personal services grouped together in national accounts as 'community, social and personal services' (CSP). CSP is demanded mainly for direct gratification of personal or community needs while most of the former category of services, which we call service-I, is linked functionally to material goods production. Chapter 7 elaborates on this relationship. On the other hand, while the intermediate demand for material goods is not much dependent on service production, as services (except transport) generally use relatively little material inputs, a very large part of the production of service-I is a *sine qua non* for material production. This sort of functional relationships are sought to be captured in the concepts of forward and backward linkages and is reflected in the values of the linkage indices discussed in Chapter 8.

The structure of an economy is a multidimensional and a somewhat amorphous construct. The idea is to have a comprehensive view of all the major aspects that characterize the economy, that is, the organization of productive activities of a nation. Production inevitably refers to social production as distinguished from natural production like growth of trees in the forest and flow of water in rivers or aquifers of the earth. Social production is cooperation among individuals to realize the forces of production in order to meet individual and collective needs. Not only does this production take place in a particular social setup, it also influences the setup; thus economic structure refers to production in relation to this social setup. Thus the structure of an economy includes the sectoral structure of employment as well as its gender composition, the distribution of income and wealth, educational structure of the workforce and even broader aspects like the stock of knowledge and resource endowments etc. There are several serious studies on all these different aspects (Kuznets, 1965; Grootaert and Bastelaer, 2002; Rangarajan, Iyer Kaul and Seema, 2009; Sen, 2010; Bhagwati and Panagariya, 2013; Hausmann et al., 2013; Stiglitz, 2013; Dreze and Sen, 2014). The scope of the present study is, however, limited to the sectoral structure of production only. Chapter 9 summarizes and concludes the study.

Notes

1. Kuznets (1954) estimated that the per capita income of underdeveloped countries in the mid-twentieth century was between one-third and one-sixth of that of the mid-nineteenth-century income levels of present-day developed countries.
2. After the Battle of Plassey in 1757.
3. It is worth noting what Lord Wavell said after he left India: 'The English would be remembered … but by the ideal they left behind of what a district officer should be' (Mason, 1985: 346). In 1857, Wood's dispatch of 1854 to the then Governor-General of India led to the creation of three universities in Bombay, Calcutta and Madras modelled on the University of London. In 1876, the Indian Association for Cultivation of Science was established in Calcutta. The spread of science education resulted in C. V. Raman's Nobel Prize winning discovery and also equally significant discoveries by J. C. Bose, S. N. Bose and M. Saha, thereby establishing Calcutta as a significant centre of modern science in the colonial days between the two world wars (Bhattacharya, 2012).
4. 'Tryst with Destiny' speech in the Constituent Assembly by Jawaharlal Nehru, delivered towards the midnight of 14 August 1947.
5. The ambitious plan (Thakurdas, 1945), signed by the leading industrialists of the time as well as the economist John Mathai, had been hugely influential in shaping the ideas of politicians immediately after independence.
6. Mahalanobis, apparently independently, reinvented the strategy that Grigory Feldman framed for the Soviet Union two and a half decades ago, in 1928.
7. A simple model by Vakil and Brahmananda (1956) has drawn much attention particularly in the light of the outcomes of the prevailing strategy.
8. Das (2002) mentions that G. D. Birla was denied permission to set up a steel plant in the 1960s.

9. Research to formulate rigorous trade cycle models also yielded, at the same time, work of the likes of Samuelson (1939) and Hicks (1971), among others.
10. Indian labour regulations, viewed as pro-worker, take effect right at the firm size of 10 workers (with use of power) and gets stringent in steps as the size goes up. Admittedly, a nascent industrializing economy feels the pangs of restrictive regulations more when compared to a relatively developed one. Particularly, the insertion of Chapter V-B (relating to separation and closure) into the Industrial Disputes Act of 1976 has made India an outlier by international standards, leaving behind China's 2006 standard (OECD, 2007). For further discussion see Ramaswami (2015) and Bhattacharya (2019).
11. Unregistered sector consists of establishments employing a maximum of 20 workers without use of power, or up to 10 workers when using power. This sector is exempt from the regulations under the Factories Act 1948.
12. In 1950–51, the public sector accounted for less than a fourth of the total gross fixed capital formation in machinery and equipment, the proportion crossed two-fifths at the end of the Third Plan and was more than half at the end of the Fifth Plan.
13. There are some signs of adjustments in firm size in this context. Hasan and Jandoc (2013) find that employment in the labour-intensive apparel sector was concentrated in the unregistered sector to the extent of about 87 per cent in 2005 whereas in China the same percentage was concentrated in medium and large firms.
14. In 1950–51, GVA in registered manufacturing was less than two-thirds of that of the unregistered part, but the ratio crossed unity in the first half of the 1980s, probably showing weakness in building up the sector adequately as complementary to the registered sector at an early stage of development.
15. Chapter 4 gives a detailed discussion of the issue.
16. Rostow (1960) marks the 1950s as the time when India launched into 'take-off'.
17. The smooth generalities essayed by theoretical models are sometimes not in conformity with the peculiarities of varied reality. Several examples of deviations from what are often supposed to be the bedrock characteristics are given by Banerjee and Duflo (2019).
18. '... early successes were seen in the creation of TVEs in rural areas, a classic development challenge of a lagging agrarian sector. TVEs injected industry and market orientation into the rural economy, which was endowed by abundant and surplus labour ... Output grew rapidly in the early 1980s ... leading to the observation that Chinese growth began in the countryside' (Yueh, 2013: 23).
19. These are industries related to defence, metals and heavy machinery, air and rail transport, power, communications and most mining (Joshi and Little, 1994: 10).
20. These are defined by the size of investment in fixed capital valued at historical cost, revised periodically. In 1990, the size was $200,000.
21. A comprehensive and illuminating discussion of all aspects of reforms may be found in Mohan (2017).
22. From this point of view a balanced development is one whereby a country does not fall into crucial dependence on imports for vital necessities of life and the production system (Dertouzos, Lester and Solow, 1990).

23. Interestingly, in the midst of this widespread structural change, there appear to be some regular patterns known as Kaldor's stylized facts, highlighted by Robert Solow (2000). These so-called stylized facts state that, subject to short-run irregularities, in advanced industrial economies labour productivity goes on increasing (at a fairly constant rate) and capital intensity goes on rising correspondingly so that capital productivity shows no systematic trend over long periods. Further, the real rate of interest remains constant.
24. Economic variables are normally measured in terms of values. So, real magnitudes are estimates at constant prices; this estimation often poses a tricky problem. A brief discussion of some relevant issues is given in Chapter 2.
25. *Economist*, 21–27 April 2012.

2

Growth and Structural Change since 1978–79

Issues in Measurement

When you have mastered numbers, you will in fact no longer be reading numbers, any more than you read words when reading books. You will be reading meanings.

—W. E. B. Dubois

Introduction

Production means activity by institutional units, as distinct from natural processes, intended to obtain a result in the form of goods or services. The process adds value to intermediate inputs with the help of primary inputs like capital and labour; this addition is gross value added. There was a time when agricultural activities were supposed to be the most crucial and there was a school of thought (the Physiocrats) that considered agricultural production alone to contribute to the national product. But this idea is not held by any significant group of economists today. Adam Smith distinguished activities in the categories 'productive' and 'unproductive' (Smith, 1776: 321). Most service activities, however lofty or revered (excluding those integrated directly with material production and distribution of the products), were classified as 'unproductive'. The idea was that the level of material production determined availability of the basic necessities of life and resources needed for economic growth, while services were fleeting. The concept of net material product (Stone, 1970; UN, 1971) of the erstwhile socialist system, which counted only goods and (material) services directly associated with them, basically owed its construct to this idea.[1] The broader concept of aggregate product, which has subsequently been formalized as the GDP,[2] is now almost universally accepted as a measure of the extent of productive activity in a country (Beckerman, 1991; UN, 2009). Basically, GDP consists of gross value added (GVA) from activities of all kinds of institutional units resulting in production of goods and services using capital, labour and intermediate inputs of goods and services. This is identical to aggregate final expenditure in the absence of product taxes.

In the course of accumulation of knowledge manifested in technical progress, practically all productive activities undergo changes. Output per unit of labour increases, and over time this increment becomes phenomenal. Although production of most commodities increases in scale with growth of population, peoples' consumption or other use (investment and export) of every commodity does not grow proportionately with income. This means the commodity composition of aggregate production changes. Though there is no general theory of development path, certain tendencies are common; these are stylized facts. How far a country conforms to such common tendencies is often taken to indicate its progress along the path of modern development or else development is idiosyncratic, which would be worthy of special study.[3]

The present chapter discusses the basic facts and issues regarding changes in the sectoral product structure of the Indian economy. From here we go to a quick summary of macroeconomic performance of the economy over the period between 1978–79 and 2012–13. The next section studies sectoral GDP shares – it presents three official estimates of sectoral shares; two are at current prices and one at constant prices. The discussion also highlights the differences between the different estimates and the consequent need to choose appropriate data depending on the objective of specific research. The section is rather long, but in view of the common reservation expressed regarding the quality of data, recording the order amidst disorder ought to be interesting. Next, we take up the conceptual problems associated with the different techniques of obtaining constant price estimates and the problem of interpretation of the estimates given by the Central Statistics Office (CSO). Then we proceed to study the trends in sectoral shares for the Indian economy and point to an apparent deficiency in the behaviour of the relative GDP-share of the manufacturing sector. Finally, we place the trend of this sector in an international perspective. The last section concludes the chapter.

India's Drive to Maturity: An Overview

India's growth trend (5-year moving average, centred in the middle)[4] shows a small bump, reaching a peak at about 5 per cent level, during the Fifth Plan (1974–79) period (Figure 2.1). The last year of that decade saw India's worst drought in several decades; agricultural production nosedived by 15 per cent and GDP by 5 per cent.[5] Then came the oil price shock along with disturbance in the northeastern state of Assam, disrupting the domestic supply of oil (Rakshit, 2009: ch. 3). The associated chain of causalities led to retardation in the growth of the manufacturing sector.

The government's response to the shocks was a break from the past tendencies – 'expansionary adjustment' with encouragement to export. Also, the country drew special drawing rights (SDR) 3.9 billion out of SDR 5 billion contracted with the IMF in spite of leftist opposition (Joshi and Little, 1994: 59). Using endogenous break-point analysis, several scholars have found a structural break in trend growth towards the end of the 1970s (see Appendix 2A), which seems to be the handiwork of the severe drought, not change in economic fundamentals. The average centred on the drought affected year was above 4 per cent, and after a couple of disturbed years since then, India's 5-year moving average rate of GDP growth did not fall much below the rate of five per cent during the next decade and a half to the mid-1990s. With some fluctuations in the annual rates, the trend growth rate moved up further over the subsequent decade and a half to create a hump above the 8 per cent level over the quinquennium 2005–10.

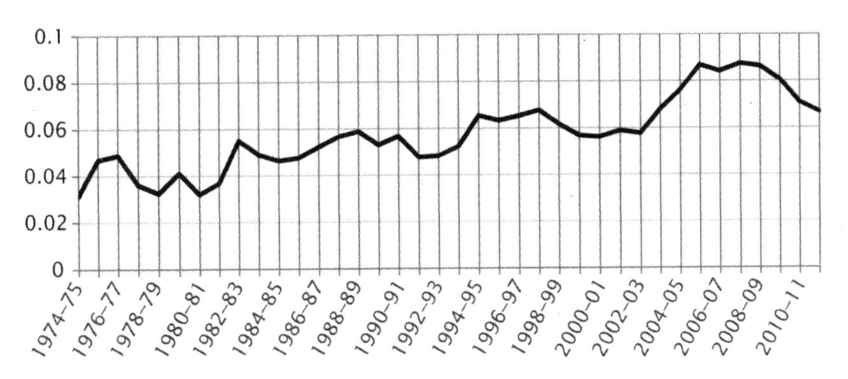

Figure 2.1 Five-Year Moving Average (Centred) Growth of GDP at Factor Cost

Source: GOI, mospi.nic.in/data, accessed in October 2018.

As one would expect, the growth of GDP is supported by increases in the rates of gross domestic saving (GDS) and gross fixed capital formation (GFCF). GDS reached 21 per cent by the end of the Fifth Plan (1978–79) when export was 6.2 per cent of GDP (Figure 2.2). Then during the aforementioned troubled years, GDS fell by as much as 4 percentage points (but GFCF overtook GDS) in the next five years. After the mid-1980s GDS moved up relentlessly reaching the 23 per cent mark in 1990–91; increase in the rate (and also that of GFCF) remained relatively subdued during the decade of the 1990s but gained vigour in the beginning of the next decade to reach almost the 37 per cent mark (somewhat lower for GFCF) in 2007–08. Export as a ratio to GDP remained stuck to a low plateau until the turn of the 1980s when it started rising moderately to reach 8.4 per cent of GDP in 1991–92, the year the comprehensive industrial policy reform was initiated with a bang. The moderate rising trend of exports was maintained until the early 2000s, but then in the next one decade the proportion doubled, and it almost touched the 25 per cent mark in 2012–13. In a nutshell, the long term GDP growth has shown an upward trend since the turn of the 1970s, though the super-performance took place in the first decade of the next century. This story is impressive, though not so much in comparison with China and some smaller East Asian countries. Real per-capita income increased more than three and a half times between 1980–81 and 2013–14, which translates to a compound annual growth rate of 4 per cent. How did this growth story reflect on the structure of production? We view that in the next section.

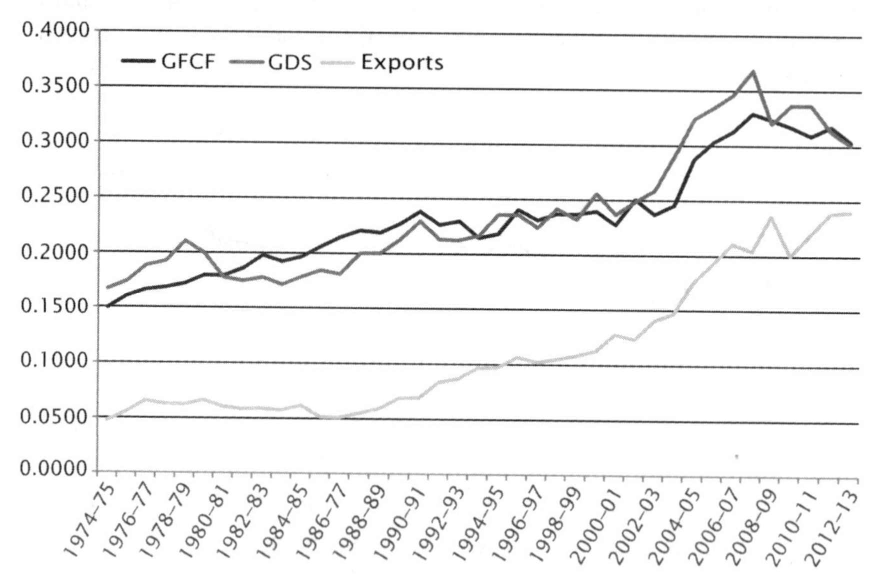

Figure 2.2 GFCF, GDS and Exports as Ratio to GDP at Market Prices

Source: GOI, mospi.nic.in/data, accessed in October 2018.

Changes in Sectoral Shares: Order amidst Disorder

In the course of the impressive growth of the GDP, the economy has grown more complex in terms of both the structure of commodities produced and the technology used in production. Naturally, the different sectors of the economy have grown at different paces. Relative growth of sectors is usually tracked by looking at their shares in GDP. The National Accounts Statistics (NAS), published by the CSO of the government of India, presents detailed data on GDP. The input–output transactions tables (IOTTs), also published by the CSO, present the inter-industry as well as final product flows of goods and services. Detailed and meticulous work to balance the flows on production and expenditure sides for each sector makes each matrix a treasure of information notwithstanding the fact that the quality of data is not always beyond question. The IOTTs for the Indian economy are available from 1968–69 (*60 sectors*), mostly at quinquennial intervals, the most recent one being that for 2007–08 (*130 sectors*). Further, the CSO has published Supply and Use tables for 2011–12 and 2012–13 so far.

Different Estimates of Sectoral Shares

Table 2.1 presents three estimates of relative sectoral shares of the Indian economy for the years consistent with availability of the IOTTs. Estimates of sectoral shares obtained from the IOTTs are at current prices. So, one might expect the IOTT-based estimates to be not very different from the current price estimates given in NAS, though common sense suggests that the third estimate, also given in NAS but at constant prices, might differ from current price estimates due to changes in relative prices over time. Apparently there is some disorder in data as shown in Table 2.1; an investigator has to take care of the suitability and relevance of data sets.

Essentially, an IOTT can be viewed as an extensive disaggregation of the production account within the system of national accounts. The commodity x commodity format is derived from the basic information contained in the (*commodity x industry*) Use or Absorption table.

The rows and columns of the Use matrix are different entities due to the lack of one-to-one correspondence between commodity and industry. Hence, adjustments are needed to transform the industry column to conform to the description of commodity by using the Supply or 'Make' matrix. This process transfers the secondary products (subsidiary products or by-products) of columns (industries) to other columns where they fit more homogeneously. The transformation needs an industry-technology assumption—the input structure of a secondary product is similar to that of the primary product of the parent industry. All this is necessitated by the theoretical requirement of showing the rows and corresponding columns as representing the same entity.

The transformation of columns from industry to commodity affects particularly the manufacturing sector where many secondary products occur.[6] But our study considers only an aggregated IOTT (*11 sectors*) with a single manufacturing sector; so, any inaccuracy arising out of the industry-technology assumption should be largely irrelevant for our results, though not fully so as adjustments often transcend major sectors (trade and transport constitute an example of services that are secondary products of many industrial sub-sectors). We will see in Chapters 5 and 6 the notable consistency of trends in inputs and GVA coefficients of the manufacturing sector obtained from the nine IOTTs. The CSO maintains that GVA and output of different sectors are largely consistent with those of NAS. But there are reasons for subsequent deviations as improvements in methodologies and data-coverage is a recurrent process and adjustments on this account are applied retrospectively in NAS estimates leaving the existing IOTTs unchanged.[7] We will check from Table 2.1 what difference all the above adjustments have made to sectoral estimates.

Table 2.1 Sectoral Shares: Three Official Estimates

Activity	1968–69	1973–74	1978–79	1983–84	1989–90	1993–94	1998–99	2003–04	2007–08	2012–13
A (Cr.P)	43.5	43.3	35.5	33.5	29.0	28.7	25.8	20.7	18.3	17.5
A (IOTT)	48.5	49.8	38.6	36.1	31.5	30.4	27.1	21.1	18.5	18.1
A (Cn.P)	40.9	39.5	36.8	35.0	29.9	28.2	24.4	20.3	16.8	13.9
M (Cr.P)	12.8	14.3	16.5	16.1	16.4	15.3	15.0	14.9	16.0	14.1
M (IOTT)	13.4	13.9	16.5	16.1	16.8	14.6	12.9	13.4	15.7	16.9
M (Cn.P)	12.6	13.6	14.6	14.7	15.2	14.6	15.4	15.2	16.1	15.8
I (Cr.P)	19.3	20.2	24.3	25.2	26.5	25.5	25.7	26.0	29.0	26.2
I (IOTT)	20.8	20.3	24.8	25.8	27.4	24.6	24.3	24.6	28.6	31.5
I (Cn.P)	24.4	24.0	25.6	25.9	27.1	26.7	27.3	27.2	28.7	27.3
S1(Cr.P)	14.0	14.7	18.3	20.2	22.5	24.4	26.8	30.1	30.6	30.6
S1(IOTT)	17.2	18.0	21.9	20.7	24.4	26.5	28.3	31.5	31.0	24.2
S1(Cn.P)	16.1	16.7	18.8	19.5	21.7	22.7	26.1	29.6	33.1	36.2
S2 (Cr.P)	23.1	21.8	22	21	22	21.5	21.7	23.2	22.1	25.7
S2 (IOTT)	13.5	11.9	14.7	17.4	16.7	18.5	20.3	22.8	22.4	26.1
S2 (Cn.P)	18.7	19.8	18.8	19.6	21.4	22.3	22.2	22.8	21.4	22.5

Source: GOI, www.mospi.nic.in/data, and different IOTTs, all published by the CSO (GOI, various years).

Note: *A (Cr. P)* = Agriculture at current price; similarly, *M* = manufacturing, *I* = industry which includes mining, construction and utilities with manufacturing, *S1* = service-I, which groups together distributive trade, transport, communication and 'banking and finance'. *S2* = service-II that includes dwellings, business services, EHPAD and other services. *Cn.P* = constant price.

Differences in observations in the panel for the manufacturing sector in the table may be disconcerting at first glance. Before 1993–94, the constant price estimates are low (we have argued in the next section why we will not use them) compared to the IOTT-based estimates; the current price NAS estimates match well with IOTTs. Afterwards, current price NAS estimates are lower than the other two (Figure 2.3).[8] All the three series show a rise in manufacturing's share over the first two quinquenniums (1968–69 to 1978–79). The two NAS series show a more or less flattening of trend after that through the end; but the IOTT-based series shows a decline and subsequent recovery. All the three series suggest that during the 1990s and thereafter the share did not reach the level attained in 1978–79.[9] The larger industry-sector, which subsumes manufacturing and includes construction and utilities, shows a rather mildly increasing trend. An important point to note here is the increased divergence between IOTT and NAS current price estimates for 2012–13 for both manufacturing and industry. It seems to be so because we got data for the year from the Use table that, apart from being at basic prices unlike the previous IOTTs that are at factor cost, shows industry rather than commodity, as discussed above, in the column showing value added. Apart from the last observation, the two current price estimates correspond reasonably well.

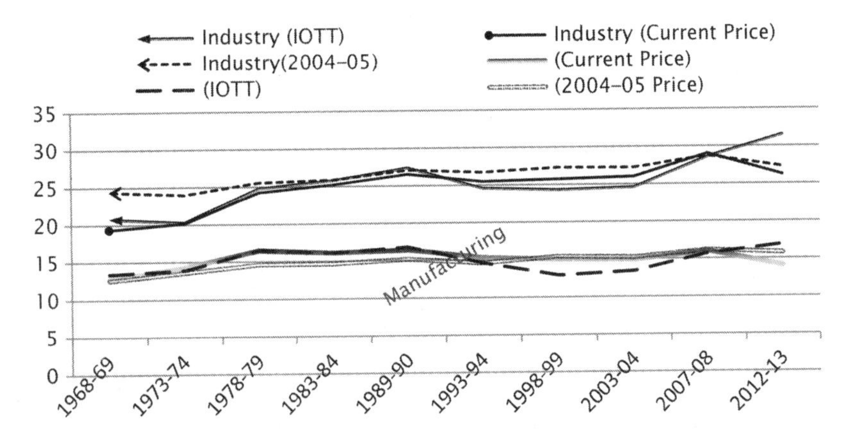

Figure 2.3 Manufacturing and Industry Shares in GDP; Different Estimates (Table 2.1)

Source: GOI, www.mospi.nic.in/data, and different IOTTs, published by the CSO (GOI, various years).

Coming to the panel for Service-I – which groups together the services distributive trade, transport, communication and 'banking and finance' – we find the divergence between the two current price estimates to be less pronounced than it is with respect to current and constant price estimates. All the three series show a rising trend up to 2007–08. The last observation (2012–13), again, is from the (commodity x industry) Use table. The columns, being industries rather than commodities, include some secondary service products, mainly trade service, in the industry sector. This causes upward bias for industry (and manufacturing) and corresponding downward bias for Service-I.[10] This is why we have not adopted the Use table for detailed inter-industry analysis in Chapter 6.

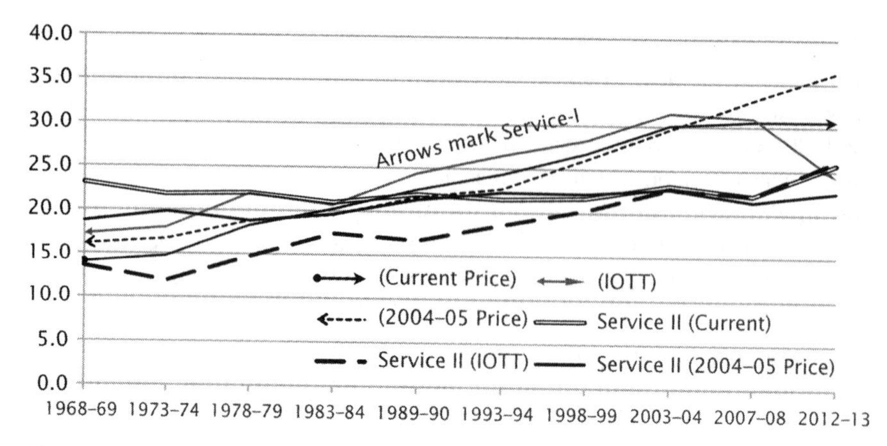

Figure 2.4 Services Shares in GDP; Different Estimates (Table 2.1)

Source: GOI, www.mospi.nic.in/data, and different IOTTs, published by the CSO (GOI, various years).

The difference between the IOTT and NAS estimates is striking for the Service-II category shown in the last panel of Table 2.1. The IOTT-based estimates were far below the other two NAS estimates in the beginning but started catching up in 1978–79. The services involved are ownership of dwelling, business services including software and legal services, 'community and social services' including education, health and 'public administration and defence' (EHPAD) and miscellaneous services. The explanation for the divergence comes from the fact that the CSO applies improvements in methodology and coverage, as they occur over time, to the past years by extrapolation. Though the revision has been applied to all the sectors it has been drastic and upward for actual and imputed income from dwellings (belonging to Service-II) in the past, resulting in the flattening of the whole NAS series. These changes were not incorporated in the IOTTs. The correction of NAS estimates has affected their comparability with the IOTTs (based on pre-correction data) mainly in the earlier part of the series. We are, however, not very concerned with the anomaly as services from dwellings remain outside the focus of the present study, though it could not be entirely avoided in Chapter 6.

Issues regarding the suitability of current or constant price estimates need to be resolved with care keeping in view the context of their use. Researchers often prefer constant price estimates – the idea is that relative price changes would lead to changes in sectoral shares even if the real economy had remained unchanged – so, to track the real economy one has to discount for price changes. But prices relate to output, not value added. In this context here we pose two points: (*a*) How should one interpret the constant price estimates of GVA as they are derived?

(*b*) To what extent is value-added related to physical production? We will take up the second point from different angles in Chapters 4 to 6. In the next section we discuss the first point.

Nature of Constant Price Estimates

The question is what does constant price (or real) value added really represent? Gross value added (GVA) is a balancing item generated out of current transactions as the difference between the value of output and that of intermediate inputs. Prices of both output and intermediate inputs are subject to vagaries of the market over time and they need not change in tandem. All sorts of forces affecting the demand and supply sides of the output of a firm, including technical change and change in market structure, come into play in determining the GVA. What is of special relevance here is that GVA includes a residual and amorphous element – profit.[11] So, *value added need not be proportional to either of the entities: output or intermediate input, or to the use of primary inputs like capital and labor; it does not have a price or volume dimension.*

GVA is conceptually bound by the national accounts identity that exists between the production, income and expenditure sides of the economy; this identity binds aggregate value added or income to aggregate final expenditure on goods and services. Specifically, the sum of value added (at basic prices) in all productive activities is equal to the sum of value of all final uses at market (purchaser's) prices[12] of goods and services produced in the economy after deduction of (net) product taxes (UN, 2009: 104–05). Assuming, for simplicity, an economy without product taxes, we can conceive in terms of an IOTT at basic prices. The IOTT necessarily maintains the identity between the (row) sum of sectoral value added and the (column) sum of final expenditure on sectoral productions[13]: the common sum is the GDP. Thus, GDP has a real representation in the sense that we can talk in terms of a basket of final (uses of) goods and services that can be indexed.[14] Since this identity is independent of prices, the notion of real aggregate GVA must also be consistent with this identity – the norm must be that real aggregate GVA equals aggregate final expenditure in real terms. Obviously, at the sectoral level such a correspondence does not exist. The sectoral production is normally only partly for final use, the other part being used as intermediate input. Since sectoral GVA is generated by the entire sectoral production, that cannot be related to sectoral final use.

When we use constant price estimates it is often erroneously supposed that an estimate of real value added from a sectoral production process should get both output and inputs evaluated at respective base year prices (double deflation). This is the procedure recommended by the CSO to be the ideal whenever achievable

(GOI, 2012: 126–27). A little reflection shows, when the whole IOTT has been thus deflated, each item by its own price, the resulting aggregate value addition from the production side (columns) is still equal to the sum total of sectoral final demands (at constant prices); this is because the identity holds independently of prices. But the problem with the double deflation procedure is that we are evaluating at base year prices the input quantities actually chosen at current year (relative) prices for current production. It does not make sense from the point of view of cost minimization that requires input substitution when relative prices change. When the current year is rather far from the base year and the relative prices change substantially leading to input substitution on a considerable scale, the method may give us fictitious results. This fear has been voiced by the CSO when it says that double deflation may even give negative value added.[15]

A hypothetical illustration may explain the point regarding negative value added rather dramatically. Suppose in some initial year gold is used as an intermediate input in the production of Y. Suppose, as price of gold rises several times over the years, technical change allows some cheaper raw material (perhaps some gold alloy) to be used in production and the product price (and quality) remains stable after the substitution. To obtain real value added by double deflation for the initial year with current year as base, we must evaluate the output at the stable price that obtains and gold input of the initial year at a much higher current year price, possibly giving the absurd result of a high negative value added for the initial year. But that is no reason to regard past production as a drag on resources at the time; production was carried out then generating enough value to pay the factors of production and possibly making a profit. Thus the double deflation procedure is fraught with conceptual problems at the sectoral levels for which it is recommended, even though it does not violate the national accounting identity at the aggregate level.

In fact, in obtaining the constant price GVA, the CSO does not follow a uniform procedure for all the sectors. It follows the double deflation procedure for agriculture and single deflation procedure for manufacturing, but for other sectors it adopts ad hoc procedures to somehow pick up some appropriate volume indicators depending on the availability of data (GOI, 2012); the focus of the estimates seems to be some sort of quantity indices. It is a different matter that such an approach inevitably makes drastic conceptual compromises, particularly in the case of services where the very concept of quantity is vague to a great extent (Hill, 1977; Kulshreshtha and Kolli, 1999), and the problem may not be much easier elsewhere because of continuous quality changes. We have to distinguish between problems associated with index numbers where one tries to achieve greater accuracy through practice and those associated with conceptual contradictions.

Blowing up the base year value added by a quantity index is the inverse process of single deflation, which deflates current price value added by the price index of output. The single deflation procedure treats value added in different sectors as different entities (like the sectoral products) to be deflated by different indices. Crucially, it fails the test of maintaining the fundamental national accounting identity between product and expenditure. When theory fails, even the best estimates are of dubious quality. Such concerns are well grounded in economic literature.[16] So, the CSO constant price estimates, obtained in different ways for different sectors, are ad hoc in nature and incapable of uniform economic interpretation.

Going back to the notion of GDP as aggregate GVA, or equivalently, aggregate final expenditure,[17] it is clear that GDP has a quantity dimension as a basket of real commodities. It is natural to view sectoral GVA as the relevant sector's command over aggregate GVA; in fact, it is commonly referred to as sectoral GDP. Now, since GDP has a real connotation in the form of a vector of goods and services (final uses), each element of which can be deflated by the relevant price index to obtain the index of real GDP, we have an implicit GDP deflator as the ratio between this real GDP and GDP at current prices. So, sectoral real GVA may be obtained by applying this GDP deflator on current price sectoral GVA[18] and this will maintain the fundamental national accounts identity between real aggregate GVA and real aggregate expenditure, both being obtained by using the same deflator. An implication of this approach is that *sectoral relative GDP shares at constant prices (using implicit GDP deflator for the numerator and the denominator) are the same as those at current prices. Sectoral real value added is a share of the real GDP-pie. From this consideration, in the present study, we work with the current price shares in aggregate GVA unless special contexts arise. Clearly, for a study of sectoral share-trends we have no need for constant price estimates.*

Trends in Sectoral GDP Shares

Figure 2.5 gives the relative GDP shares of major sectors of the Indian economy from the mid-1970s to the early 2010s. Several observers have identified the return of Indira Gandhi to power in January1980 as a watershed moment for India's political economy (Little and Joshi, 1994; Kohli, 2006; Desai, 2009) in the sense that attitude towards the private sector started changing.[19] Also, as Figures 2.1 and 2.2 show, the growth rate of the economy inched up since the mid-1980s, and the same is true of saving and investment rates (mainly due to the private sector; see Rakshit, 2007). Liberalization in 1991 came as a sharp break from the past; central planning became a subsidiary exercise with the private sector being given prominence and freedom to discover their enterprise. Early signs of change came from performance on the export front. The manufacturing sector remained apparently idiosyncratic[20] whereas Service-I, which basically serves industry, combined with IT-enabled services (World Bank, 2004) to bring a phase of unprecedented growth of GDP – not so much in the 1990s, but vigorously in the next decade.

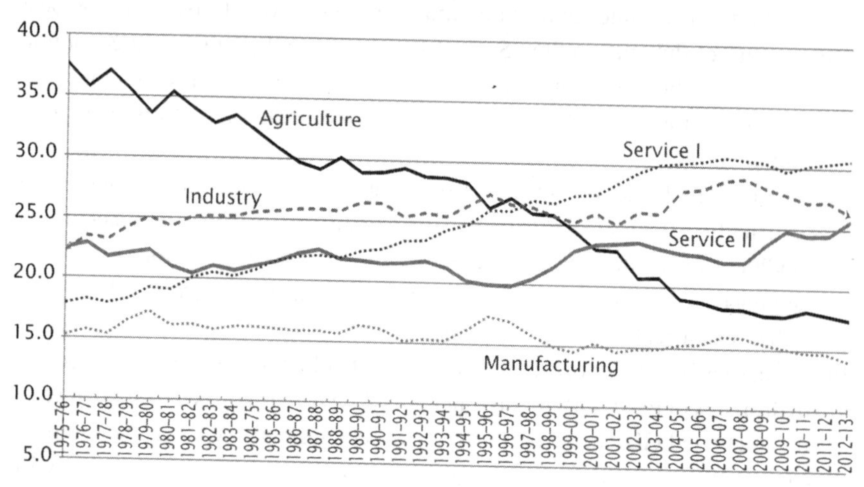

Figure 2.5 Sectoral Shares in GDP at Factor Cost

Source: GOI, www.mospi.nic.in.data, GDP by Economic Activity, sectoral shares at current prices, accessed in October 2018.

Figure 2.5 shows that over a period of almost three and a half decades from 1978–79, agriculture's share in GDP at factor cost maintained a trend of decline; going down by 18 percentage points (in 2012–13). Service-I maintained a reverse trend, filling up two-thirds of the space vacated (12 points) by agriculture. More than half of the remaining points have gone to construction, which is included in industry, and a couple of points is the net gain of all other sectors. Specifically, manufacturing gained nothing. In fact registered manufacturing has maintained its share while unregistered manufacturing has lost marginally. This observation does not conform to the stylized facts in the Clark-Kuznets tradition, which lead to the expectation that manufacturing should raise its relative share substantially in the initial phases of development through which India had been passing.

Service-I consists of services that are directly associated with material (or goods) production. For example, demand for distributive trade services is wholly a derived demand and, further, there is enough evidence that trade in intermediate goods (basically of industry) is the dynamic component of trade services (M. Datta, 2001: 77), which saw an increase in relative share from less than 10 per cent at the turn of the 1970s to more than 15 per cent (increase of almost 6 percentage points, not shown in Figure 2.5) in the early 2010s. This accounts for half of the increase in the relative share of Service-I. What is true of trade is to a great extent true of other components of Service-I. One would naturally ask: how can this category of services grow so fast when manufacturing, which accounts for the lion's share of industry, is apparently stagnant (relative to GDP)? This question will occupy our attention in the following chapters. Here it should be interesting to cast a glance around and see how manufacturing's share performed in major developing countries in recent times.

Manufacturing's Relative Share in Major Developing Countries

Perhaps there is no clear answer to the question: what should be the right share of manufacturing in the GDP of a country at the particular stage of development the country is going through? Much depends on the 'economic complexity' that the country has achieved (Hausmann et al., 2013), the organization of production (Caselli and Pastrello, 1992) and much more, including the accounting tradition (Xu, 2009). But the well-known stylized fact is that in the course of development from an early stage the share of manufacturing in GDP rises until a considerable level of industrialization has been achieved, and then it declines (Fisher, 1935; Clark, 1940; Kuznets, 1971; Chenery and Taylor, 1968).[21] This broad pattern makes development synonymous with industrialization.

On the basis of recent evidence, manufacturing's share goes up to nearly 25 per cent, possibly far beyond, before taking a downturn. Table 2.2 gives the example of the performance of eight major developing economies[22] in recent times. While the relative share of manufacturing for Bangladesh has been growing,[23] that for India seems to have peaked much before coming near 20 per cent (Figure 2.5). Mexico reached 20 per cent but other countries went much beyond that mark before the share declined. That India's experience is unusual, given the country's size, is borne out by the findings of more detailed studies pursued in Chapter 3.

Summary and Conclusion

After slow growth for two and a half decades since the early 1950s, the Indian economy accelerated during the Fifth Plan period (1974–79). The next couple of years were choppy due to external shocks in the form of severe drought, surging oil prices and domestic socio-political disturbances. India brought attitudinal changes to jettison long-held inhibitions about private capital, first incrementally and then gradually more substantially. The private sector responded and it was reflected in the shift to a higher trajectory of GDP growth as well as increases in private

Table 2.2 Share of Manufacturing in GDP, Percentage, at Current Prices

Country	1970	1975	1980	1985	1990	1995	2000	2005	2010
Brazil	27.4	31.3	31.3	31.6	25.5	17.2	16.2	17.4	15.0
China#	26.4	29.8	32.50	28.3	27.80	31.0	30.90	32.1	31.6
India*	13.7	16.0	18.2**	16.3	16.5	16.3	14.7	15.3	15.1
Indonesia	9.6	9.4	12.4	16.4	20.8	24.0	25.2	24.7	22.6
Philippines	27.0	27.7	27.4	26.7	26.6	24.4	24.7	24.0	21.4
Mexico	19.6	19.8	19.2	19.6	20.5	20.0	19.9	16.4	16.2
South Africa	22.6	22.4	21.4	21.6	23.4	20.9	18.6	18.1	14.4
South Korea	18.8	21.9	24.3	26.6	27.3	27.8	29.0	28.3	30.7
Bangladesh	8.4	11.3	17.0	15.1	13.4	15.3	15.	16.5	16.3

Source: Basic data from http.www.unstats.un.org/unsd, Main Aggregates, accessed in May 2018; for India: GOI (2011, 2012).

Notes: Data for different countries are not strictly comparable as national accounting practices vary (see next chapter). Also, data are often revised; so, the table only gives an idea of the order of magnitude.

China groups mining, manufacturing and utilities together up to 2003. We have segregated manufacturing by extrapolation, using ratio observed in the later period.

* Refers to the year ending in March of the year. ** A bit misleading; due to severe drought, GDP declined sharply.

as well as aggregate saving and investment. Inevitably these changes brought in corresponding changes in the sectoral structure of the economy.

A careful study of sectoral structures leads one to three alternative sets of estimates of sectoral relative shares having somewhat different conceptual bases. Hence, it is important to distinguish between the concepts. It is important to note that value added is a concept defined at current prices and it is value or purchasing power, independent of its industrial origin. Constant price GVA can have meaning only when deflated uniformly by the GDP deflator. We have further argued that constant price value added, as prepared by the CSO of India, is inappropriate and unnecessary[24] for study of changes in sectoral relative shares in GDP over time. That leaves us with two sets of estimates: current price NAS estimates and the IOTT-based estimates. Both the sets give us the same trend except in the case of Service-II, more specifically in respect of income from dwellings.

The major observation is stagnation of relative share of manufacturing on the one hand and steady increase in that of Service-I on the other. This is paradoxical for two reasons: first, the steady increase of Service-I, which mostly derives its demand from the manufacturing sector, does not match with the stagnation of manufacturing; secondly, stylized facts as well as the recent experience of major developing countries do not match with the Indian experience. We need to explain these points for a proper understanding of structural changes in the Indian economy.

Appendix 2A Structural Break Analysis

There have been several studies seeking to identify break points in the Indian macroeconomic time series but there still is a lack of consensus about the conclusiveness of the analysis (Wallack, 2003; Panagariya, 2004; Balakrishnan and Parameswaran, 2007a, 2007b; Dholakia and Sapre, 2011). Most often the idea behind finding a break point is to check the effectiveness of some action like a change in government policy or, more broadly, transition to a different regime in terms of economic fundamentals. When there is a series of changes, as it often happens, and researchers' expectations of their effectiveness vary, objectivity becomes very important. Also, in some circumstances, one may be interested in finding the sequence of changes to reflect on causality. In order to preclude any prior judgement of a break date researchers look for endogenous determination of multiple breaks making full use of the information content of data by applying modern econometric techniques (Bai and Perron, 1998, 2003). But techniques cannot overcome conceptual fuzziness; the difficulties are as follows:

The Bai-Perron method leaves the choice of the minimum break-free segment length (h) to the investigator. Since trend breaks are to be distinguished from short term or random fluctuations, a minimum segment needs to be defined and at the same time, robustness demands that the identification of the precise break date should not be too sensitive to the chosen length of the segment. Evidence suggests that such robustness is often missing, exposing the limits of endogeneity, as it stands now.

It is also desired that the observed break dates should be robust to the extension of the time series concerned. Balakrishnan and Parameswaran (2007b) find a single break in GDP growth in 1978–79 when data from 1950–51 to 2003–04 is investigated (with h = 8). But extension of the series by just two years up to 2005–06 produces a second break point at 1990–91. Dholakia and Sapre (2011) gives multiple instances of changes in breaks due to extension or change in the base-year of the series. Since a break is supposed to distinguish between distinct regimes, sensitivity to factors unrelated to changes of regimes creates uncertainty in judgement.

If a break is desired to be linked to changes in economic fundamentals then care should be taken to somehow correct for external shocks. Let us explain. The year 1978–79 has been found to be a break point for different choices of 'h' by several studies, signaling transition to a higher growth regime. However, it was the result of a sharp decline (–5.2 per cent) in GDP in 1979–80, caused by the worst drought after Independence. If, heuristically, we assume there were only a moderate shock keeping the growth rate for the year to just 1 per cent, which would make the growth rate for the subsequent year (1980–81) also roughly 1 per cent if we keep the GDP for the year unchanged, the changed line for 5-year moving average of growth rates is shown in Figure 2A.1 by dotted lines against bold lines for the original series. Now, 1978–79 is no longer the break point, having been deprived of a deep trough in annual growth the next year. The revised moving average (centred) is higher in three consecutive years prior to 1978–79 than it is for three subsequent years; and what is more, the observations for the next four years also do not significantly surpass what was achieved earlier. So, definitely, there is no signal of transition to a higher growth regime, contrary to what is generally suggested. The above exercise shows that external shock undermines the improved growth trend in the later part of the 1970s for no adverse change in economic fundamentals (see Figure 2.2). The moving averages suggest transition to a higher growth regime in the mid-1980s, which seems to be more in conformity with the perception of regime shift.

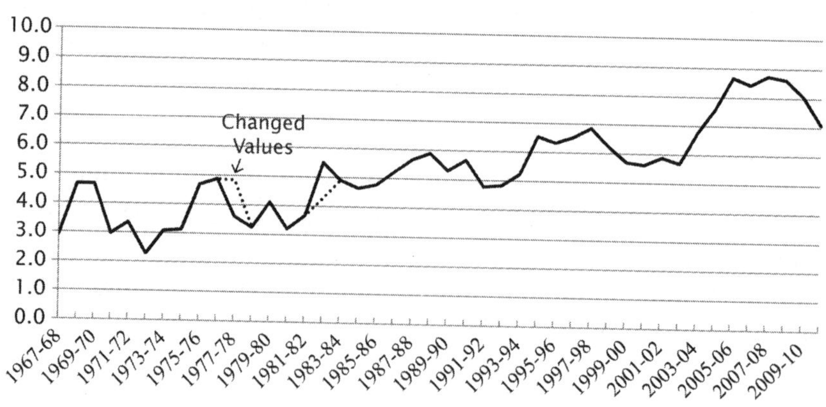

Figure 2A.1 Five-Year Moving Average of GDP Growth Rates

Source: GOI, www.mospi.nic.in/data, GDP by Economic Activity at 2004–05 prices, growth rates, accessed in October 2018.

In view of the above considerations, too much should not be made of the precise endogenous identification of a break date. Thus, for a GDP series, when the economic fundamentals are visibly changing and a break in trend is discernible, one must be alert about external shocks undermining the fundamentals.

Notes

1. Marx discussed 'productive' labour in the context of capitalist production and emphasized on the criterion of generation of 'surplus'. He considered Smith's

'vendibility' criterion a distraction (Marx, [1863] 1963: 152), but in the socialist context the criterion of 'surplus' generation lost its importance (M. Datta, 1989: 38).

2. Though the concept has been formalized with major contributions by Richard Stone under the influence of Keynesian macroeconomics only towards the end of the first half of the last century, the broad contours of the concept can be traced back to the works of William Petty (1665). This is quite extraordinary in view of the subsequent narrowing down of the concept (Studentski, 1958: 13; Schumpeter, 1954: 213).
3. The structure of an economy is a multidimensional and perhaps a somewhat amorphous construct involving many aspects associated with productive activity, as already pointed out in Chapter 1.
4. Refers to GDP at factor cost at 2004–05 prices.
5. A drastic fall in GDP depresses the 5-year moving average for five years and the trough of the trend need not be in the year of lowest performance.
6. We have to keep in mind the great transformation we are making: the basic data is on establishments or enterprises, but we align the information with commodities.
7. In NAS, aggregates according to production and expenditure approaches, obtained independently, do not balance. This is referred to as statistical discrepancy. For an IOTT, however, it is essential that the discrepancies be dissolved to balance row and column totals. The overall discrepancy is absorbed in various categories of final demand using different balancing techniques, including manual balancing. This exercise only uses best judgement to distribute the discrepancy between expenditure categories, leaving the production account relatively unaffected. The CSO obviates this problem by resorting to the publication of Supply and Use tables.
8. The divergence of IOTT estimates for 1998–99 is sharp and we do not know why exactly. We have not used this matrix as a basis for our comparison in Chapter 6.
9. Figure 2.5 shows that annual data at current prices supports this observation, only, the peak shifts to 1979–80. For further discussion the reader is referred to GOI (2012), particularly Chapter 28.
10. It is possible to make an adjustment for this anomaly using Supply table so far as output is concerned but not for GVA, which is not separately available for multiple products without making assumptions.
11. Defined as the difference between net revenue and the full opportunity cost of the factors used in the production of output concerned, including the cost of using the owner's capital. It is different from the accountant's measure of profit.
12. We can ignore separately invoiced product taxes, without any loss of generality. Note that product taxes include taxes on imports.
13. The reader may see Table 3.1 in the next chapter which is not free from product taxes though. Here reference is to the last but one row and column.
14. This, of course, abstracts from the difficulties of measurement, particularly of services (Griliches, 1992). But these difficulties relate to the problems of estimation, not the concept of real value added.
15. The CSO warns at the same time as it recommends the double deflation procedure. 'In such case, there are guidelines to use only the output price index as the single

deflator for obtaining both value of output and GVA at constant prices. This procedure is known as single deflation method' (GOI, 2012: 127). Claiming double deflation to be ideal in the same breath is not clear thinking.

16. In a related discussion, Berndt and Hulten (2007) refer to Koopmans' (1947) concerns regarding measurements without a theoretical basis.
17. Assuming absence of product taxes.
18. This assumes that the constant price estimate of GDP should be arrived at by deflating final uses; sectoral real value added can be estimated only at the next step after obtaining the GDP deflator.
19. Kohli (2006) quoted the Finance Minister (from 1982 onwards):

    > An area of strength for the industrial sector today is the highly favourable investment climate, which has prevailed since 1980.… The annual budgets for the years 1980–85 have a distinct philosophy. The government has actively encouraged the corporate sector to mobilize the financial resources…. The total amount of capital issued by the private corporate sector increased from a little over Rs. 300 crore in 1980–81 … to Rs. 809 crore in 1983–84 … an expansion of 170 percent in three years.

20. In fact great changes were underway that were not reflected in the growth of value added in the sector, as discussed in detail in Chapter 5.
21. Fisher and Clark used the terms primary, secondary and tertiary. The terminology was supposed to be descriptive of the nature of the activities grouped together in these categories. Kuznets deviated from this practice.
22. Chenery and Taylor (1968) identified three distinct development patterns for the group of large countries, small primary-oriented countries and small industry-oriented countries. Our focus is on large countries, so we exclude many small but highly industrialized countries from the sample.
23. We have excluded Pakistan as the country seems to have faltered in its industrialization effort.
24. Instead, it should be more useful to focus on constructing quantum indices.

3

Sectoral Shares in Indian GDP

How to Regard It?*

'What would life be without arithmetic, but a scene of horrors?' To Miss…, 22 July, 1835

—Rev. Sydney Smith, Holland (1855)

Introduction

The manufacturing sector of the Indian economy has been widely held to be an underperformer, defying the traditional idea contained in stylized facts summarized by Kuznets (1971) and Chenery and Taylor (1968) (henceforth, K-CT) regarding the evolving pattern of sectoral shares in GDP in the development process of an economy. The World Bank (2004) has described India's recent experience as a services revolution. In more informal discussions, this development is often viewed with some degree of reservation – the feeling is that services are fleeting while material goods last; therefore, growth with a declining share of the secondary sector in GDP is not considered as solid growth. Even if one does not subscribe to this idea (we have discussed the point in detail in the next chapter), it still remains an interesting question from the point of view of structural changes. In this context we discuss the question: what really is the share of manufacturing or industry in Indian GDP and how should we regard it?

The K-CT line of thinking would suggest that the trend of industry's share in India should have been rising and placed at a higher level than what it is now. Comparison with China makes the point particularly stark and this point has appeared time and again in the literature (Bosworth and Collins, 2007; Kochhar et al., 2006). We raise some pertinent questions here regarding data and methodology

*Discussion in this chapter draws heavily on Datta, Neogy and Sinha (2015).

in use, because underestimation in one case and overestimation in the other would make comparison very hazardous. Then, keeping these points in view, we proceed to evaluate India's standing with regard to levels and trends of relative shares of industry, manufacturing and services in the context of recent development experience of countries above a minimum size.

In the following section we take a hard look at the Chinese data on sectoral shares in view of wide misconceptions that prevail and take a quick look at the Indian data with respect to its nature and appropriateness for comparison with other nations. Then we present a brief discussion of the concepts underlying factor cost and market price estimates and point out how market price estimates of relative GDP shares of the manufacturing and industry sectors would be higher than that at factor cost in the presence of indirect taxes. Following this discussion we discuss an alternative procedure for the estimation of relative shares based on IOTTs available at hand. We have argued that this alternative estimate of industry's relative share may be taken as a rough approximation of that at market prices which is not provided by the CSO. Further, we have juxtaposed in the course of this discussion estimates at factor cost given in the NAS and the alternative estimates obtained from our analysis, for comparison. The subsequent section takes up an evaluation of the sectoral structure of the Indian economy in the present international context after incorporating corrections required for international comparison and controlling for China-influence, explained in detail in the next section. The last section summarizes and concludes.

Nature and Comparability of Data

China is known to be struggling, particularly since 1993, to improve its services data which has been in a miserable state due, basically, to the country's mooring to the material products system (MPS) of erstwhile socialist countries. Now China has decidedly veered towards the system of national accounts (SNA) and improved its data in line with SNA, though much remains to be done still (Dongyou, 2009). There have been several revisions of data, each time reducing the industry share and raising the services share. One revision made in 2004 raised the GDP by 17 per cent, and the services share from 31.9 to 40.4 per cent mainly through revision of estimates for material services[1] (Xu, 2009); this upward revision means a corresponding decline in industry's share. China is in the process of developing a reliable mechanism (proper sample surveys) to account for (material) service activities like distributive trade and transport below a certain threshold which is quite high.[2] The relevant activities are probably inadequately accounted for separately. However, these activities are traditionally merged with the value generated in the material products sector, of which the industry sector constitutes the major part under the MPS. Thus, national product under the MPS, that is, the net material product (M. Datta, 1989; Beckerman, 1991), is not so much affected; but industry (and manufacturing) share tends to be overestimated, and services underestimated, vis-à-vis the SNA.

China published GDP data as a supplement to its MPS accounts up to 1993 when the country adopted the SNA as the accounting system. Due to conceptual moorings to the system of material product accounting many important service sector activities remained bound to material goods production and their separation was a tardy process. China's first economic census took place only in 2005 and then, for the sake of historical comparison, data has been revised several times. Despite all these efforts China is still some distance from full adoption of the SNA (Xu, 2009). We take up this brief discussion to put the India–China comparison, or views on India's low industry-share, in proper perspective.

Indian national accounts, by comparison, have been much better integrated with the SNA, with a network of censuses and sample surveys in place. That things are not all rosy in spite of a long history and a sophisticated statistical network is pointed out by none other than the National Statistical Commission (2001) citing frequent revisions (though revisions are not unknown even in developed countries). The Commission points out:

> Indian national accounts data are based on a mish-mash of income, production and expenditure methods as well as combinations of data referring both to the relevant year as well as extrapolations from past years.... [Estimation] often requires the use of certain norms, rates and ratios and other assumptions ... based on data from a remote past. (Quoted from Srinivasan, 2003)

The points made remain valid even now (GOI, 2012). While the above criticism underlines the in-exactness of the data and a constant need to improve it, is the inadequacy is rooted in the nature of the estimation under limited information and the approach of extrapolation is more or less resorted to by all countries under similar circumstances.

The estimation of aggregate product in different countries is beset with a maze of procedural complications and this makes international comparison a bit tricky. International agencies like the UN, IMF, World Bank and the OECD have undertaken great efforts to standardize estimation procedures resulting in the SNA being accepted in principle by almost all the countries. Nevertheless, the statistical systems of different (particularly less developed) countries are not fully ready to implement the SNA in a uniform way. So, the degree of accuracy and also the orientation of the accounts vary quite a great deal. Many less developed countries (LDCs),[3] including India's two neighbours China and Bangladesh, provide estimates of sectoral shares at producer's (or market) prices (see UN, 2013) while the OECD countries, and also India, provide these estimates at basic prices (or at factor cost) along with estimates of final expenditures at market prices. Market price estimates differ from factor cost estimates in the treatment of indirect taxes. Excise and customs taxes are product taxes and they constituted more than ninety percent of central government's indirect tax collections, with excise duty playing the major part, in the Indian economy prior to the last decade (when service tax started gaining weight).[4] Herein lies the seed of non-comparability between the estimates of sectoral shares at factor cost and those at market prices, particularly for industry and manufacturing. We will take up the point in greater detail below.

Current Price Estimates of Sectoral Shares: Factor Cost versus Market Price

Value Added at Factor Cost and at Market Prices

We briefly go through the basics of national income accounting to emphasize some finer distinctions. The existence of varied structures of indirect taxes in different (developing) countries makes the precise conceptualization of GDP from the production side somewhat complicated. Since the UN Statistics Division (UNSD) presents national accounts of different countries either at factor cost or at producer's or market prices, we need to distinguish between the different ideas of GDP for proper international comparison. The basic categories of indirect taxes are those on products and other taxes incidental to production. The latter category consists of taxes like those on buildings or payroll, license renewals, and so on; quantitatively, this is generally not very important, but it makes the difference between factor cost and basic prices. For simplicity we will ignore this difference and not make a distinction between factor cost and basic prices without any significant analytical inconvenience.

Traditionally taxes on products have been basically excise and sales taxes, taxes on imports and others like service and value added taxes. For intertemporal comparisons going back beyond the present decade, excise duty played an important role in India though the diverse types of indirect taxes were gradually being subsumed under goods and services tax until all major indirect taxes have been integrated into value added tax (VAT) in 2017, which is generally separately invoiced and passed on to the purchaser. For comparisons over the past through the 2000s, it is not inappropriate to ignore VAT. In that case producer's price, which is basic price plus product taxes not separately invoiced to purchasers, becomes equivalent to purchaser's price (what the users actually pay); the only complication arises due to distributive services. Trade and transport services are considered as a separate item in sectoral accounting, which would otherwise be a part of purchaser's price of commodities. So, for sectoral accounting we will not distinguish between producer's and purchaser's prices.[5] Further, instead of purchaser's price we will use the term market price as the term is traditionally in use, ignoring practical accounting difficulties.[6] This simplification takes us to the standards by which accounts of different countries are presented by the UNSD.

The *gross value added at factor cost is output valued at factor cost*[7] *less intermediate consumption valued at market prices.* ... (I)

Similarly, *gross value added at market prices is the value of output at market prices less the value of intermediate inputs also at market prices.* ... (II)

With reference to the IOTT framework (Table 3.1 presents an abridged IOTT for the Indian economy for the year 2003–04), the relevant *market price excludes margins for* trade and transport services as these are shown as separate production processes (part of Service-I in Table 3.1). We will work extensively with IOTTs in the subsequent chapters, so it should be helpful to go through a detailed discussion of the basics. Our objective here is to check what difference it makes for relative sectoral shares as we go from factor cost to market price basis of accounting. This is important for comparisons as different countries present their accounts at different price bases.

Given the two concepts of value added defined above, we can write the following relations with reference to the IOTT framework where *all the entries are at factor cost, that is, exclusive of net indirect taxes (NIT)*:

Gross *value added at market prices* in sector 'j',

$$V_j = (X_j + T_j) - (\Sigma_i x_{ij} + \tau_j) \quad \text{... (1)}$$

Subscripts 'i' and 'j' stand respectively for row and column of the IOTT while X and x stand for output and intermediate consumption respectively (so, X_j is the jth output and x_{ij} is input from the ith sector used in the jth sector; all evaluated at factor cost) . T_j stands for product tax (does not appear in the IOTT) on the jth production process while τ_j stands for NIT incorporated in intermediate inputs of the jth production process[8] (shown in the row NIT in Table 3.1). Clearly, the second term on the right hand side of equation (1) is total intermediate consumption at market prices in the jth production process (*vide* definition II earlier).

Further, from definition I, *value added at factor cost* in sector 'j' is:

$$U_j = X_j - (\Sigma_i x_{ij} + \tau_j) \quad \text{... (2)}$$

Clearly, comparing equations (1) and (2),

$$V_j = U_j + T_j \quad \text{... (3)}$$

Table 3.1 Input–Output Transactions Table: Indian Economy, 2003–04 (Unit: INR Billions)

	Agri	Mng	Mnfg	Cons	EGW	Serv.I	Serv.II	II Use ($\Sigma_j x_{ij}$)	F.Use (F_i)	Total (X_i)
Agri	1,505	0	1,334	55	4	352	6	3,255	4,470	7,725
Mng	0	6	1,608	181	183	4	0	1,983	-1,108	875
Mnfg	545	103	5,881	1,380	233	1,874	318	10,334	6,963	17,297
Cons	42	20	152	107	27	138	114	600	3,815	4,415
EGW	86	25	510	100	401	213	18	1,352	205	1,558
Serv.I	548	52	2,765	789	274	1,839	212	6,478	7,386	13,864
Serv.II	12	10	259	1	3	174	311	769	4,752	5,522
($\Sigma_i x_{ij}$)	2,739	215	12,508	2,613	1,126	4,593	979	24,773	26,483	51,256
NIT (τ_j)	−387	172	1,369	8	−139	−37	3	τ = 989	1,172	(T+z)[#] = 2,161
GVA (U_j)	5,373	488	3,421	1,795	570	9,350	4,497			**U = 25,494**
Output (X_j)	7,725	875	17,297	4,415	1,558	13,864	5,522	51256		**GDP = 27,655**

Source: Aggregated from CSO, *Input–Output Transactions Table 2003–04*, New Delhi.

Notes: The matrix is presented at factor cost basis.

Abbreviations: *Serv.I* = transport, communication, trade and financial services. *Serv.II* = rest of services; Agri = agriculture; Mng = Mining; Mnfg = Manufacturing; Cons = construction; EGW = Utilities. IIUse = intermediate input use, FUse = final use.

[#] (T+z) is aggregate collection of product tax.

The equation states the distinction between market price and factor cost.

As we are dealing with a *commodity x commodity* matrix, row must be equal to column sum, that is, total uses net of imports must equal total production. This overall balance between product and expenditure sides is expressed in the following equation: From (2),

$$\Sigma U_j = \Sigma X_j - \Sigma_j (\Sigma_i x_{ij} + \tau_j) = \Sigma_i (X_i - \Sigma_j x_{ij}) - \Sigma_j \tau_j = \Sigma F_i - \tau \quad \ldots (4)$$

(writing F_i as final use of the ith commodity at factor cost and $\Sigma \tau_j = \tau$, total indirect tax collected from intermediate consumption; we have omitted subscripts from Σ where it is obvious)

Clearly, in the presence of indirect taxes, *aggregate value added at factor cost is not equal to aggregate final demand evaluated at factor cost.* This happens because NIT on intermediate consumption (τ) (which is actually cost incurred by producers) is a part of price and final expenditure at factor cost, but excluded from value added at factor cost. The national accounting identity (or production–expenditure balance) requires aggregate value added at factor cost (or GDP at factor cost) to be equal to aggregate final demand evaluated at factor cost less aggregate NIT incorporated into intermediate consumption (τ).

Market price accounting also needs some care to satisfy the accounting identity between the product and the expenditure sides. To see this we first note that GDP is the aggregate final expenditure (net of imports) at market prices. Then, in order to obtain the aggregate from the production side we must add import taxes[9] to aggregate sectoral value added at market prices, as this item cannot be allocated to production sectors. Adding these taxes (z, say), which are left out of sectoral value added at market prices (V_j), we have: GDP at market prices, often written simply as

$$GDP = \Sigma V_j + z$$

$$= \Sigma_j [(X_j + T_j) - (\Sigma_i x_{ij} + \tau_j)] + z$$

$$= \Sigma_i (X_i - \Sigma_j x_{ij}) + \Sigma(T_j - \tau_j) + z; \qquad \text{(from [1])}$$

Or, $$\Sigma V_j + z = \Sigma F_i + (T + z - \tau); \ [\text{writing } \Sigma T_j = T] \qquad \ldots (5)$$

(This may be verified from the column of final use in Table 3.1. GDP = 26,483 + 1,172 = 27,655)

The right hand side term in (5) is aggregate final demand at market prices, as ($T + z - \tau$) is the net indirect tax on final uses = 2,161 – 989 = 1,172 (row NIT in Table 3.1).

So, we can write aggregate value added at market prices:

$$\Sigma V_j = \Sigma F_i + (T - \tau) \qquad \ldots (6)$$

This can also be directly obtained from (3) and (4).

Clearly, jth sector's relative GDP share at market prices is $V_j / (\Sigma V_j + z)$, for all j's. They do not add up to unity unless we consider shares in aggregate value added (ΣV_j) (*vide* equation [6]). Strictly speaking, these are not shares in GDP but it is only an academic point that can be ignored for practical purposes.

Now we can go back to equation (3); indirect tax collected from sector 'j' (T_j) is added to the sectoral value added at factor cost (U_j) in order to arrive at sectoral value added at market prices (V_j). Since import tax (included in 'z') is not collected from production, excise duty basically forms T_j.[10] *The important point for our present discourse is that T_j is unevenly distributed; excise duty is almost wholly collected from products belonging to industry, particularly manufacturing.* Under such circumstances, it is clear that manufacturing's (and industry's) relative share, when value added is taken at market prices, will be higher than that at factor cost. (Taking industry's share in GDP at factor cost to be 26 per cent, an addition of 4 percentage points to both the numerator and the denominator on account of excise tax would take the relative share near 29 per cent; and this is true of manufacturing, constituting the lion's share of industry, *a fortiori*.) This point should be kept in mind while making international comparison in order to avoid being misled as different countries present their estimates at different price bases (UN, 2013).

The present day concept of GDP has evolved after an intense debate particularly during the second quarter of the last century (Frisch, 1955; Syrquin, 2011). Variation in country practices has been largely disciplined by fiat, so to say, starting with the publication of the UN SNA, 1953, and continuing with refinements thereafter. The concept of GDP as aggregate final expenditure at market prices is suited to the Keynesian framework. The basic idea is that the production side is the dual of the expenditure side; balance between the two sides is a fundamental national accounting identity.

We have seen that indirect tax is considered to be a part of value added at market prices of the sectors paying the tax to the government. This is a convenient accounting ploy having nothing to do with tax incidence. We know no general statement can be made about the precise tax incidence in reality. However, taxes are generally passed on to the purchasers, at least partially, if not fully. So long as the purchasers are producers themselves, that is, the uses of the relevant goods are intermediate consumption, the taxes are paid by the users at the cost of what would otherwise be counted as their own value added. Thus when '... a tax is collected between two stages of production, how can it sensibly be allocated to either?' (Nicholson, 1955). One might well treat value added in basic-price (factor cost) accounting to include taxes paid by the producing sector on its intermediate inputs (τ_j) rather than taking taxes collected on their outputs (T_j) in market-price definition. In fact, the whole objective of negative tax on agricultural inputs is to depress the cost of production and raise the value added at factor cost of the taxpaying sector, making value added not a purely technological act with 'invisible hands'. It is in this perspective that IOTTs suggest an alternative that is very convenient for input–output analysis, *though not for national income accounting*, and for our specific purpose to be stated in the next section.

Alternative Estimates of Sectoral Shares

In view of the above discussion an alternative is to account for net indirect tax paid on intermediate consumption (the row NIT in Table 3.1) in the value added of the concerned sector. Let us define modified value added (W_j) based on IOTTs as

$$W_j = U_j + \tau_j.$$

Then, going back to equation (4):

$$\Sigma U_j = \Sigma X_j - \Sigma_j (\Sigma_i x_{ij} + \tau_j)$$

Or, $$\Sigma W_j = \Sigma(U_j + \tau_j) = \Sigma_i (X_i - \Sigma_j x_{ij}) = \Sigma F_i \qquad \ldots (7)$$

The basic idea with equation (7) is that it makes aggregate value added identical to aggregate final expenditure (in factor cost accounting) without any further adjustment—thus satisfying an essential requirement of input–output analysis for tackling queries like the size of sectoral multipliers caused by a specific expenditure.

From equations (3) and (7):

$$V_j = U_j + T_j = W_j + (T_j - \tau_j)$$

Or, $$\Sigma V_j = \Sigma W_j + (T - \tau) \qquad \ldots (8)$$

Equation (8) shows the adjustment needed to obtain aggregate gross value added at market prices from ΣW_j, which is aggregate final expenditure at basic prices (factor cost).

It is to be noted that industry (and, particularly, manufacturing) is by far the most intensive user of its own products as intermediate inputs (see NIT row in Table 3.1). Thus, industry itself pays a good part of the indirect tax it collects. Thus for practical purposes, remembering that τ_j includes import taxes, we can take the tax paid by industry (τ_j) as a first approximation for the total tax on the industry's product (T_j). Inclusion of import tax in τ_j may be taken, albeit roughly, as an offset for the part of T_j left out of τ_j, which industry collects from final uses. *This consideration suggests that industry's (or manufacturing's) share in aggregate (modified) value added (W_j) obtained by exploiting IOTTs, as discussed above, should be a rough approximation of the corresponding market price share when it is not provided by the statistics office.*[11]

Relative Sectoral Shares: From NAS and IOTTs

Table 3.2 presents two estimates of relative sectoral shares in the GDP[12] of the Indian economy for the years for which IOTTs are available; one is current price estimates at factor cost given by the CSO in its annual National Accounts Statistics (NAS) and the other is relative sectoral shares obtained from the IOTTs based on modified value added as explained above. Observations suggest that current price NAS estimates vary quite a great deal from the IOTT-based modified estimates, which we take as an approximation of the corresponding market price estimates, in the cases of manufacturing and industry. We must note here that the CSO makes all efforts to make its IOTTs roughly compatible with the NAS. The basic reason for the observed discrepancy is that we have included the net indirect tax (NIT) paid by producing units, on their purchases of intermediate inputs, in the value added by the same producing units,[13] as explained earlier.

Table 3.2 Relative Sectoral Shares: Alternative Current Price Estimates

Sector		1968–69	1973–74	1978–79	1983–84	1989–90	1993–94	1998–99	2003–04	2007–08
Manufactures	NAS	12.8	14.3	16.5	16.1	16.4	15.3	15.0	14.9	16.1
	IOTT	15.1	16.4	19.4	19.5	21.2	16.7	17.5	18.1	17.4
Industry	NAS	19.3	20.2	24.3	25.2	26.5	25.5	25.7	26.0	29.2
	IOTT	22.7	23.0	28.1	29.6	32.0	27.0	28.6	29.0	30.7

Source: mospi.nic.in/data, and IOTTs published by the CSO.

Note: NAS indicates current price estimate obtained from National Accounts Statistics and IOTT indicates estimates based on input–output transactions tables.

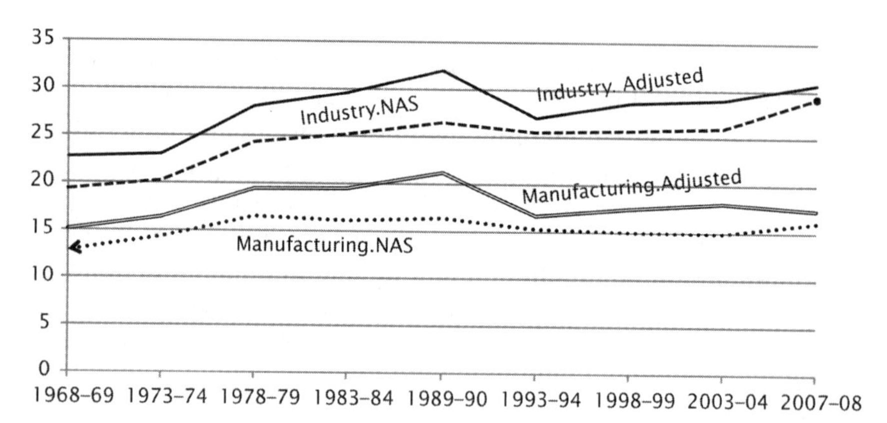

Figure 3.1 Alternative Estimates of Sectoral Shares

Source: Table 3.2.

The observations have been plotted in Figure 3.1. It is clear that IOTT estimates are higher all along both for manufacturing and industry, though the difference gets narrow at the end point (2007–08). A measure of the average difference between the two estimates is root mean square difference which is found to be 2.85 for manufacturing and 3.42 for industry.[14] Our conclusion is that in international comparisons of manufacturing sector's share in GDP, available official estimates should be taken with caution. For comparison with developing countries like China and Bangladesh that present their estimates at market (or producer's) prices, India's share for manufacturing or industry should be raised by about three percentage points to make it comparable with those of other countries. We make this correction in our comparative study in the following section.

India's Sectoral Shares in International Perspective

Figure 3.1 shows the difference in the relative GDP shares of industry and its largest sub-sector, manufacturing, as per the alternative estimates. Taking cue from the above discussion we have added a flat three percentage points to India's relative shares for 1981 and 2001 and two percentage points for 2011, in view of narrowing of the gap between estimates at factor cost and producer's price, for industry and manufacturing. Also, we have deducted two percentage points from India's service sector shares to roughly adjust the sum of sectoral shares to unity. Even after the correction, India is far behind China with respect to observed share of manufacturing in GDP. Part of the difference must be ascribed to overestimation in China on the yardstick of SNA, as discussed earlier. To address this issue we have reported results of a regression exercise for the group of countries that leaves China out.

In order to check how India compares with other countries with respect to the sectoral structure[15] we have run cross-country regressions (with heteroskedasticity robust standard errors) of sectoral shares on per-capita GDP (designated as y), its square and population[16] (both variables in logarithm) and a dummy standing for *India indicator*, for three years – 1981, 2001 and 2011. We have excluded tiny countries below the size of 75,000 square kilometres in geographical area. This leaves us with a group of around 100 countries; we refer to them as 'all countries'.[17] Then we have taken a more homogeneous group after leaving out the richest countries judged by the criterion of per-capita purchasing power parity (PPP) income in 1981. After excluding countries having per-capita PPP income above or equal to that of the UK we get the group designated G-I. Since rich countries industrialized much earlier and have gone along the way much farther than the present-day developing countries, their sectoral dynamics may not match well with presently industrializing countries; so, G-I is of greater interest to us rather than the larger sample of 'all countries'. Finally, in order to control for the China influence, we have excluded China from G-I to obtain the group designated G-II, that excludes the rich countries along with China, and check the results of regression for the two groups.

The regression results are presented in Table 3.3. For each of the dependent variables, which is a sectoral share (for either manufacturing or industry or services), we have run regressions twice; once with adjusted data after incorporating corrections for India's sectoral share only, as mentioned above, and again with given official data. Thus we obtain two different estimates of India indicators; *indicator1* for regression with adjusted India-shares, and *indicator2* for given shares. These indicators are our basic instruments for analysing how India deviated from the international norm. About the choice of dependent variables the following points may be noted:

1. In explaining manufacturing's share in GDP, apart from income in logarithm, (ln y), population plays an important part. Coefficients for both the variables are statistically significant at 1 per cent level in all the regressions. This is consistent with the hypothesis that a large domestic market is advantageous for initial progress of industrialization (Chenery and Taylor, 1968: 395). Indeed, dropping population as an explanatory variable reduces R-squared dramatically (results not presented)[18] while the incorporation of an additional explanatory variable in the form of (ln y)-squared improves the power of regression, in explaining the case of 'all countries' that includes the richest countries, marginally, without affecting the indicator considerably. This additional variable is not helpful in the other two cases – for the groups G-I and G-II. In view of our interest in G-I and G-II, which exclude rich countries, we have focused on the simpler regression presenting the more general version in the appendix (Table 3A.1) for interested readers.
2. Population does not play any important role in explaining relative shares for industry or services, the relevant coefficients always being statistically insignificant; and, contrary to what we have seen in the case of manufacturing, inclusion of population in these regressions does not help much with R-squared. The explanation is easy. Major non-manufacturing components of industry are mining and construction. Many relatively small countries (by population) with poor manufacturing base have highly developed mining activity based on foreign demand and also a high level of construction activity. This factor discounts the influence of population on industry. As for services, development of a part of the sector (Service-I) may be linked to mining and construction and the sector, in general, does not seem to be very dependent on economy of scale, and hence size of the domestic market.
3. Our specific focus is on results with adjusted data after controlling for China effect (indicator1/G-II); we call it *our case*. This result is compared with that for given data and without controlling for China effect (indicator2/G-I), what we call the *standard case*. It shows how issues with estimation influence the conclusion. While we have presented regression results for groups G-I and G-II in Table 3.3, the corresponding results for all countries are given in the appendix (Table 3A.2).

Interpretation of Results

A. Consider the case of industry. The *standard case* (indicator2/G-I) shows India as an average country in 1981 but going down to be a negative outlier (statistically significant at 1 per cent level) in 2001 and remaining so a decade later. But after correction of Indian data and exclusion of China, *our case* (case1/G-II) shows India to be an outstanding performer, a *positive* outlier, (at 1 per cent level of significance) in 1981and from the high position India goes down to be a *negative* outlier (at 1% level of significance) in 2011.

B. Coming to manufacturing, the *standard case* is that India was a negative outlier at all the three points of our observation. The picture for *our case* (that is, after data adjustment and exclusion of China, indicator 1/ G-II) is, again, different. India's performance was almost an average one in 1981. However, the country was a *negative* outlier (at 5 per cent level) in 2001. In 2011 indicator1 (G-II) was insignificant (even at 10 per cent level) though negative and rather considerable. Thus, compared to the *standard case*, *our case* presents a picture much less out of tune with international experience. The difference with industry-experience is that India never attained a high position of being a positive outlier and the decline as a manufacturing economy over the subsequent decades was less sharp. Thus India's performance looks more out of tune with international experience if Chinese data is taken into account (*standard case*) for whatever comparability it may have.

Table 3.3 Sectoral Share Regressions with India Indicator

Dependent Variable: Relative share of a sector in GDP at current prices#						
Independent variables	G-I Countries			G-II Countries: China Excluded		
	1981	2001	2011	1981	2001	2011
	Sector: Manufacturing					
ln(y)	2.90	2.94	3.87	3.38	2.92	3.73
	2.75	*5.17*	*5.22*	*3.21*	*5.16*	*5.00*
ln(pop)	3.02	2.23	1.84	2.41	2.04	1.59
	3.85	*5.48*	*3.39*	*3.57*	*4.78*	*2.76*
Indicator1	−4.62	−4.86**	−4.24*	**−1.24**	**−3.94****	**−3.05**
(adjusted data)	*−1.21*	*−2.52*	*−1.75*	*−0.40*	*−1.96*	*−1.19*
Indicator2	**−7.62****	**−7.86*****	**−6.24*****	−4.24	−6.94***	−5.05**
(given data)	*−1.99*	*−4.07*	*−2.57*	*−1.37*	*−3.45*	*−1.97*
Observations	52	89	68	51	88	67
R-squared	*0.42*	*0.34*	*0.37*	*0.40*	*0.31*	*0.33*

Table Contd.

Table Contd.

Dependent Variable: Relative share of a sector in GDP at current prices#						
Independent variables	G-I Countries			G-II Countries: China Excluded		
	1981	2001	2011	1981	2001	2011
	Sector: Industry					
ln(y)	−10.19	50.56	51.37	4.51	48.99	50.46
	−0.40	*2.98*	*2.36*	*0.19*	*2.88*	*2.32*
ln(y)-sqr	1.31	−2.87	−2.76	0.35	−2.77	−2.71
	0.76	*−2.68*	*−2.10*	*0.21*	*−2.58*	*−2.06*
Indicator1	4.64**	−2.79*	−6.01***	**6.15*****	**−2.58**	**−5.85*****
(adjusted data)	*2.08*	*−1.76*	*−3.06*	*3.15*	*−1.60*	*−2.95*
Indicator2	**1.64**	**−5.79*****	**−8.01*****	3.15	−5.58***	−7.85***
(given data)	*0.73*	*−3.65*	*−4.08*	*1.61*	*−3.47*	*−3.96*
Observations	61	90	72	60	89	71
R-squared	*0.43*	*0.28*	*0.26*	*0.49*	*0.28*	*0.26*
	Sector: Services					
ln(y)	48.18	−4.38	−17.01	40.49	−3.38	−16.13
	2.48	*−0.23*	*−0.93*	*2.09*	*−0.18*	*−0.88*
ln(y)-sqr	−3.15	0.69	1.32	−2.65	0.63	1.27
	−2.33	*0.60*	*1.18*	*−1.96*	*0.54*	*1.14*
Indicator1	−2.08	5.40***	6.58***	**−2.85***	**5.26*****	**6.42*****
(adjusted data)	*−1.32*	*3.52*	*3.74*	*−1.86*	*3.37*	*3.62*
Indicator2	**−0.08**	**7.40*****	**8.58*****	−0.85	7.26***	8.42***
(given data)	*−0.05*	*4.82*	*4.88*	*−0.55*	*4.66*	*4.74*
Observations	62	90	72	61	89	71
R-squared	*0.15*	*0.30*	*0.19*	*0.11*	*0.30*	*0.20*

 # Results for separate regressions: one with adjusted data and indicator1; the other with given data and indicator2. All coefficients, except indicators, remain unchanged as sectoral shares for India are adjusted.

Constant term not shown in the table. Figures in italics below the coefficients are robust t-statistics. * stands for 10%, ** for = 5% and *** for 1% level of significance.

Source: World Bank, www.data.worldbank.org, accessed in April 2014.

C. The picture for services is almost a mirror image of that for industry. The *standard case* shows India moving forward from an average country to the status of a *positive* outlier in 2001 (at 1 per cent level) and maintaining that position a decade later. *Our case* is, again, a bit different not regarding the trend but regarding the level. From being a *negative* outlier (at 10 per cent level, though) in 1981 India rose to be a *positive* outlier at (1 per cent level) in 2001 and maintained that position a decade later.

Summary and Conclusion

Some countries (including China) provide their sectoral product estimates at market (or producer's) prices while others (including India) give those estimates at factor cost (or basic prices) making international comparison tricky. Input–output transactions tables compiled at factor cost for the Indian economy allow value added at factor cost to be adjusted for indirect taxes (that are not separately invoiced to the purchasers), like excise duty, import tax, and so on. Since the manufacturing sector itself pays a good part of these taxes in purchasing its own intermediate inputs, a first approximation of the sector's value added at market price can be obtained by treating these payments as part of value added at producer's prices. Consequently, in the presence of substantial excise duties, producer's price estimates of relative sectoral shares will be higher than that at factor cost in the case of manufacturing and industry, and correspondingly lower for services.

For a proper international comparison, relative GDP shares of Indian industry or manufacturing sectors need to be adjusted upward, and this implies a corresponding correction for the service sector downward. Even after this correction there are wide differences in sectoral relative shares between India and China. A part of the explanation must be aberrations in Chinese estimates by the yardstick of the SNA though China has been working to bring their estimates in line with international standards. This suggests a case for studying the Indian performance after controlling for the Chinese influence. Our conclusion from the study is the following.

In light of the international comparison exercise, India's position in terms of sectoral relative share in manufacturing has always been below the average, though not by far in 1981; the position declined further to make India an outlier on the lower side in 2001 with not much improvement in 2011. For the broader industry sector, India was above the average, an emphatic positive outlier, in 1981; the position declined over the next three decades, so much so that India was a negative outlier in 2011. The case of services was a mirror image of that of industry. If we do not adjust the Indian data for comparability and, further, do not control for the aberrations in Chinese estimates, as in our standard case, India's performance looks much more dismal. We will investigate in subsequent chapters how real this appearance is.

Appendix 3A Tables

Table 3A.1 Sectoral Share Regression for Manufacturing with ln(y)-sqr as an additional independent variable

	All Countries			G-I Countries			G-II Countries		
Manufacturing	1981	2001	2011	1981	2001	2011	1981	2001	2011
ln(y)	16.55	17.01	23.30	16.59	15.77	6.11	30.88	14.94	5.32
	2.37	*4.02*	*3.81*	*0.92*	*2.42*	*0.58*	*2.09*	*2.26*	*0.49*
ln(y)-sqr	−0.91	−0.89	−1.22	−0.95	−0.81	−0.14	−1.90	−0.76	−0.10
	−2.10	*−3.54*	*−3.37*	*−0.77*	*−1.95*	*−0.20*	*−1.84*	*−1.80*	*−0.14*
ln(pop)	3.10	1.78	1.64	3.06	2.18	1.84	2.37	2.01	1.59
	4.54	*4.99*	*3.39*	*3.80*	*5.73*	*3.37*	*3.70*	*5.02*	*2.75*
Indicator	−4.50	−3.71	−4.41	−4.56	−5.35	−4.37	−0.52	−4.48	−3.14
	−1.23	*−2.15*	*−2.02*	*−1.13*	*−2.82*	*−1.74*	*−0.18*	*−2.23*	*−1.18*
Observations	64	107	73	52	89	68	51	88	67
R-squared	*0.47*	*0.33*	*0.33*	*0.43*	*0.36*	*0.37*	*0.44*	*0.33*	*0.33*

Note: Constant term not shown in the table. Figures in italics below the coefficients are robust t-statistics.

Table 3A.2 Regressions of Table 3.3 Applied to All Countries

Dependent Variable: Relative Share of a Sector in GDP										
Indepnd.	Manufacturing				Industry			Services		
Variables	1981	2001	2011		1981	2001	2011	1981	2001	2011
ln(y)	2.33	2.00	2.43	ln(y)	22.48	46.99	61.51	11.90	−0.70	−25.37
	3.10	*4.75*	*3.43*		*1.84*	*4.10*	*4.24*	*1.21*	*−0.05*	*−2.05*
ln(pop)	3.08	1.84	1.66	ln(y)-sqr	−1.09	−2.65	−3.37	−0.50	0.46	1.82
	4.69	*4.95*	*3.09*		*−1.41*	*−3.83*	*−4.02*	*−0.79*	*0.61*	*2.52*
Indicator	−5.46	−3.28	−3.02	Indicator	3.98	−2.56	−5.74	−1.45	5.17	7.21
	−1.66	*−1.81*	*−1.25*		*1.72*	*−1.84*	*−3.41*	*−0.88*	*3.67*	*4.64*
Obsvn	64	107	73	Obsvn	79	108	77	80	108	77
R-squred	*0.43*	*0.28*	*0.26*	*R-squred*	*0.34*	*0.24*	*0.26*	*0.24*	*0.44*	*0.32*

Note: Constant term not shown in the table. Figures in italics below the coefficients are robust t-statistics.

Table 3A.3 Summary Statistics for the Group of All Countries

Dependent Variable: Relative share	Obs	Mean	S.D.	Min	Max	India	China
Industry, 1981	84	32.66	13.15	6.74	70.89	25.12	46.11
Industry, 2001	110	30.72	11.78	4.23	78.65	25.08	45.15
Industry, 2011	80	32.47	13.12	8.34	76.63	26.73	46.59
Manufacturing, 1981	69	15.08	8.19	0.96	38.32	16.25	38.32
Manufacturing, 2001	110	14.73	7.05	1.57	34.12	14.64	31.64
Manufacturing, 2011	76	13.23	7.48	0.94	36.56	14.39	32.46
Services, 1981	85	46.89	11.21	22.01	68.51	40.81	22.01
Services, 2001	110	51.60	14.02	13.30	80.74	51.99	40.46
Services, 2011	80	50.97	12.95	19.99	85.93	55.72	43.37
Independent Variable							
ln(y), 1981	87	7.73	1.24	5.46	11.06	6.18	5.66
ln(y), 1981	110	8.34	1.32	5.48	11.03	7.40	7.87
ln(y), 1981	107	8.79	1.30	5.97	11.37	8.21	9.03
ln(pop), 1981	119	15.97	1.80	9.42	20.72	20.39	20.72
ln(pop), 1981	120	16.35	1.75	9.87	20.96	20.78	20.96
ln(pop), 1981	120	16.51	1.76	9.93	21.02	20.92	21.02

Source: www.data.worldbank.org.

Abbreviations: Obs = observations.

Notes

1. Material services under the MPS refer to such services as are incorporated in material goods at the point of their use. These are basically trade, transport and financial services used by industry up to the final delivery of its output to the user.
2. For wholesale trade, the threshold is enterprises employing 20 or more workers or having annual sales of at least 20 million yuan. For retail trade, it is 60 or more workers or annual sales of 5 million yuan (Xu, 2009: 453).
3. The abbreviation LDCs is often used to mean 'least developed countries'. We, however, stick to the traditional use of the abbreviation in the broader sense of 'less developed countries'. We have used LDC interchangeably with 'developing countries'.
4. In 2007–08, while still the most important source of central government's indirect tax revenue, excise duty declined to account for somewhat less than half, and service tax close to a fifth of total collections. Customs duty accounted for the rest (GOI, 2014).
5. In the absence of VAT the distinction collapses. On the contrary, when VAT or GST is the all-important form of tax, the distinction between basic and producer's prices

collapses. In that case GDP = Aggregate gross value added at basic prices plus all taxes (less subsidy) on products (UN, 2009: 104).

6. See UN (2009: 102).
7. For simplicity, as already explained, without any quantitative or qualitative significance for our present analysis, henceforth we ignore the difference between factor cost and basic price, as also between producer's price, purchaser's price and market price.
8. It is to be noted that though indirect tax is deducted from prices in factor cost accounting, the intermediate-input cost actually includes indirect taxes. This cost to the producer is separately shown in the row for NIT.
9. Also non-deductible VAT has to be added, but we have assumed it out of analysis.
10. This is true of the period covered in the study. The relative importance of excise duty has declined in India very recently as other forms of taxation are being implemented.
11. An important point to note here is that this approximation cannot be applied to disaggregated manufacturing sectors as neither intermediate input intensity nor tax incidence on intermediate inputs is uniform.
12. Here we refer to GDP rather loosely. As we have pointed out, for factor cost estimates the shares are in what is referred to as GDP at factor cost, but for the IOTT estimates the denominator is the corresponding aggregate value added (ΣW_j).
13. It is here that explanation is to be found for equality in relative shares of industry in Bangladesh and India despite much lower level of industrialization in the former country. Bangladesh, as also China, expresses its accounts at market prices while India expresses it at factor cost.
14. Means of absolute differences, all the differences being positive, in the two cases are 2.7 and 3.2 respectively.
15. We do not aim at a comprehensive study of influences on the relative shares (Chenery and Taylor, 1968; Chenery and Syrquin, 1975). Our objective here is to take a broad view of the Indian position after correcting for non-comparability.
16. For given per-capita income, population stands as a proxy for market size.
17. We may note that for all of these countries data on sectoral shares are not available for all the points concerned. Summary data are shown in the appendix, Table 3A.3.
18. The indicator also changes dramatically. Interestingly, it shows India to be an emphatic positive outlier all through but with a very bad fit.

4

Sectoral Growth

GVA–Output Dichotomy

> I only took the regular course … different branches of Arithmetic – Ambition, Distraction, Uglification and Derision.
>
> —'The Mock Turtle's Story', in *Alice's Adventures in Wonderland* (Carroll, c. 1930)

Introduction

Sustained and rapid growth of GDP with a steadily declining share of agriculture and a stagnant share of manufacturing inevitably draws one's attention to the service sector. Our discussion in Chapter 3 has shown that given the state of development of the Indian economy in 1981, the performance of the service sector, when judged by gross value added (GVA), was quite below the average by the yardstick of the global development experience. However, the sector subsequently performed well so that in the course of the next two decades it surpassed the K-CT norm[1] by far to become an outlier, and thereafter further strengthened its position as a super-performer in 2011. Just the reverse is true of the industry sector by the same yardstick. The manufacturing sector, which is supposed to be the mainstay of industry, did not show a spur; the rising trend of the past decades of its relative share flattened out after the turn of the 1970s. By the global standard, the sector's performance judged by GVA was far below the norm insomuch as it qualified as an underperforming outlier in 2001 and almost so in 2011. This has been the case in spite of all product market reforms, discussed earlier, aimed at boosting the sector. Since manufacturing ability is a reflection of the stock of productive knowledge amassed by a country, the apparent stagnancy in manufacturing has caused some dismay and serious reflection. In this backdrop, the rapid growth of the economy has been judged to have been made possible by the impressive growth of the service sector; the observation is statistically incontrovertible.

But what were the services that grew and what were the more dynamic components of the sector? A fundamental question is about the relevance of gross value added (GVA) as a measure of the level of activity in a sector. Value added is a monetary measure and it has a lot to do with the movement of relative prices, which may be caused by either the demand side or the supply side. In this context, keeping in view even the problems of measurement of volume of service output, one may ask if the trend in domestic output gives the same picture as that in GVA. The same question is relevant about expenditure on domestic final products originating from different sectors. The import of the questions posed above is a need to tackle the scepticism about the GVA as a reliable measure of the level of activity of a sector.

In the following discussion we first look at the picture of sectoral GVA growth and trend of shares in GDP. Service-I is found to grow leaving manufacturing far behind. In this context, the next section takes up the issue of interrelationship between gross output, value added and prices while the subsequent section focuses on the growth of sectoral gross outputs. The discourse then delves into the nature of goods and services and raises some relevant questions regarding the measure of sectoral productivity. The section also takes a broad view of income elasticity of demand for goods and services in light of the findings of the UN International Comparison Project. The last section summarizes the discussion of the chapter.

Growth of Sectoral GVA

For a comparative picture of the underlying real economy, the growth rates must be based on constant price estimates. Our earlier discussion on deflation of estimates for intertemporal comparisons (Chapter 2) suggests that the appropriate deflator for GVA for all the sectors has to be the common GDP deflator, which should be the ratio between the estimates of aggregate final expenditure at current and constant prices. But comprehensive sectoral break-ups from the expenditure side are available only in the IOTTs at, more or less, quinquennial intervals. So, we do not have the above deflators (where expenditure, not value added, is deflated by the relevant price deflator) for all the years. For an annual real GVA series, therefore, we have adopted the second best alternative given by the CSO constant price estimates, which have been arrived at by different ad hoc methodologies.[2]

Figure 4.1 shows average growth rates (of GVA at 2004–05 prices) of the major sectors other than agriculture for more than three decades since the turn of the 1970s. Since we intend to take a long view, not focus on year-to-year fluctuations, we have taken the 5-year moving average. The figure clearly shows the trend line for Service-I, which comprises trade, transport, communications and 'banking and finance', to be above manufacturing and industry lines all along, barring a short phase in the mid-1990s when the growth rate of manufacturing shot up temporarily from a very low level. This fact is reflected in the relentless rise in the share of Service-I in GDP over the whole period (Figure 4.2), starting low but going beyond all other sectors towards the end of the 1990s. During the 1980s, Service-II, which includes dwelling and business services apart from 'community, social and personal services', grew neck to neck with Service-I only to fall behind afterwards. Growth of industry as well as manufacturing also accelerated along with the GDP during the decade, with industry's curve remaining above manufacturing's for most of the time due to the rapid growth of construction. Thus, industry raised its share during the decade though manufacturing could not.

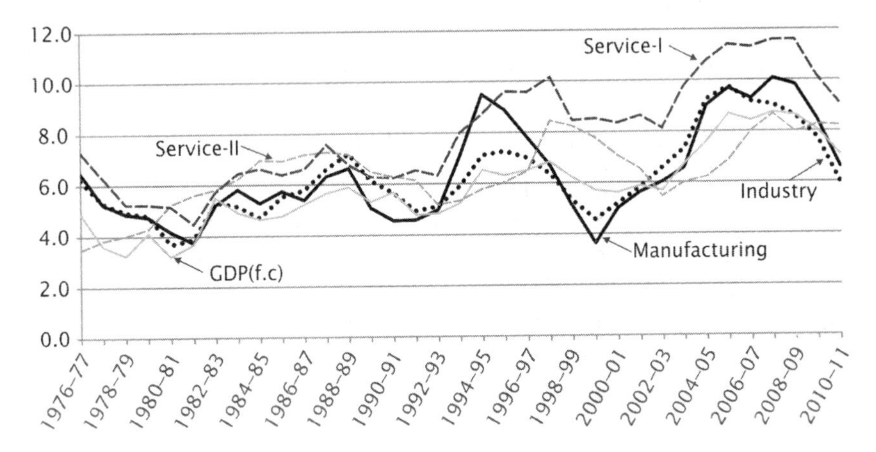

Figure 4.1 Five-Year Moving Average Growth Rates of GVA

Source: www.mospi.nic.in/data, sectoral shares at 2003–04 prices.

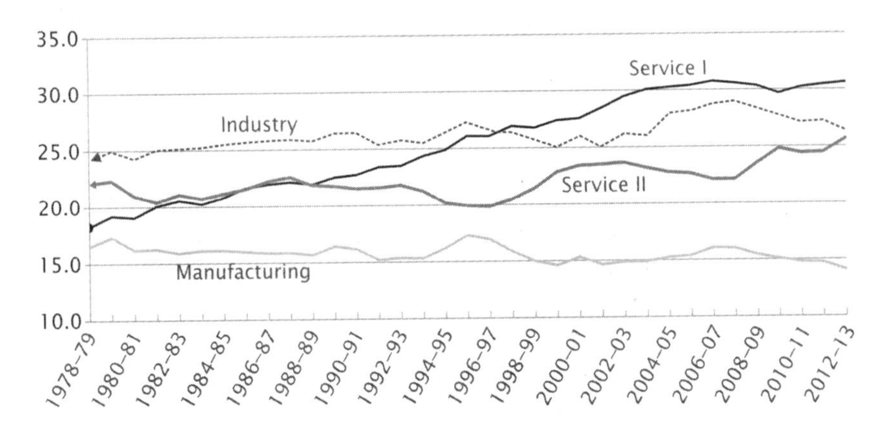

Figure 4.2 Sectoral Shares in GDP at Factor Cost, Current Prices

Source: Figure 2.5 is reproduced here after deleting the line for Agriculture for the convenience of comparison.

During the 1990s, growth rates of all the sectors fluctuated much more than they did during the previous decade and this is clearly visible from 5-year moving averages too. It is also clear that fluctuations have been the greatest for the manufacturing sector and the least for Service-I. Agriculture declined to the same extent as in the previous decade but this time industry could not capture any part of it. It happened in spite of a great spurt in manufacturing's growth in the early 1990s; that shows the churn the sector went through after reform. In the latter part of the 1990s, the sector's growth rate dropped and shot up again early in the next decade. Decline in growth rate was experienced by all the sectors, more or less, towards the end of the 1990s; again the least affected sector was Service-I. During this decade the growth trend of Service-II was much below that of Service-I, barring a jump in 1996–97 caused by the implementation of the pay commission award.[3]

Table 4.1 GDP-Shares of Major Sectors and Sub-sectors; Current Prices, Percentages

Sector	1980–81	1985–86	1990–91	1995–96	2000–01	2005–06	2010–11	2012–13
Agriculture, etc.	35.4	30.9	29.0	26.3	23.0	18.8	18.2	17.5
Manufacturing	16.2	16.0	16.2	17.3	15.3	15.4	14.8	14.1
Industry	24.3	25.7	26.5	27.4	26.0	28.1	27.2	26.2
Trade, hotels, etc.	11.6	12.9	12.7	13.9	14.5	16.7	17.3	17.2
Transport &Communication	4.4	5.4	6.1	6.8	7.6	8.2	7.3	7.5
Communication	0.6	0.6	0.9	1.4	1.5	1.6	1.1	1.1
Banking & Insurance	3.0	3.4	3.9	5.4	5.4	5.4	5.7	5.9
Service I	*19.1*	*21.6*	*22.7*	*26.1*	*27.6*	*30.4*	*30.2*	*30.6*
Dwellings, Business Services etc.	8.2	8.5	8.4	7.4	8.7	9.1	10.4	11.4
CSPS	12.8	13.0	13.2	12.5	14.7	13.5	14.0	14.3
PAD	5.1	5.6	5.9	5.4	6.5	5.6	6.1	6.0
Service II	*21.0*	*21.5*	*21.5*	*19.9*	*23.4*	*22.7*	*24.4*	*25.7*

Source: www.mospi.nic.in/data.

Note: Sectoral shares do not add up to 100 due to rounding-up error. CSPS = community, social and personal. services. Its major components are education, health and PAD (EHPAD).

The major story for the first decade of the new millennium is that manufacturing's growth rate picked up from a couple of points below that of the GDP at the start and went past the rising GDP growth rate by mid-decade. Industry's curve neither dipped as much as manufacturing's nor did it rise as much. However, at current prices, manufacturing could not make up for the loss of GDP share in the previous decade. Service-I again remained above all other sectors. An important development of the new decade is the coming to prominence of composite business services.[4] It is mainly based on these services that the growth of Service-II picked up after falling quite a bit; nevertheless, the sector's growth trend remained below that of GDP, which also picked up.

To conclude the above discussion of GVA growth trends, we first note that Service-I is apparently the leading sector of the Indian economy. Its growth curve has remained above those of industry and manufacturing over most of the three decades since 1978–79 (the year will be a point of reference in the next two chapters for the additional convenience of having an IOTT for the year). The same cannot be said of Service-II. In terms of sectoral shares in GDP expressed as percentage points, agriculture has lost 17 points over three decades since 1980–81 (Table 4.1). Service-I has gained 11 of these points and the rest have been equally shared by industry and Service-II. Manufacturing actually lost two points! But demand for Service-I is derived from the demand for goods, basically manufactured goods.[5] Then how come Service-I consistently grew so much faster than manufacturing? Particularly, distributive trade accounts for more than half of GVA in Service-I, and demand for this service is entirely derived demand, mostly from manufacturing. Claiming that trade is the engine of growth for manufacturing is putting the cart before the horse.[6] Does valuation of output have something to do with the overriding growth of Service-I? With this doubt in mind we will examine the relationship between output, value added and prices of the different sectors.

Output–Value Added Symbiosis

Output is an elementary concept of economics, but contrary to common perception the concept is involved enough to bear a careful consideration. The ultimate purpose of production is to make goods and services available for use outside the production process. Thus, for a production unit the purpose of production is to make the results (output) available for use (or sale) outside the unit. The gross output (or, simply output, interchangeably) of the electricity generating sector is what flows out of the sectoral production process for use outside the sector; this amount excludes the generated electricity used up by the sector itself for running the machinery and lighting up the plants concerned. In this simple example with only one product (let us say) gross output may be viewed in physical units as there is no need to add up heterogeneous quantities. But, for broad sectors with more than one product we need to resort to measures in value terms. Clearly, the gross output of a broad sector, say manufacturing, viewed as a group of subsectors (say, leather goods, metals, transport equipment, chemicals, and so on), is not just the sum total of outputs of the sub-sectors in value terms, as output of the broader sector must exclude intra-sectoral intermediate uses of products of sub-sectors.[7]

> It is not difficult to see that the inclusion of intra-industry flows of intermediate products adds identically to both the input and output side of an industry production function.... This is a form of double counting and in principle, output and intermediate inputs can be made larger and larger by basing industry aggregates on increasingly smaller statistical units.... (OECD, 2001: 31)

The import of the above discussion is that the manufacturing sector's output is goods made available for final use (like consumption, investment or export) and also for intermediate use outside the sector. This is what the sectoral production process generates, using inputs from other sectors, for use outside the sector; we will take this definition of output throughout the discourse in this book.[8] Sectoral 'net output' or GVA (meaning that depreciation of fixed capital has not been accounted for) is its (gross) output less intermediate inputs taken from outside the sector.[9] At the sectoral level, it is often a maintained assumption, particularly when we do not look beyond a few years, that intermediate input of a process is proportional to its output, that is, the intermediate input coefficients are stable. A subtle assumption here is that relative prices are stable. On this basis GVA has been used as a proxy for output in productivity studies. This line of thought suggests that GVA and output should follow the same trend, which implies the trend of GVA in the manufacturing sector, say, should reflect the trend of output of the sector. But things often do not turn up so conveniently; GVA and gross output may diverge in trend. In that case ambiguity arises about which of the two variables would better represent growth of the sector? Let us look at the matter a little further in detail.

The Importance of Relative Price for Relative Shares of GVA

For simplicity, let us conceive of a simple production setup with only M (manufacturing) and S (services) sectors. We may write the production functions as:

$$Y_M = F_M(f_M, S_M) \quad \text{... (11)}$$

$$Y_S = F_S(f_S, M_S) \quad \text{... (12)}$$

Here subscripts are used to denote sectors, Y stands for output, F represents production function and f stands for primary factor of production, M and S with relevant subscripts stand for intermediate input uses. Thus S_M is service input in the manufacturing process.

An important point to note here is that a production function is a relationship among real variables. So, we take all the variables in (1) and (2) as real quantities.

However, value added is a monetary quantity expressed at current prices. So, writing V for GVA and following the definition:

$$V_M = P_M Y_M - P_S S_M = (P_M - P_S \mu)\, Y_M \quad \text{... (13)}$$

$$V_S = P_S Y_S - P_M M_S = (P_S - P_M \lambda)\, Y_S \quad \text{... (14)}$$

where, μ and λ are factors of proportionality between output and the relevant intermediate input.

Clearly, $(V_M / V_S) = [(P_M - P_S \mu) / (P_S - P_M \lambda)](Y_M / Y_S)$ ... (15)

Assuming μ and λ to be constant, it is clear from (5) that depending on the trend in relative prices the trend in relative value added may deviate from that in relative real output. Particularly, if relative price of manufactures falls consistently, value added in manufactures relative to that in the services sector will go on declining even if outputs of the two sectors remain unchanged. Clearly, it is a real possibility that systematic price movements would whittle away value added from a sector (and add that up to another sector) making relative sectoral GVA an improper proxy for the relative size (level of activity) of the sector in real terms.[10] A more general representation of the production setup could include agriculture and divide the tertiary sector into groups – Service-I and Service-II. But the simplified setup does not constrain us here. Equation (5) shows the relative price as the essential issue involved in obtaining a transformation factor from relative real output to relative value added and thus shows the limitations of conclusions regarding relative sectoral growth based on GVA calculus. We will discuss later and in the next chapter how systematic price movement may be generated.

Trends in Output Growth

Since (gross) output of a sector is what comes out of the sectoral production process to cater to final demand as well as intermediate input demand from other sectors, output of manufacturing is aggregate final demand for manufactures plus intermediate consumption demand coming from non-manufacturing sectors net of imports of manufactures. The IOTTs provide the relevant information, only they need to be aggregated and deflated appropriately to convert to a constant price base. The methodology for obtaining the price indices has been given in the appendix to the next chapter.

Table 4.2 presents output estimates at constant prices for the Indian economy. The table and also Figure 4.3 show growth trends of outputs of manufactures and Service-I as almost convergent.[11] The convergence of output trends stands in sharp contrast to GVA trends that diverge, as we have seen from growth rates and relative shares (Figure 4.1, Figure 4.2 and Table 4.1). In fact, most of the components of Service-I are very closely connected with M-sector production, so much so that it is sometimes difficult to segregate them from the M-sector's process.[12] This is the basic logic why they used to be called material services in the MPS of erstwhile socialist countries. Very close growth paths of manufactures and Service-I are reflected in their exponential trends. The best-fit log-linear curves to the output data give the growth factors (base of the discrete time exponent) as shown at the bottom of Table 4.2. Even for the period of fastest growth of services (1993–94 to 2007–08), due to the 'service revolution' ushered in by IT-enabled services, the growth of output of manufacturing did not lag behind very much; but during the next quinquennium manufacturing's growth surpassed that of services. The findings are contrary to the widespread perception of stagnation of the sector in general, and the puzzle of an unresponsive manufacturing sector to the comprehensive product market reforms of the early 1990s in particular (Gupta, Hasan and Kumar, 2009; Srinivasan, 2009).

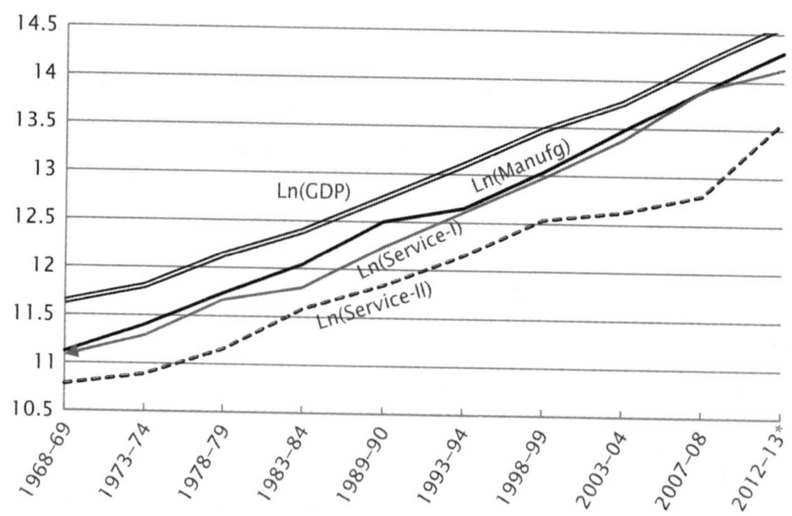

Figure 4.3 Natural Logarithm of Output

Source: Table 4.2.

It is interesting as an aside that the index of industrial production (IIP), which includes mining and electricity but gives about 80 per cent weight to manufacturing and lacks in coverage for reasons including non-response of producing units, is found to be remarkably consistent with the above manufacturing output trend. After conversion to 1993–94 base, the indices become as shown in Table 4.3. Back of the envelope calculations show the closeness of trends.

Table 4.2 Gross Output of Selected Sectors and GDP at Factor Cost

(INR Crores, at 1993–94 Prices)

	Manufactures	Serv-I	Serv-II	Serv-I + Serv-II	GDP
1978–79	124,951	116,667	69,843	186,510	399,855
1983–84	170,519	133,533	106,964	240,497	489,296
1989–90	268,970	205,995	137,990	343,985	651,032
1993–94	311,571	298,378	189,965	488,343	830,557
1998–99	459,254	433,052	278,779	711,831	1,114,885
2003–04	715,174	647,226	304,509	951,735	1,436,499
20007–08	1,088,581	1,094,589	364,729	1,459,318	2,083,810
2012–13*	1,629,212	1,372,026	789,541*	2,161,567	2,958,506
Growth factors obtained from best-fit log-linear function					
1978–1999	1.067	1.071	1.069	1.070	1.053
1978–2008	1.075	1.081	1.059	1.073	1.058
1978–2013	1.078	1.081	1.066	1.076	1.061
1993–2008	1.093	1.095	1.045	1.079	1.066
1993–2013	1.093	1.084	1.063	1.077	1.069

Source: Computed by author from the IOTTs already cited.

Note: Output excludes intra-sectoral intermediate input uses.

*Estimates for 2012–13, based on SUT, are not fully comparable with those of the previous years, which are obtained from (commodity x commodity) IOTTs.

Table 4.3 Index of Industrial Production

Year	1983–84	1989–90	1993–94	1998–99	2003–04	2007–08	2012–13
IIP	52	86	100	149	197	338	412

Source: RBI (2017–18: 68).

Service-II provides a contrast with a growth rate about two percentage points slower than that of Service-I since 1978–79.[13] An interesting point to note here is that India's 'service revolution' was in full force since the mid-1990s with fast growth of information technology related services, as already mentioned. These services are mostly classified with business services and included in Service-II. Two points need to be noted here. First, the rapid growth phase of these services needs to be viewed in the context of the very low base from which it spurted so that even after fast growth for a decade and a half, 'computer related services' accounted for just more than three per cent of GDP (at constant prices) in 2007–08 (GOI, 2010:

15,161). Second, this phase of fast growth only compensated for the stagnation, or even decline (though not in nominal terms), of EHPAD since the mid-1990s. As a result Service-II, as a whole, managed to grow at just about the same pace as GDP (Table 4.2) did over the three decades since 1978–79.[14]

To sum up, the most notable finding is the contrast between growth rates of GVA and output of the manufacturing sector. Output growth appears to be equal to that of the fastest growing sub-sector, that is, Service-I, while GVA growth is slower than that of GDP as is evident from the trend of relative share of the sector (Table 4.1). This is an apparent paradox of the Indian economy, as per national accounts, since the turn of the 1970s and this point will keep us engaged in the next two chapters. At this stage let us delve into the nature of goods and services that we are dealing with.

Nature of Goods and Services

What we have been measuring are values. Goods are tangible and so are a bit easier to deal with by national accounts statisticians, compared to intangible services. Consider the famous quotation from Bernard Shaw (1928):

> When a village carpenter makes a gate to keep cattle out of a field of wheat, he has something solid in his hand which he can claim for his own until the farmer pays him for it. But when a village boy makes a noise to keep the birds off he has nothing to shew, though the noise is just as necessary as the gate.

A service is the result of some useful application of labour that does not produce a tangible result. On a positive note the labour works on, or brings some transformation or satisfaction for, the recipient who pays for the service (Hill, 1977). There has to be a market intent: a payment, be it a compensation to the agent by a principal (payment to a lawyer or a broker) or for direct purchase of a commodity (payment for a software or for trade service). A session with a physician (even though it may not help sometimes), attending a class in a school (even though the benefit may depend on the student and in this way the recipient herself is an active participant), movement of goods from workshop to home (rendering trade and transport services), deployment of security personnel (irrespective of whether the service is actual or perceived), and so on, are examples of generation of service. The important point is involvement of an institutional unit to bring about a result that has a market, otherwise we do not have an economic service as distinct from a natural process (UN, 2009: 96).

Obviously, the scope of services is very wide and, moreover, the distinguishing line can often be fuzzy. Thus, while an automobile assembly plant is a manufacturing establishment, an automated modern automobile repair shop is a service establishment. Janitorial service generated within a manufacturing firm by its own management is counted with manufacturing, but when rendered by a different company contracted in by the manufacturer it is not manufacturing. So, splintering of the activity away from manufacturing affects the value added pie of the manufacturing sector. Examples can be multiplied. Thus a hair-splitting judgement of the nature of a service activity is often not practical. A less nuanced but practical approach may be to consider services to be a residual category (tertiary) of activities not viewed as material production as in agriculture, mining, manufacturing, construction or utilities.

The problem for the statistician interested in real flows is to distinguish between price and quantity, taking into account quality. Measurement of quality in goods may be as problematic as that in service; it does not help much discussing the degree of difference. For a perfectionist the constant appearance of a bewildering variety of new products with real and perceived quality differences and disappearance of old ones may pose a maddening statistical challenge. This is true of services as well as goods. But services are intangible and fleeting – visibly more difficult to grasp and challenging to measure. For durables like cars, computers and mobile phones we know the number of units being purchased but wonder about the precise quality index. But for many services it is not clear what should be measured or even how much is being charged to the customer for what service. Think of the service a customer gets from her bank, or of the service that the government's economic adviser renders.

Griliches (1992: 6) notes:

> Many of the service industries produce intermediate products in areas with very little direct price coverage, such as computer programming, advertising, and information.... Because of this lack of data, a number of service industries series are deflated by makeshift deflators, and real output is assumed to grow proportionally to some measure of input and to lead to no observed productivity growth by assumption. The latter is true for the whole government sector, the contribution of various nonprofit organizations, such as universities, and such difficult-to-measure sectors as banking and business services.

These problems cannot be avoided and we have discussed in the appendix to the next chapter how we tackled our problem in this context.

With the progress of information technology, collection of data has improved but even that is not sufficient for the economist's problem because of the nature of the question raised. For example, consider the problem of productivity measurement. The economist does not bother about the scientific technology until it is reflected in output or use of inputs. Several technologies have not seen the light of day because the market did not accept them even though the researchers' services in generating knowledge is demanded, for which they got their salary that was counted as a part of GDP. The economist measures technological improvement in terms of inputs used and output obtained, and most situations in the case of hard-to-measure services cannot be easily framed in terms of these requirements. The researcher has to look for appropriate proxies for important variables. More specific discussion on the subject will take us beyond our present objective. However, the present discussion will remain deficient unless we go back to the significance of our observation of the incongruity between GVA and output of the manufacturing sector in the context of productivity studies.

The incongruity shows that even in the case of a closely observed and widely studied sector, concepts can be tricky. Researchers on productivity growth in Indian manufacturing often treat the GVA of the sector as the measure of the output variable of the production function and go on measuring productivity against the use of factor inputs. But when there is a systematic drift of GVA away from gross output, as we have seen plausible, this approach is bound to give a systematically biased result (see Chapter 6). On the contrary, if gross output measure is adopted as the appropriate output variable then care needs to be taken in measuring it after exclusion of intra-industry intermediate inputs and inclusion of other intermediate inputs as an argument in the underlying production function (OECD, 2001). This invariably requires information from IOTTs and proper deflation of different sectoral products. For the Indian economy, as we know, IOTTs are available only at about quinquennial intervals, thus limiting the number of observations. Great ingenuity is required to overcome this problem even when keeping in mind that 'ingenuity cannot fully or effectively compensate for lack of basic information'.[15] The results of Indian productivity studies[16] should be viewed in this context.

Demand for Goods and Services

Goods and services produced in any period are used either as intermediate inputs in the production process or for the satisfaction of final demand. A sector producing a large volume of output may cater only to input demand but that demand must be motivated by some ultimate final demand as nothing is produced for its own sake. Thus the structure of final demand has a crucial importance in the study of the structure of production. However, as value addition takes place in production and production need not directly cater to final demand, structure of final demand need not correspond to structure of value added. A prominent example is the mining sector whose output is scarcely reflected in final demand (unless, as exports). However, because of the nature of commodities some broad correspondences can be traced. Keeping this correspondence in view we have divided the service sector into Service-I and Service-II. Demand for Service-I is basically derived from demand for something else. Distributive trade is the best example; it is not used for its own sake. The same is true to a very large extent for transport and finance (see Chapter 7). So, it is appropriate to look at this category of services as mainly intermediate services. In the same way Service-II, comprising education, health, public administration and defence (EHPAD), dwelling and business services, is mainly final service.[17] And, by the nature of things, these services take very little intermediate inputs. Thus, practically, the total supply of Service-II has a close correspondence with total demand for its final uses and its value added.

Manufacturing, on the other hand, takes inputs from all sectors like agriculture, mining, Service-I and, most prominently, itself. So, final demand for manufactures affects all these sectors. Demand for Service-I comes from, apart from manufactures, agriculture, mining and construction too. It is, therefore, not difficult to visualize that final demand for manufactures, comprising consumption, investment and export demands, influences not only the size of the manufacturing sector but also that of Service-I.

What sort of demand should a country face in the early phase? Hoffman (1960) gives an apt description:

> … it must increase its production and consumption – that is, its workers must produce more food, clothing, shelter, and the other necessities and amenities of life. This means greater output per worker on the farm and in the factory. It means adding mechanical horse power to muscle power. This requires new techniques and increased investment.

Emphasis is mainly on the firm and the factory. For a large country in terms of total population, it is easier to reach a minimum threshold to reap the benefits of economy of scale. Given the above interrelations it is fairly understandable why manufacturing's GVA-share should increase at least in the initial phases of development. Again, since services are basically non-tradable, their demand has to be met mainly domestically. Manufacturing's interrelations with Service-I should explain why it should not lag much behind; and Service-II, being constituted of vital services like EHPAD, cannot remain suppressed as per-capita income grows. This is what happened in India until the turn of the 1970s. The question before us is, why does the service sector grow much faster leaving manufacturing far behind in India since the early 1980s?

Let us consider a common answer: it comes in terms of income elasticity for services, which is taken as greater than unity. It is not a very convincing answer as Engel's law quite allows the elasticity for manufactures to be greater than unity too at the same time. Expansion of the frontier for white goods has ensured that there is always scope for expenditure on luxury goods (Cohen, 2003). In fact, there is no clear evidence that income elasticity of demand is consistently, or even on the average, higher for services than for commodities. On the contrary, a path-breaking study (Kravis, Heston and Summers, 1978; Heston and Summers, 1992) on international comparison of real demand for services with respect to real income concludes the existence of a flat relationship between the real final service share in GDP and GDP per capita.[18] Analyses were done for three benchmark years – 1970, 1975 and 1980. Heston and Summers (1992) mention strikingly consistent findings among these studies:

> ... when the relative price of services is taken into account, there is virtually no change, or a small decline, in the share of services in GDP as GDP per capita goes up; and there is a consistent but small rise in the consumption service share as consumption per capita goes up. One is tempted to conclude from this that, contrary to Wagner's Law and much-received doctrine on the increasing role of government, the real share of government declines slightly with income....[19]

Kravis, Heston and Summers (1978) have explained their findings in the light of rising nominal share of services in GDP in terms of the productivity differential model.

> As a first approximation it may be assumed for purposes of explaining the model that the prices of traded goods (mainly commodities) are the same in different countries. With similar prices for traded goods in all countries, wages in the industries producing traded goods will differ from country to country according to differences in productivity – a standard conclusion of Ricardian trade theory. In each country the wage level established in the traded-goods industries will determine wages in the industries producing non-traded goods (mainly services). Because international productivity differences are smaller for such industries, the low wages established in poor countries in the low-productivity traded-goods industries will apply also to the not-so-low-productivity service and-other-non-traded-goods industries. The consequences will be low prices in low-income countries for services and other non-traded goods.[20]

The authors conclude:

> Across countries, productivity is, of course, lower in poor countries relative to rich countries in both services and commodity-producing sectors, but it is lower by a larger margin in commodities. (The possibility that these differences may reflect mainly superior remuneration of the factors of production in service industries

> is rejected.) … When it comes to cost reduction for existing products or services technological change is more frequent and more powerful in its effects in the commodity sector.

That causes a systematic pattern of rising relative price of services vis-à-vis commodities. Though the International Comparisons of Real Product and Purchasing Power (ICP) project focused on final services the productivity differential logic may extend to intermediate services too. So, while their demand is tagged to demand for manufactures and other commodities, their costs and value added rise faster as for final services. A parallel explanation based on differential technological progress but not explicitly on trade theory, is given by Baumol's Cost Disease discussed in the next chapter.

Summary and Conclusion

The Service-I sector has been a consistent top performer in terms of GVA growth since the turn of the 1970s. Service-II matched this performance in the 1980s; then the sector fell far below, showing a short spurt only in the late 1990s. During the 1980s, manufacturing's GVA-growth trend was below that of the services, but not by far. During the early 1990s, manufacturing picked up pace but let off steam over the second half, with the GVA-growth rate of Service-I remaining several notches higher. During the next decade, manufacturing's GVA-growth again shot up but remained considerably below that of Service-I all through. Considering that demand for Service-I is mostly derived from demand for goods, basically manufactured goods, how come Service-I consistently grew so much faster than manufacturing? Did movement of relative price play a role here?

Sectoral GVA has been used as a proxy for sectoral gross output in much of economic analyses and productivity studies. But GVA and gross output may systematically diverge in trend. In that case ambiguity arises about the appropriate variable to describe the growth of the sector. Our estimates using IOTTs show the growth rates of output of the manufacturing sector to be at par with that of Service-I; this trend runs counter to the GVA growth trend as reflected in the trend of manufacturing sector's GDP shares. This is a paradox of the Indian economy, which assumes significance in the context of the widespread perception that the sector did not respond to the sweeping reforms of the 1990s. Output growth trends for manufacturing as well as Service-I, indeed, got a boost post reform.

From international comparison projects, there is strong evidence that in poor countries productivity is lower in both commodity and services production compared to rich countries, but the gap is larger in commodities. Trade theoretic arguments translate this phenomenon for intertemporal comparison as well.

Technological change is more frequent and powerful in the commodity sector leading to rising relative cost for services over time, as a country moves from poverty to affluence; that would cause costs and value added for the service sector to rise faster. The next two chapters will explore this possibility for the Indian economy.

Notes

1. Refers to the Kuznets-Chenery and Taylor norm discussed in Chapter 3.
2. We have discussed constant price estimates in some detail in Chapter 2.
3. Rakshit (2007) has made this point.
4. Receipts on account of miscellaneous invisibles, representing exports of software, business services, financial and telecommunication services went up as percentage of GDP from 1.7 in 1998–99 to 4.5 in 2008–09 and then declined to 3.5 during 2010–13. The peak growth rates, around 35 per cent per annum, of these services were achieved during 2003–06 (RBI, 2018: 184). This remarkable achievement has been hailed as the service revolution (World Bank, 2004). It is to be noted that financial and communications services, for which we do not have separate estimates, belong to Service-I.
5. This point has been dealt with in detail in Chapter 7.
6. This point has been treated in detail in Chapter 7.
7. This norm of output measurement is different from that of arriving at 'total output' in IOTTs which is essentially a row or column sum.
8. This point is often not carefully tackled in productivity analyses based on output production functions. We will have occasion to comment on this point further as we proceed.
9. At the level of the economy as a whole, the net output is the GDP or the sum of final uses (expenditures) like consumption, investment and exports out of domestic production less imported intermediate inputs.
10. It may be noted here that obtaining real GVA is not a solution in practical situations. A 1 per cent change in price may change GVA by several percentage points depending on the importance of intermediate inputs and their price changes. Further, as the CSO has warned, double deflation procedure may result in negative value added for a vibrant industry. For a detailed discussion see Chapter 2.
11. Output estimates for the two sectors happen to be very close but this point is not important for our present consideration. It may be noted that we can obtain output estimates only from the IOTTs after taking into account intra-industry transactions; so, we present data only for the years for which the IOTTs are available.
12. Trade service is very often a subsidiary product of a manufacturing process. This is reflected in the Supply Table (2012–13) published by the CSO.
13. Fitting an exponential curve to the output path of Service-II is not very enlightening; we did it just to get a proximate compound annual growth rate imposed on the data.
14. The other very rapidly growing service since the turn of the1980s is 'communications' which is classified with Service-I in the present study.

15. Kuznets (1941: 111), quoted by Griliches (1992).
16. There are several studies. Kathuria, Rajesh Raj and Sen (2014) provide a collection. The book also includes a study of the literature by Goldar (2015). Also see Datta (2014).
17. 'Business services' is included in this category only because the relevant data used to be merged with dwellings though they are recently being provided separately. But we do not have a reasonably long time series.
18. The 1980 project undertook the Herculean task of standardizing qualities and prices of services in sixty countries and obtaining PPP income levels. With all the inevitable inadequacies of data, the relation obtained from for 1980 is: Real service share = 0.397 – 0.003 GDP per capita (in thousands) with standards errors (0.014) and (0.002) respectively.
19. Datta (2001) provides a detailed study of Wagner's Law in the context of the Indian economy.
20. A general equilibrium formulation of the explanation has been given by Bhagwati (1984a).

5

Manufacturing Sector in the Indian Economy

Paradox of Growth and Stagnation*

... to do development theory, one must have the courage to be silly, writing down models that are implausible in the details in order to arrive at convincing higher-level insights.

—Krugman (1998: 15)

Introduction

Stories abound about how India treated its private enterprise before the comprehensive reform was launched in 1991. Entrepreneurs, who were pioneers in their own fields, used to get the feeling that they were being treated as greedy pursuers of monetary gains; they had to run from pillar to post wasting time, energy and money, to get sanctions for crucial business matters. The public sector emerged to provide a good foundation of basic and heavy industries, but in this process, the animal spirit of the private entrepreneurs was caged in a network of license and permit legislations. Inadequacies of the public sector became increasingly evident as time wore on and presumably the first real step to break out of the public sector mindset was allowing the entry of Suzuki Motors in India in 1983, in an eloquent declaration of intent to let the caged animal spirits fly.

Development under successive Five Year Plans over the past decades was, however, quite significant though below potential. By the turn of the 1970s, the industrial sector achieved some depth by developing the basic and heavy industries, as is evident from their being comfortably placed by international comparison of sectoral weights (Chapter 3). The Green Revolution of the 1970s reduced the extent

* This chapter draws heavily on Datta (2019a).

of agriculture's dependence on weather and resolved the problem of recurrent food crises. The service sector was not very dominant at this stage; rather, it was an underperformer by the K-CT norm, as already discussed. During the 1980s, the GDP growth shifted to a higher trajectory and the private sector started showing animation with signs of change in government attitude. The three-year averages of gross fixed capital formation (GFCF) as a percentage of GDP were similar for the public and private sectors during 1977–80 (a little below 9 per cent); but just before the reform, during the three years to 1991, the private sector investment surpassed that of the public sector by almost two percentage points (12.3 versus 10.5). The situation before the reform has been aptly summarized by Rakshit (2009: 64):

> The financial repression, the inward looking trade strategy, exclusion of private enterprises from the major spheres of economic activity and the long shadow of the 'licence-permit-quota raj', all, it is generally emphasized, tended to create gross distortions, promoted rent seeking at the expense of productive economic endeavour, and severely eroded the country's export competitiveness. A reflection of this loss of competitive edge in the world market was the steep fall in India's share in global trade, from 1.0 percent in the early 1950s to 0.5 percent in 1990.

The cool draughts of incremental change of the 1980s developed into a big storm that hit the land in 1991. The reform and its subsequent pursuit, replacing dirigisme by market mechanism – in domestic production, banking and finance as well as international trade – corrected market distortions very substantially, bringing new challenge to domestic producers accustomed to regulations. It meant that the hitherto largely protected industries encountered growing competition. The manufacturing sector was suddenly exposed to intense competition from domestic and international rivals and the resulting heightened quality consciousness. Surviving under competition required dynamism and flexibility.[1] Under the circumstances, as one would expect, a great churning got underway. By 2016 almost two-thirds of the top-50 companies of 1991, by market capitalization, were pushed off the elite list to make way for companies that were either non-existent or unlisted in 1990.[2] The balance of average GFCF as a percentage of GDP got skewed to stand at 7.1 for the public sector against 26.0 for the private sector during 2010–13.

Did Indian entrepreneurs respond adequately to the initial halting moves of liberalization in the early 1980s? To hear from someone closely invested in the process, Baba Kalyani (2017) of Bharat Forge:

> With the entry of Suzuki Motor Company … indigenous components manufacturers for the first time were exposed to Japanese manufacturing processes and practices. This resulted in improved productivity.… Indian components manufacturers did not lag behind and started manufacturing products that were, in some cases, even

> superior to the imported ones.... More importantly, the belief that we could develop and manufacture our own products without overwhelming reliance on imports began to gather momentum.

(Also see Bajaj, 2010; Tata, 2010; Banik and Bhaumik, 2010.) Then, with the big blow of 1991, the economy experienced mind-boggling developments. There are several anecdotes of creative destruction unleashed by the liberalization of 1991 (Gopalakrishnan, 2017).

In spite of the churn, there seems to be a sort of consensus that though the reform targeted basically the manufacturing sector (henceforth, M-sector) the growth of the Indian economy since then has been led by the service sector (henceforth services or S-sector). This opinion (Panagariya, 2004) is fundamentally based on the fact that the trend of the share of the M-sector in aggregate value added (GDP at factor cost) has not moved upwards since 1979–80 even as the economy charted a much higher growth path over the next three and a half decades.[3] The relative share of agriculture rapidly declined with the S-sector basically filling up the space thus vacated. One of the major explanations given in the literature for the super-performance of services comes from the rapid export-led growth of information technology enabled services (ITES), in which respect India's revealed comparative advantage[4] soared (World Bank, 2004; Rakshit 2007) for a decade since the mid-1990s. The ITES story, however, gives only a partial explanation as the apparent stagnation of the M-sector stretches back to the 1980s during which decade, Indian economic growth picked up and the 'service revolution' was only in the making, not yet the news (Basant, 2008). The primary objective of the present chapter is to resolve this riddle.

The nature of the present study demands extensive use of the input–output transactions tables (IOTTs) for the Indian economy. IOTTs are available mostly at quinquennial intervals, starting from 1968–69 up to 2007–08, and then supply and use tables have been published for 2012–13. The tables are published by the Central Statistics Office (CSO) of India, which makes utmost lot of effort to attain compatibility of the tables with the National Accounts Statistics (NAS) of India. So, we have data on detailed inter-industry transactions at ten points from 1968–69. It is well known that conversion from current to constant prices involves many challenges and these are particularly tricky for services (Griliches, 1992; Hill, 1977). Nevertheless, following the system of national accounts (SNA), the CSO tries to make sense by carefully getting the best out of a bad job. The base year of constant price estimates provided in NAS shifts periodically. So we had to convert them to a common base year, 1993–94, by splicing as it is normally done. We have used the ratio of current and constant price sectoral GDP (instead of the net domestic product [NDP], as the CSO uses in its suggested implicit price indices) as the corresponding sectoral price indices (justification is given in Appendix 5A.3) for deflation of the IOTTs aggregated to nine sectors.[5] It is only for public administrative services that we have modified the CSO constant price estimates, as discussed in Appendix 5A.3. In spite of all the statistical discrepancies and worries regarding the quality of data, our premise is that the observed trends reveal important information. Our analysis of data reveals a general decline in relative price of manufactures vis-à-vis the GDP deflator causing slippage of value added from manufactures; and that is the catch.

In the following discussion, we first examine the trend of GVA share of the manufacturing sector and then look at the sector's growth both from the supply and the demand sides. That the relative cost of production may systematically go in favour of services and against manufacturing, is the subject matter of our discussion in the next section. This discussion is the key to our understanding of the paradox of growth and stagnation in the M-sector in India. Then, in the subsequent section we proceed to show that the relative price of manufactures (vis-à-vis the GDP deflator) actually declined almost steadily and quite significantly since the late 1970s over the next three and a half decades, which means that value added over the period underestimates the trend of real output. Just the opposite seems to be true of some services like education, health, public administration and defence (EHPAD). Finally, we take up the issue of the low sectoral share to point to the unique and restrictive path that India has taken when viewed in the context of rapid growth of the East Asian countries and China. The last section concludes the chapter.

The GVA Trend in Manufacturing

M-sector's share in aggregate value added was rising till the turn of the 1970s, crossing 17 per cent in 1979–80, but then it moved ambivalently around a band of 15–16 per cent. The relative share reached the previous peak level just once after almost two decades in 1995–96, but then again declined to move around the band. However, the relative share of Service-I went up relentlessly (Figure 5.1). In popular perception M-sector's stagnant share in GDP at factor cost is taken to indicate that it has failed to maintain its drive. A popular perception is that income elasticity of demand for final-use services is greater than unity, which causes its rapid growth. But we have argued in the last chapter that there is no persuasive evidence that the same elasticity for final-product manufactures is less than unity or even less than that for the services, particularly at an early stage of development. Notably, the services that have grown rapidly in India are basically intermediate-use services like distributive trade, transport and finance (Service-I). [6] Growth of final-use services, basically Service-II, has been relatively muted (Figure 5.1).

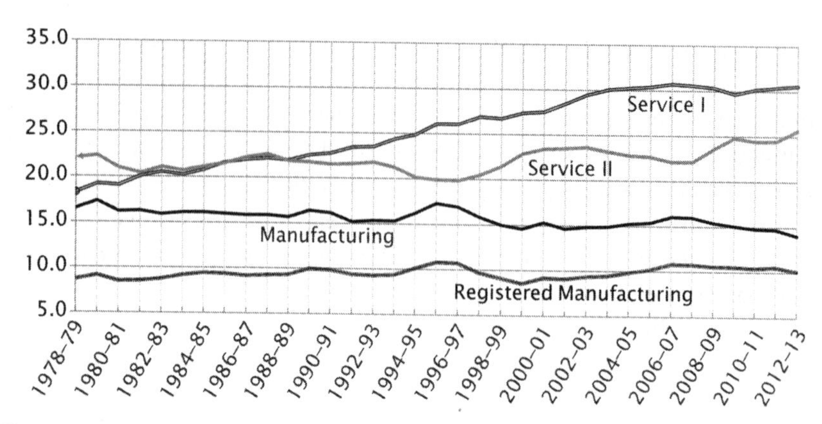

Figure 5.1 Sectoral Shares in GDP at Factor Cost

Source: GOI, www.mospi.nic.in.data, GDP by Economic Activity, sectoral shares at current prices, accessed in October 2018.

We have already referred to the anecdotal evidence that the M-sector responded with enthusiasm to the incentives provided by the economic liberalization. In fact, a careful look at the trend shows that the share of registered manufacturing within the manufacturing sector had been mildly upward in the 1980s, and then this trend abated but did not turn negative; the unregistered segment has declined.[7] Did the segment fail to cope with the technical progress of the registered segment? Restrictive labour laws did not apply to this segment, and yet the sector could not flourish.

The picture of relative sectoral growth is quite different when viewed from another angle. As we have discussed earlier, gross output (henceforth, we use simply 'output' interchangeably with 'gross output', unless the context demands otherwise) of overall manufacturing has grown in tandem with that of Service-I and these two have been the fastest growing sectors (Table 4.2). Viewed in this light, these sectors together responded positively to the reforms of the early 1990s. The contrarian behavior of output (vis-à-vis GVA) of the manufacturing sector (but not that of Service-I) has remained a gray area, which we try to shed light on here.

The Supply Side Scenario

Investment in Manufacturing

Table 5.1 shows that GFCF in the M-sector as a proportion of GDP more than doubled over roughly the four decades since the mid-1970s when the sector's share in aggregate value added did not rise at all. Over the same period the trend of capital to gross output (obtained from IOTTs) ratio[8] of manufacturing remained almost flat (Figure 5.1). More specifically, let us focus on the two decades of the 1980s and the 1990s. Compared to the second half of the 1970s, GFCF to GDP ratio was considerably higher during the period and, quite significantly, capital formation in manufacturing as a proportion of economy-wide capital formation (GFCF[M]/GFCF) increased during the 1980s[9] before taking a big jump in the second half of the 1990s (Table 5.1). This led to more than doubling of capital formation in manufacturing as a ratio to gross value added in the sector (GFCF[M]/GVA[M]). If GVA(M) is taken as an indicator of output of the sector, given the fact that capital-output ratio (the denominator being gross output, not value added) remained constant, the growth rate of output of manufactures would have doubled by the

Table 5.1 Mean* Quinquennial GFCF Ratio and GDP Growth

	1975–80	1980–85	1985–90	1990–95	1995–2000	2000–05	2005–10	2010–13
GFCF/GDP	18.1	18.9	21.8	23.5	25.1	26.4	35.8	35.5
GFCF(M)/GFCF	26.5	29.7	29.8	31.6	39.4	27	29.2	24.9
GFCF(M)/GDP	4.80	5.61	6.50	7.43	9.89	7.13	10.45	8.84
GFCF(M)/GVA(M)	29.6	37.6	44.2	49.6	63.5	48.6	64.6	56.4
Average Annual GDP Growth Rate	4.9#	5.5	5.7	4.8	6.8	5.8	8.7	6.7

Source: GOI (2011, 2014).

Notes: *Geometric mean of yearly numbers. # Refers to period 1974–75 to 1978–99.

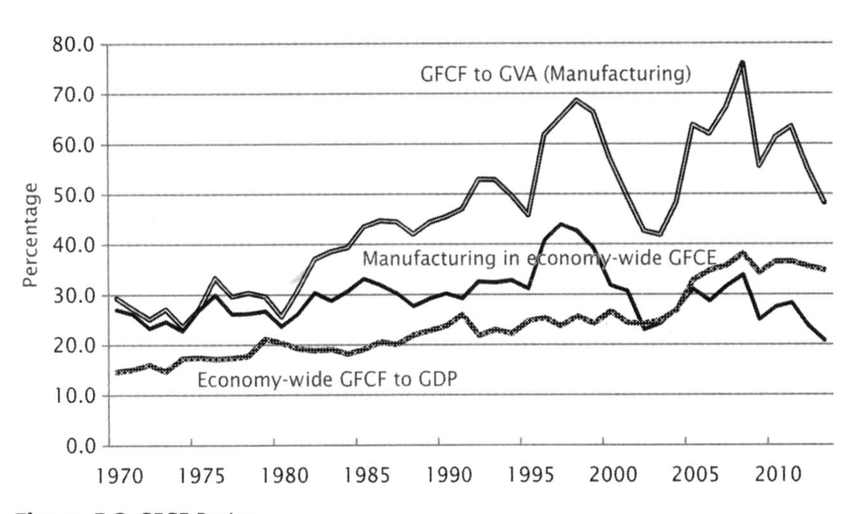

Figure 5.2 GFCF Ratios

Source: GOI (2011, 2014).

end of the 1990s compared to that in the late 1970s. But actually GVA(M) grew by the same order of magnitude as the GDP which grew at 6.8 per cent during the second half of the 1990s as compared to 4.9 per cent two decades earlier. Thus, it seems, there is some missing growth of value added in the manufacturing sector.[10] It seems, the explanation for the stagnancy of M-sector's value added share should be sought in the divergence between output and value added.[11] This is the hypothesis we will seek to establish in the subsequent discussion.

Trends in Sectoral Output

The question that arises from the above discourse is: what should we take as the suitable indicator of growth for the manufacturing sector – is it the growth in value added or that in output? Output of a sector, as we have discussed earlier, is what comes out of the production process to cater to final demand and intermediate input demand from other sectors.[12] Thus output of the M-sector is aggregate final demand for manufactures plus intermediate consumption demand coming from non-manufacturing sectors met out of domestic production. The IOTTs provide the relevant information.

Table 5.2 presents output growth estimates for manufactures and services. The interesting observation is the close compound growth rates for manufactures and services, which belies the widespread perception of stagnation of manufacturing (relative to GDP) since the turn of the 1970s. Output of the M-sector grew 1.4

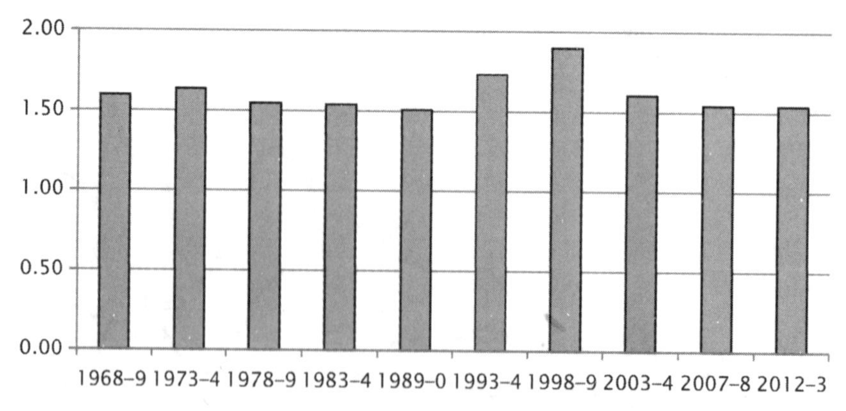

Figure 5.3 Capital to Gross Output Ratio in Manufacturing

Source: Computed by author based on the relevant IOTTs and GOI (2011).

Note: In measures of capital–output ratio one normally takes value added as a measure of output in the denominator. We have taken gross output, which excludes the sector's own intermediate inputs produced within the sector. The computation is based on IOTTs published by the CSO.

Table 5.2 Growth Factors# for Outputs of Selected Sectors and GDP at Factor Cost

	Manufactures	Service-I	Service-II	Service-I+II	GDP
1978 to 1999	1.067	1.071	1.069	1.070	1.053
1978 to 2008	1.075	1.081	1.059	1.073	1.058
1978 to 2013	1.078	1.081	1.066	1.076	1.061
1993 to 2008	1.093	1.095	1.045	1.079	1.066
1993 to 2013*	1.093	1.084	1.063	1.077	1.069

Source: Table 4.2.

Note: Output excludes intra-sectoral intermediate input uses.

*Estimates for 2012–13, based on Supply and Use Table (SUT), are not fully comparable with those of the previous years.

#Base of the exponent in discrete time compound growth function.

percentage points faster than GDP during the two decades since the turn of the 1970s and the difference is even larger if the horizon is pushed forward. Particularly, if we look at the period just after the comprehensive reform, the difference becomes around 2.5 percentage points. Clearly, if value added had grown in proportion with output, M-sector's relative share would have increased significantly. To be more specific, with the rates of growth obtained during the period 1979 to 2008 (Table 5.2), manufacturing's relative share would have increased from 16 to 25 per cent. This observation supports our basic hypothesis, to be explained below, of dissociation between output and value added in the sector.

An interesting point to note here is that India's service revolution was in full force since the mid-1990s with fast growth of information technology related services. These services are classified here with business services and included in Service-II. Two points need to be noted in this context. First, the rapid growth of these services needs to be viewed in the context of the very low base from which it spurted so that even after unprecedented growth for a decade and a half, 'computer related services' accounted for a little more than 3 per cent of GDP (at constant prices) in 2007–08 (GOI, 2010: 15, 161). Second, this fast growth only compensated for the stagnation, or even relative decline (though not in nominal terms), of EHPAD since the mid-1990s. As a result, Service-II (mostly final-product services) as a whole managed to grow just a tad faster than GDP over roughly three and a half decades since 1978–79. The other very rapidly growing service since the mid-1990s is 'communications' which is classified with Service-I in the present study.

Let us take a view from another angle. Growth of income and inequality in its distribution in a poor economy leads to rapid decline in the share of agriculture in both private final consumption expenditure (PFCE) and aggregate final expenditure. This may well leave room for growth of shares of both manufactures and services in aggregate expenditures. Ultimately the economy's (net) output is its GDP which is equivalent to the aggregate final uses (demand) net of imports. Comparing in real terms, total final demand for manufactures expressed as a proportion of GDP at constant prices, increased no less than that for the more dynamic part of services – Service-I – over the whole period concerned; the lead of manufactures over Service-I did only marginally narrow down (Figure 5.5; Table 5A.1) in the mid-2000s, when India's service revolution was in full swing and one would expect services to take the lead. How should we explain this phenomenon in the light of stagnation of manufacturing's GVA-share in GDP?[13] This apparent paradox of the *steady growth of manufacturing's share in aggregate final demand along with stagnation in the sector's GVA-share conceals an important development of the Indian economy.*

Further, Figure 5.4 shows that Service-I and manufactures have grown hand in hand so far as their shares in PFCE are concerned. The share of Service-II shows a decline in both PFCE and aggregate final uses after 1993–94, *reconciling with the conclusion that in terms of relative share in aggregate expenditure manufactures increased by no means less than services taken as a whole* (Table A5.1). The finding goes perfectly with the absence of any clear evidence that income elasticity of demand is consistently (or even on the average) higher for final-product services than for final-product commodities (Heston and Summers, 1992).

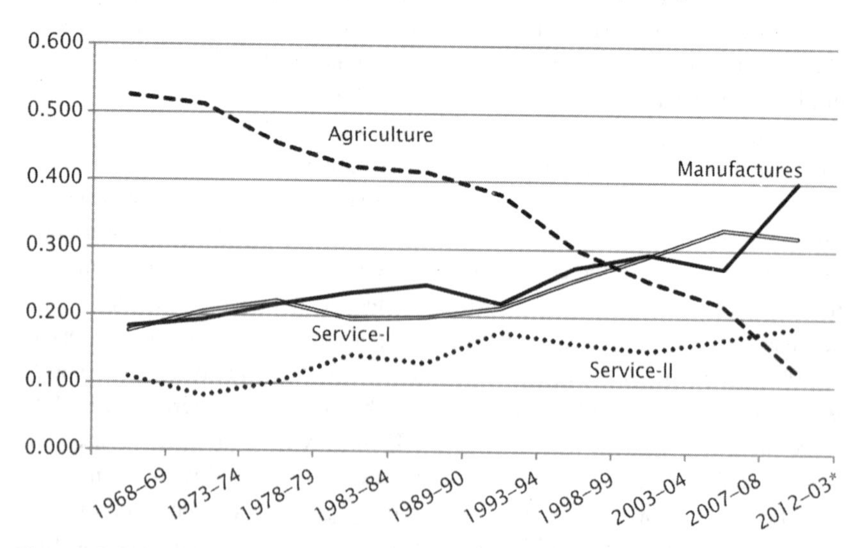

Figure 5.4 Sectoral Shares in Aggregate PFCE at 1993–94 Prices

Source: IOTTs for the respective years, deflated to 1993–94 base.

Note: Methodology is given in Appendix 5A.3. Estimates for Service-I and Service-II for 2012–13 are not strictly comparable with those for previous years due to reclassification; the totals for services, however, are comparable.

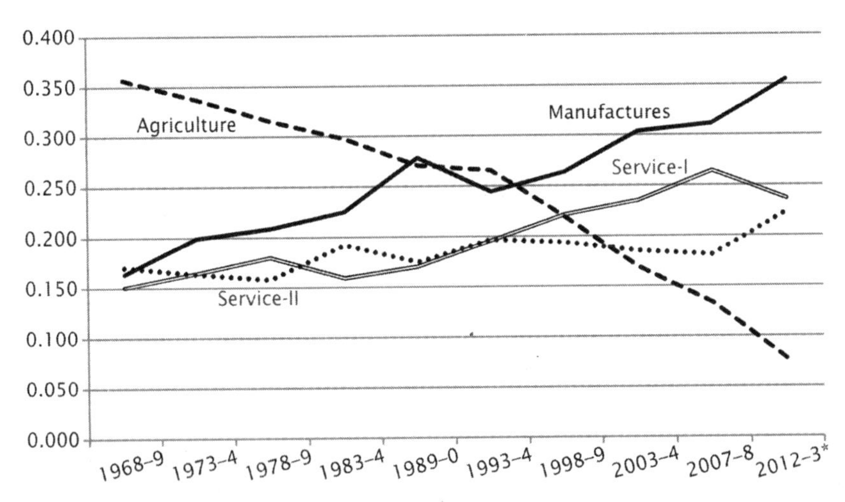

Figure 5.5 Sectoral Shares in Aggregate Final Use at 1993–94 Prices

Source: IOTTs for the respective years, deflated to 1993–94 base.

Note: Methodology is given in Appendix 5A.3. Estimates for Service-I and Service-II for 2012–13 are not strictly comparable with those for previous years due to reclassification; the totals for services, however, are comparable.

A Model of Missing Growth of Value Added in Manufacturing

Manufacturing has traditionally been the most fertile ground for adoption of new technologies while the flip side of the picture, perhaps, is provided by certain services (like performing arts, teaching, medical care and public administration) that are by nature akin to the labour of the service provider. While reality is not a static bundle of rules and revolutionary changes in technology in several fields have changed the nature of many activities, several studies have attested to the validity of the basic notion of differential productivity changes favouring the manufacturing sector generally (Nordhaus, 2006; Fagerberg, 2000). William Baumol (1967) presented a very simple construct using the assumption that economic activities can be classified into basically two types: one is technologically progressive in that it experiences more or less sustained productivity increases[14] while the other type is technologically stagnant in the sense that productivity increases are relatively small and sporadic (the model was extended and empirically tested later in Baumol, Blackman and Wolff, 1985). Here we make a simple restatement of Baumol's original model using the input–output (I-O) structure to easily fit into our analysis (Baumol's original model is introduced in Box 5.1). Our objective is to understand how uneven labour saving technologial progress leads to divergent trends in relative prices, suppressing the growth of value added in the progressive sector.

Box 5.1 Baumol's Unbalanced Growth Model

The model was motivated by an insight that certain activities, be they essentials like education and health services or life's luxuries like a live concert or theater performance, that are essentially service of labour, are not amenable to frequent or substantive productivity improvements as we find happening in other cases, typically in the manufacturing sector, where innovation, capital accumulation and economy of scale relentlessly raise the productivity of labour. Though Baumol does not mean that all the activities can be neatly classified between the two extremes of stagnant and progressive activities, and is conscious that different activities fall between these black and white categories in all shades of grey, the extreme two-way classification helps to develop the insight of differential productivity improvements and their implication.

The rudimentary model with a powerful message has an absolutely stagnant and a progressive sector represented by the following production functions:

$$Y_{1t} = aL_{1t} \quad \text{... (i)}$$

and

$$Y_{2t} = bL_{2t}e^{rt} \quad \text{... (ii)}$$

where, Y represents output and L labour, the numbers 1 and 2 represent sectors, a and b are constants, t stands for time.

The model abstracts from the use of capital for simplicity, and toward the same goal it assumes wage (w) equalization though what is required is that wages move more or less the same way across sectors.

Obviously, unit cost (C) in the two sectors will work out in terms of the common wage rate.

$$C_{1t} = (wL_{1t}) / Y_{1t} = wL_{1t} / aL_{1t} = w/a \quad \text{... (iii)}$$

and

$$C_{2t} = (wL_{2t}) / Y_{2t} = wL_{2t} / bL_{2t}e^{rt} = w/ be^{rt} \quad \text{... (iv)}$$

Clearly, at any time, the relative price of sector-1's output in terms of that of sector-2 is:

$C_{1t}/C_{2t} = be^{rt}/a$, which goes up cumulatively over time. This is Baumol's proposition-1.

Moving one step further, if we take prices in the two sectors as proportional to respective unit costs, then relative price of the stagnant sector's output in terms of that of the progressive sector rises relentlessly. Baumol has derived three other propositions but those are not directly relevant for our purpose. We have sought to build on proposition-1 in our restatement of Baumol's model.

Source: Published in *American Economic Review* in 1967. Development of Baumol's thought on the subject is captured in two other papers written jointly with other authors (see References) in the same journal, one earlier in 1965 and the other in 1985.

Let there be two sectors: M and S. Manufacturing being traditionally viewed as the foremost example of the progressive sector, we denote the progressive sector by M; and certain services, as mentioned above, being the prime examples of comparatively stagnant activities, we denote the stagnant sector by S. We denote x_{ij} = intermediate use of the ith commodity in the jth sector, and X_i = output of the ith sector (i, j = 1 and 2 respectively for M and S), this norm is maintained all through the present discussion. Also, we denote l_i = labour used in, and f_i = final demand for, the ith sector. The I-O structure is:

	M	S	Final Demand	Output
M	x_{11}	x_{12}	f_1	X_1
S	x_{21}	x_{22}	f_2	X_2
Labour	l_1	l_2		

I-O flows are real flows per production cycle defining the underlying technology. In practice, the observations are conveniently recorded as money values. At any point of time, we may take advantage of defining units of measurement to do away with the distinction between physical quantities and money values. Accordingly, we choose units of measurement suitably to set prices of both the commodities to unity; so we may treat the observed values as real quantities. The assumption here is that technology is characterized by fixed coefficients: $a_{ij} = x_{ij}/X_j$. We use the following notations using brackets for matrices, braces for vectors and superscript 'T' to denote transpose:

$$x = [x_{ij}];\ A = [a_{ij}];\ X^T = \{X_1, X_2\};\ F^T = \{f_1, f_2\};\ L^T = \{l_1, l_2\}$$

Thus, for given A, $X = (I - A)^{-1}F$,

$(I - A)^{-1}$ being the Leontief-inverse matrix with a typical element, α_{ij}, representing the total (direct and indirect) requirement of the ith commodity for production to satisfy one unit of final demand of the jth commodity.

All the elements in the vectors and matrices must be non-negative in order to be economically meaningful. While A, F and L are given; conditions for obtaining $X \geq 0$ are the well-known Hawkins-Simon conditions:

$$(1-a_{ii}) > 0,\ i = 1, 2;\ \text{and}\ \det(I - A) > 0. \quad \ldots (1)$$

Looking at the uses of products, we have the following relations among inputs, outputs and final demands:

$$X_1 - x_{11} - x_{12} = f_1,\ \text{and}\ X_2 - x_{21} - x_{22} = f_2 \quad \ldots (2)$$

We assume initially that there is a single (primary) factor of production, labour, and no fixed cost; so, in a competitive setup, price equals average (and marginal) variable cost. An assumption[15] of the model is that *the wage rate is equal across sectors*[16]. Then the price equations are:

$$(p_1)x_{11} + (p_2)x_{21} + wl_1 = (p_1)X_1, \text{ and } (p_1)x_{12} + (p_2)x_{22} + wl_2 = (p_2)X_2 \quad \text{... (3a)}$$

We put the prices in parentheses to highlight the relations among quantities, which are also values in the beginning, as prices are set to unity. In this economy, since labour is the only factor of production, $l_1, l_2 > 0$, it follows from (2) and (3a), putting $p_1 = p_2 = 1$, that aggregate wage payment equals aggregate final uses ($f_1 + f_2$), which is equal to the GDP of the economy. Thus, the real wage rate can be found from the accounting identity:

$$\text{GDP} = f_1 + f_2 \equiv w\,(l_1 + l_2) \quad \text{... (4)}$$

More generally, $(p_1)f_1 + (p_2)f_2 \equiv w\,(l_1 + l_2)$ ... (4a)

Using vector-matrix notations we can write (3a) as:

$$P^T x + wL^T = P^T Z \quad \text{... (3b)}$$

where, $P^T = \{p_1, p_2\}$ and Z *is diagonalized 2x2 matrix form of* X. Further, let us write the labour coefficients as $\lambda_i = l_i/X_i$, so that, $L^T = \lambda^T Z$, *for* $\lambda^T = \{\lambda_1, \lambda_2\}$.

Clearly, (3b) gives[17]:

$$P^T = wL^T(Z - x)^{-1} = w\,\lambda^T(I - A)^{-1} \quad \text{... (5)}$$

Writing in full form[18]:

$$p_1/p_2 = (\lambda_1(1 - a_{22}) + \lambda_2 a_{21}) \,/\, (\lambda_1 a_{12} + \lambda_2(1 - a_{11})) \quad \text{... (6)}$$

Now, so long as λ_i*'s* are independent of a_{ij}*'s,* we have:

$$\delta(p_1/p_2)/\delta\,\lambda_1 = \lambda_2\,[(1 - a_{11})\,(1 - a_{22}) - a_{12}a_{21})] \,/\, [(\lambda_1 a_{12} + \lambda_2(1 - a_{11}))]^2 \quad \text{... (7)}$$

Similarly,

$$\delta(p_1/p_2)/\delta\,\lambda_2 = \lambda_1[a_{12}a_{21} - (1 - a_{11})\,(1 - a_{22})] \,/\, [(\lambda_1 a_{12} + \lambda_2(1 - a_{11}))]^2 \quad \text{... (8)}$$

Using the two Hawkins-Simon conditions on (7) and (8), we have $\delta(p_1/p_2)/\delta\,\lambda_1 > 0$; and $\delta(p_1/p_2)/\delta\,\lambda_2 < 0$. So, *if labour saving technical progress takes place in the technologically progressive M-sector without affecting* a_{ij}*'s (which are fixed by assumption here); so, the labour coefficient in the M-sector* (λ_1) *is now reduced, leaving that for the S-sector unchanged, the relative price of the M-commodity will decline and vice versa.*

Clearly, from (3a), labour saving technical progress reduces the cost of production in the M-sector by reducing l_1 for unchanged F. Under competitive conditions the benefit of cost reduction is fully passed on to the users through lower price[19]. Intuitively it is clear that, so long as the same final demand vector is being produced, the real GDP remains unchanged, now being produced using less labour due to productivity increase in the M-sector. By assumption, real wage rises uniformly (equation 3) in the two sectors. The result is *relocation of value added through change in relative price in favour of the stagnant sector*[20] *and corresponding change in value added per unit of output, again in favour of the stagnant sector. This leads to a decline in the progressive sector's relative share in GDP even without any change in real output of the two sectors* as the sectoral GDP is proportional to the sectoral employment.

In fact, no assumption of unchanged final demand vector is necessary to show the direction of change in relative price which is independent of final demands (equation 6). In reality, how the structure of final demand changes will depend on several factors affecting the price and income elasticities. The basic point is economizing on the use of resources through productivity improvement, no matter from which source it comes and distribution of the gain across sectors through uniform wages causing adjustment in relative price and sectoral value added. So long as the progressive-stagnant classification remains effective and technical progress goes on reducing the opportunity cost of production of the progressive sector, decline in relative price of the progressive sector, and a corresponding rise in that of the stagnant sector, will go on cumulatively without respite. This message of the model forms the basic notion that has come to be known as the Baumol disease.

The objective here is not to build a comprehensive model of the economy, but to develop a macroeconomic insight even at the cost of precision, as models always do more or less. Working out the equilibrium would inevitably require consideration of the demand side (Echevarria, 1997; Kongshamut, Rebelo and Xie, 2001). Our model is admittedly oversimplified, as was the original Baumol (1967) model; only, we have introduced intermediate inputs and thus used the input–output framework simply to show that cost in the progressive sector reduces even though the cost of its intermediate inputs from the stagnant sector rises. Regarding this progressive-stagnant classification of the entire economy Baumol, Blackman and Wolff (1985: 807) clarifies: 'Outputs, firms and industries do not fall into black and white categories of stagnation and progressivity – they are all shades of grey. Even the most stagnant sectors of the economy have undergone some technological change, varying from one period to another.' We deliberately ignore agriculture and other informal sectors, and other shades of gray. Skill requirement in these sectors is generally of a lower order and tendency to wage equalization does not work. With this clarification, our model may be viewed as an instrument to highlight the intuition that so far as benefits of productivity gains tend to get diffused more or less uniformly across the sectors and one sector experiences labour saving technological progress more consistently and intensively than the other, and so long as prices remain tied to cost, the relative price of the progressive sector will fall.[21] The literature on the subject focuses on differential cost and price changes and growth rates while the present discussion focuses on value added adjustment.[22] It is possible to introduce greater generality to the model, without complicating matters much, by introducing cost-plus pricing and still maintain the insight (Appendix 5A.3). This extension would free the model of the apparent labour theory of value format. One implication of this extension would be that productivity gains necessarily do not translate into wage gains.

Labour Productivity: The Evidence

Anecdotes and hard evidence suggest that the manufacturing sector of the Indian economy has gone through a vigorous process of labour saving technical progress over the period concerned. Within a decade after liberalization (roughly, the 1990s) Tata Steel successfully transformed itself by downsizing its workforce by half while the company's output of saleable steel increased by three fourths.[23] The story is not peculiar to Tata Steel. Even public sector companies responded to the challenge to raise efficiency by substantially reducing labour intensity. We take the case of public sector oil refineries; they were being taken out of the administered pricing mechanism at the turn of the century. Average output and workforce over nine years to 1999–2000 and nine years after that are shown in Table 5A.3. Out of the five large companies only in Kochi Refineries Limited (KRL) employment rose in tandem with output. In three companies (Chennai Petroleum Corporation Limited [CPCL], Bharat Petroleum Corporation Limited [BPCL], Indian Oil Corporation [IOC]), while output increased by about 30 per cent, employment remained practically stagnant; in Hindusthan Petroleum Corporation Limited (HPCL) employment declined drastically. At the aggregative level, organized sector employment as measured by Director General of Employment and Training shows a steady decline from 1.94 to 1.80 crores, during 1999 to 2005, in the public sector as a whole. This sort of development has been referred to as jobless growth. Indeed, for the whole of the manufacturing sector (registered and unregistered), employment elasticity with respect to GVA steadily declined during the decades of the 1980s and the 1990s from 0.67 to 0.26; and improved marginally to 0.34 in the next quinquennium (Rangarajan, Kaul and Seema, 2007). It should be noted that this has been so in spite of the widening gap between output and value added, as discussed above.[24] So, definitely, labour productivity has increased considerably in general and phenomenally in particular cases.

Indeed, technological progress cannot be limited to manufacturing alone. With revolution in information and communication technologies the service sector in general must have seen productivity improvement too; and some parts may have experienced spectacular improvement. But the tenor of our argument above suggests that there are other parts that are less amenable to technological change.

On the whole, our argument maintains that the manufacturing sector should show greater productivity improvement compared to services. We have made some gross productivity calculations based on comparable data after carefully distinguishing between value added and gross output. The results (presented in Table 5A.6) confirm that labour productivity growth since 1993–94 in the manufacturing sector far outpaces that in the service sector as a whole. Our employment data are based on usual principal and subsidiary status, which means some workers have worked for varying periods over the year under reference; a more satisfying measure should be based on output per day's work, though estimation is challenging. Ghose (2016) has obtained measures of value added per day's work for the two broad sectors and found the productivity growth with respect to value added to be 4.4 and 5.2 per cent per annum respectively for manufacturing and services from 1999–2000 to 2011–12. We must be very careful in jumping to a conclusion from this result. For a proper measure, those figures must be corrected for decline in value added per unit of gross output in manufacturing. IOTTs are available for the years 1998–99 and 2007–08 (we avoid SUTs for some aspects of non-comparability), which show the ratio to fall from 0.27 to 0.21 for the manufacturing sector; the corresponding change being insignificant for the service sector.[25] Though the years do not tally, to get a rough approximation we apply those ratios for correction to obtain productivity growth for the manufacturing sector to be 6.6 per cent per annum; considerably higher than the corresponding rate for services.[26] This correction highlights the underestimation of productivity estimates for the Indian manufacturing sector in studies that use value added as a proxy for output.

The important question here is: with differential sectoral productivity growth did wage equalization across sectors happen? We do not know of a comprehensive study on the question. However, we can point to some relevant considerations. Government plays a very important role in effecting wage equalization in the organized sector by using central and state pay commissions, Board of Public Enterprises as well as statutory and non-statutory wage boards for the private sector, including one for even working journalists. This mechanism goes on along with competition in the labour market. The guiding principles of all central pay commissions have been: (i) pay should be sufficient to attract and retain high quality staff and it should motivate staff to work hard; (ii) pay levels should be consistent with long term fiscal sustainability (GOI, 2018). The Islington dictum accepted by the government before Independence continues to be the underlying spirit: 'Government should pay so much … as was necessary to obtain recruits of the right stamp and to maintain them in such degree and comfort and dignity as would shield them from temptation and keep them efficient.' In this context, and considering the predominant role of the government in the service sector, it seems the assumption of wage equality across sectors is a reasonable one for the Indian economy.

Declining Relative Price of Manufactures

It follows from our argument in the previous section that while labour saving technical progress is a reality and observers of the Indian economy have talked about jobless growth in organized manufacturing in India, decline in relative price may be caused by factors other than labour saving technical progress, like increasing competitiveness caused by increasing openness of the economy leading to a decline in the mark-up. While this possibility may indeed be relevant for the Indian economy particularly since economic liberalization in 1991, intensive competition must also have encouraged productivity improvement.[27] Thus the narrative of potential cumulative decline in relative price in the progressive sector seems to fit well with observations on the Indian economy.[28]

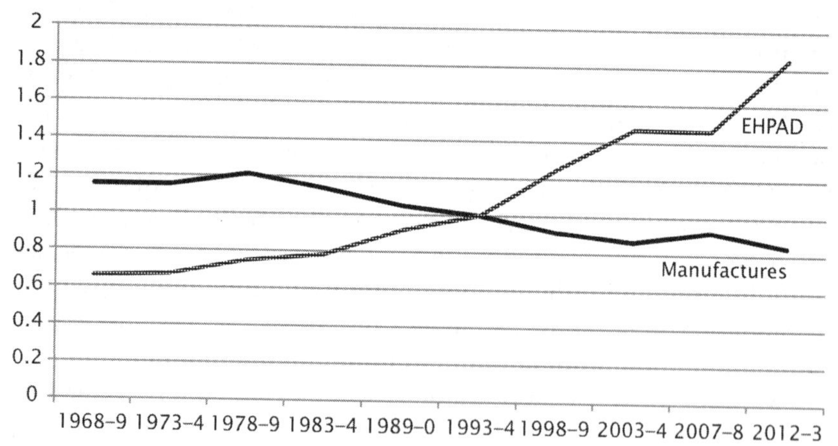

Figure 5.6 Sectoral Price Relative to the GDP Deflator

Source: Table A5.4.

Figure 5.6 (Table 5A.4) shows the trend in price of manufactures relative to the GDP deflator and that of the composite sector 'Education, Health, Public Administration and Defence' (EHPAD) belonging to Service-I during the reference period. The relative price is obtained as ratio between current and constant price relative shares in aggregate final uses. The major story for the Indian economy is systematic decline in relative price in the manufacturing sector and systematic rise in EHPAD. A sector experiencing a significant and sustained fall in relative price will lose in GDP share disproportionately to its output trend and that has really happened to the manufacturing sector of India since the turn of the 1970s. All the findings marshalled above counter the perception of stagnation generated by the flat share of the sector in GDP.

Low Sectoral Share

While we reject the perception of relative stagnation, the low sectoral GDP-share is a fact that remains and does not fit well with the stylized facts of development. Productivity growth-differential, and dissemination of the benefit between manufacturing and services, need not be a unique phenomenon for India; though, of course, there is no presumption that the whole process should apply for all countries the same way. We do not know of studies in this regard for other emerging countries. In this perspective, it is in order that we pause and consider how the Indian manufacturing sector compares with that of other countries.

It should be useful to start with a brief summary of our discussion in Chapter 3. The country that stands most prominently for comparison with India is China. Service activities seem to be inadequately accounted for in Chinese accounts, though they are implicitly merged with the value generated in industry, or the material product sector in general. The country's first economic census took place only in 2005 and it is still some distance from full adoption of the SNA (Xu, 2009); so that the Chinese sectoral shares are not properly comparable to India's or other countries' that traditionally follow the SNA. Further, many countries, including India's two neighbours – China and Bangladesh, provide estimates at producer's (or market) prices while the OECD countries, and also India, provide these estimates at basic prices (or at factor cost). Producer's price estimates differ from factor cost estimates in the treatment of indirect taxes. These taxes affect industry basically and herein lies a source of non-comparability across countries. Careful consideration suggests that manufacturing's share for India should be raised by about three percentage points to make it comparable with those of other countries like China and Bangladesh.[29]

The question is: where does India stand after taking the above points into account? To answer the question, we have run cross-country regressions (with heteroskedasticity robust standard errors) of sectoral shares on (all in logarithm) per-capita GDP, square of the variable, population and a dummy standing for *India-indicator*, apart from a constant term, for three years: 1981, 2001 and 2011. In order to obtain a relatively homogeneous group we exclude tiny countries below the geographical size of 75,000 square kilometers and rich countries of the level of the UK and beyond. Further, we exclude China. That leaves eighty-eight countries in the group as per World Bank data. Table 5.3 reproduces the estimated India-indicators (and corresponding t-statistics) from Table 3.3.[30] It is seen that in 1981 India was a mainstream country, though on the lower side, so far as manufacturing's share is concerned but a super-performer in industry-share and an under-performer in services. In spite of stellar growth performance in terms of gross output (*vide* Table 5.2) over the next two decades, the India-indicators become largely negative for manufacturing but positive for services, both being statistically significant, in 2001. After another decade, manufacturing's underperformance remains substantial though, now, statistically insignificant, because of rise in income. If India's manufacturing did grow rapidly, then in what respect did it dither so as to get deflected from the mainstream of countries? Comparison with specific countries is beyond our scope here; we would attempt only at a broad answer.

Table 5.3 India Indicators in Sectoral Share Regressions

	Manufacturing			Industry			Services		
	1981	2001	2011	1981	2001	2011	1981	2001	2011
Indicator	**-1.24**	**-3.94***	**-3.05**	**6.15****	**-2.58**	**-5.85****	**-2.85**	**5.26****	**6.42****
	-0.40	*-1.96*	*-1.19*	*3.15*	*-1.60*	*-2.95*	*-1.86*	*3.37*	*3.62*

Source: Regression results collected from Table 3.3.

Note: Figures below the coefficients are robust t-statistics. * for 5% and ** for 1% level of significance.

Lewis (1954) viewed capital and natural resources to be the real constraints to development of a labour surplus economy; generation of skill is ensured by the capitalists and their government, perhaps with a lag, as capital formation proceeds. Indian state-capitalists, with their ambitious industrialization dreams, foresaw the lag and provided to preclude it. The government spent huge amounts on tertiary education, even to the neglect of primary and secondary education, from the beginning. Kochar et al. (2006) note that even in 2000, India spent per student in tertiary education substantially more in PPP adjusted dollar than China and even Korea with only two-thirds of China's and less than a tenth of Korea's per-capita (PPP) income. The result was early skill formation that was utilized for the country's development programme. The authors regressed the relative skill intensity of registered manufacturing for eighty countries on their per-capita income, its square, country size and an India-indicator apart from a constant term. The exercise was for the year 1981; the India indicator was substantial, positive and highly significant,[31] Given this experience, Kochar et al. pursued the course taken in this regard by India and a group of comparator countries over the next decade and a half. Strikingly, India's graph shows a somewhat rising trend and lies above those of China or Indonesia all along. The relative skill intensity reached levels achieved by Malaysia or Korea at much higher levels of per-capita income. The authors conclude that unlike the East Asian economies that drew employment from agriculture to manufacturing at a rapid pace, India, with plentiful availability of highly skilled but relatively cheap labour and an import substitution strategy, ventured to invest at an early stage of development in areas that are typically not a poor country's comparative advantage. Has this very unique course given the country some advantage in pursuing its subsequent drive for industrialization?

The pattern of industrialization has been reflected in India's export of skill-intensive goods with manifestation in the Economic Complexity Index (ECI) developed by Hausmann et al. (2013). In a path breaking study the authors seek to measure the amount of knowledge embedded in the production structure of an economy based on information gathered from what countries export. Like any other index ECI has its drawbacks; the principal one being that it considers only merchandise exports ignoring services. This puts India at a disadvantage as service export is its strength. Nevertheless, in terms of ECI in 2010, the country is put in the class of Brazil, Greece, Argentina, Philippines, Botswana and Indonesia; all these countries commanded per-capita PPP gross national income several times that of India. Going a step ahead, the authors have developed Complexity Outlook Index (COI), which puts a value to the 'option to move into more and more complex products, given how far they are from a country's current position in the product space' (Hausmann et al., 2013: 56). In this regard India is right on top, by far (both in 2000 and 2010), which may be taken to mean that the country is most comfortably placed in its class to launch more and more complex products than it currently produces. Stagnation in GDP-share is no dampener in this respect.[32]

The flip side of this skill-based development has been that firm size distribution in India has a 'missing middle'. Among all firms, there is an overwhelming concentration in the size class below 10 workers and a relative rarity in the size class between 50 and 199 workers. This is reflected in the employment distribution (in 2009): about 84 per cent of workers in Indian manufacturing are employed in enterprises with fewer than 50 workers,[33] while a paltry 5.5 per cent are employed in the middle size category. The corresponding figures for China are 25 and 23 per cent. Other East Asian countries fall between the two extremes (Hasan and Jandoc, 2013). The phenomenon of 'missing middle' has been sought to be explained by labour regulations, whether that be the reason per se or seen as a proxy for broader attitude towards industry (Bhattacharya, 2019). The import of the finding is that the middle category of establishments suffered the most from restrictions and attitude towards industry; large firms with sufficient clout survived and even flourished. While reforms encouraged and even boosted these large firms,[34] much has been lost over the past several decades in the form of initiatives and investments in small and medium firms. This lost opportunity, apart from hysteresis, should explain to a great extent the continuation of the missing middle and the low peak of the share of manufacturing in GDP.

Summary and Conclusion

Our findings contradict the widespread impression that the service sector of the Indian economy is a super performer while manufacturing is a laggard. Service-I, the part of services that are closely associated with manufacturing, has grown quite fast since the turn of the 1970s; and this has been the more dynamic part of the overall service sector. In our view the growth of Service-I is mainly a manifestation of the vibrancy of manufacturing. Output (not value added) estimates given by input–output tables show manufacturing's growth matched that of Service-I; and this statement applies equally to expenditure on GDP (in real terms) originating in the two sectors. What really lagged behind is growth of employment in organized manufacturing; and the unorganized segment declined relatively. Capital formation in the sector, as a proportion of aggregate capital formation, progressed at an accelerating pace particularly over the two decades of the 1980s and the 1990s. Even during this period, and later, the trend of manufacturing's GVA share remained stagnant.

The apparent stagnancy of manufacturing conceals the story of growth of output of the sector with slippage of value added away from the sector through decline in relative price. Thus value added is not a reliable indicator of the level of activity in the sector and conventional measures of productivity using value added as a proxy for output systematically underestimate productivity growth. Nevertheless, the point still remains that the sector's low share in GDP marks India as an outlier by international comparison. Was the relative price trend a unique Indian experience? Though we do not have a clear answer, there are, indeed, some unique aspects of Indian industrialization.

From the very beginning, a labour surplus and capital-scarce newly independent India chose the path of skill based planned industrialization while looking at private entrepreneurs askance. The attitude toward private capital and stringent labour laws, that still survive, have created a void in the middle firm-size segment of relatively low-skill large industry, unlike in the counties of East Asia or China. The void reflects lost opportunity and should explain to some extent the low peak in manufacturing's relative share. However, that does not mean growth of manufacturing (output) lagged behind that of services, either quantitatively or qualitatively.

Appendix 5A.1 Tables

Table 5A.1 Sectoral Shares in Aggregate PFCE (1993–94 Prices)

Year	1968–69	1973–74	1978–79	1983–84	1989–99	1993–94	1998–99	2003–04	2007–08	2012–13
Agr	0.526	0.512	0.455	0.421	0.413	0.381	0.301	0.253	0.218	0.121
Manf	0.183	0.194	0.216	0.234	0.246	0.220	0.273	0.294	0.273	0.400
Service-I	0.177	0.205	0.222	0.196	0.199	0.213	0.254	0.292	0.331	0.320
Service-II	0.109	0.082	0.102	0.142	0.131	0.178	0.161	0.151	0.168	0.187
M-S Ratio*	0.642	0.675	0.669	0.692	0.746	0.563	0.657	0.664	0.547	0.789

Sectoral Shares in Aggregate Final Uses (1993–94 Prices)

Year	1968–69	1973–74	1978–79	1983–84	1989–90	1993–94	1998–99	2003–04	2007–08	2012–13
Agr	0.356	0.337	0.315	0.298	0.270	0.265	0.219	0.169	0.133	0.077
Manf	0.163	0.199	0.209	0.225	0.278	0.244	0.263	0.304	0.311	0.355
Service-I	0.150	0.165	0.180	0.159	0.170	0.196	0.221	0.235	0.264	0.236
Service-II	0.170	0.163	0.158	0.192	0.174	0.197	0.193	0.185	0.181	0.224
M-S Ratio*	0.510	0.608	0.618	0.640	0.807	0.623	0.635	0.722	0.815	0.772

Sources: GOI (1978, 1981, 1989, 1990, 1997, 2000, 2005, 2008 and 2016). Also, GOI, http://www.mospi.nic.in/download-reports (accessed February 2018). IOTTs deflated to 1993–94 base by the author; methodology given in Appendix 5A.3. Division of services between service-I and service-II in SUT (2012–13) may not be in full conformity with IOTTs.

Note: *Refers to the ratio of manufacturing's share to the sum of shares of Service-I and Service-II.

Table 5A.2 Intermediate Input Coefficients* in Manufacturing, at 1993–94 Prices

	1978–79	1983–84	1989–90	1993–94	1998–99	2003–04	2007–08
Agriculture	0.145	0.133	0.098	0.091	0.099	0.067	0.074
Manufactures	0.308	0.304	0.332	0.320	0.315	0.340	0.367
Services	0.169	0.155	0.166	0.185	0.173	0.164	0.181
Total Input	0.722	0.684	0.693	0.697	0.683	0.683	0.733

Source: Computed by author from the IOTTs after conversion to constant prices.

Note: *Intermediate input per unit of output.

Table 5A.3 Average Output and Workforce in Public Sector Oil Refineries*

	CPCL	BPCL	HPCL	IOC	KRL
Output: APM REGIME	6,006	7,367	9,540	25,050	6,069
Post-APM REGIME	7,848	9,527	13,533	36,535	7,098
Workforce: APM REGIME	1,149	2,672	3,357	11,065	1,009
Post-APM REGIME	1,172	2,723	2,480	11,215	1,250

Source: Datta and Neogi (2013).

Note: *Nine Year average before and after 1999–2000.

Table 5A.4 Price of Sectoral Final Uses Relative to GDP

	1968–69	1973–74	1978–79	1983–84	1989–90	1993–94	1998–99	2003–04	2007–08	2012–13
Manuf	1.15	1.15	1.21	1.14	1.05	1.00	0.91	0.87	0.92	0.84
EHPAD	0.66	0.67	0.75	0.78	0.92	1.00	1.25	1.47	1.46	1.85

Source: Same as Table 5A.1.

Note: Obtained as the ratio between sectoral shares in aggregate expenditures at current and constant prices.

Table 5A.5 Sectoral Value Added per Unit Output, Major Sectors, at 1993–94 Prices

Year	Agr	Manf	Trnsp	Comn	THR	B I F	EHPAD	Services
1978-9	0.76	**0.43**	0.55	0.78	0.57	1.03	**0.58**	**0.68**
1983-4	0.72	**0.39**	0.45	0.6	0.66	1.03	**0.64**	**0.68**
1989-0	0.68	**0.34**	0.52	0.76	0.67	0.81	**0.80**	**0.69**
1993-4	0.72	**0.30**	0.49	0.84	0.72	0.85	**0.86**	**0.71**
1998-9	0.77	**0.27**	0.49	0.67	0.69	0.71	**0.98**	**0.69**
2003-4	0.65	**0.24**	0.49	0.3	0.7	0.69	**1.31**	**0.73**
2007-8	0.54	**0.21**	0.49	0.2	0.68	0.53	**1.60**	**0.70**

Source: Author's own estimates, based on IOTTs cited earlier.

Note: Output values are obtained from IOTTs after deflation by sectoral price indices. Details of price indices are given in Appendix 5A.3.

Abbreviations: Agr = agriculture, Manf = manufacturing, Trnsp = transport, Comn = communication, THR = trade, hotels and restaurants, BIF = banking, insurance and finance, EHPAD = education, health, public administration and defence, Services = all services.

Table 5A.6 Gross Output, Employment and Labour Productivity

Year	Gross Output Rs. Crores; at 1993–94 Prices		Employment: UPSS '00,000		Labour Productivity (gross output per UPSS worker)	
	Manufacturing	Services	Manufacturing	Services	Manufacturing	Services
1993–94	311,571	488,343	425	737.6	73,311	66,207
1998–99	459,254	711,831	439	910	104,614	78,223
2007–08	1,088,581	1,459,318	524	1,129	207,744	129,258
	CAGR 93–94 to 2007–08:				**7.72**	**4.89**
	CAGR 98–99 to 2007–08:				**7.92**	**5.70**

Sources: Employment figures are taken from NSSO surveys, reported in Rangarajan, Paul and Seema (2007, 2014). Gross output figures are taken from Table 4.2 of present volume.

Notes: Employment Figures for 1998–99 are obtained by interpolation of figures for 1993–94 and 1999–2000; those for 2007–08 are obtained by interpolation of figures for 2004–05 and 2009–10.

Appendix 5A.2 Missing Growth of Value Added – Cost-plus Pricing

To see this, let us introduce overhead cost. This is reflected in price through a mark-up over cost depending on the market power of the producer. It is supposed to give a reasonable return on investments, though we have not introduced capital in our model explicitly. So, generally it will vary across sectors.[35] We apply a factor, $\mu_i >$ 1, to the average variable (and marginal) cost, where (μ_i -1) is the mark-up for the relevant sector. We proceed in the same way as in the simpler case, setting prices to unity by choosing units for quantities of commodities. Obviously, units are different now unless $\mu_1 = \mu_2 = 1$; in which case we are back to average (variable) cost pricing. However, since comparing the two cases is not our objective, for simplicity we continue to use the same notations for inputs and outputs; the only change in notations is in the case of prices: p' for p. The price equations are now:

$$\mu_1(p'_1x_{11} + p'_2x_{21} + wl_1) = p'_1X_1, \text{ and } \mu_2(p'_1x_{12} + p'_2x_{22} + wl_2) = p'_2X_2 \quad \dots (9)$$

Solving (9):

$$p'_1/p'_2 = (\lambda_1(1/\mu_2 - a_{22}) + \lambda_2 a_{21}) / (\lambda_1 a_{12} + \lambda_2(1/\mu_1 - a_{11})) \quad \dots (10)$$

Writing the price equations (9) in terms of the coefficients:

$$p'_1(1/\mu_1 - a_{11}) = p'_2a_{21} + w\lambda_1, \text{ and } p'_2(1/\mu_2 - a_{22}) = p'_1a_{12} + w\lambda_2,$$

For $p'_1 = p'_2 = 1$, that defines the units of measurement and, therefore, the coefficients, we have: $(1/\mu_1 - a_{11}) = a_{21} + w\lambda_1$, and $(1/\mu_2 - a_{22}) = a_{12} + w\lambda_2$. Since $w, \lambda_1, \lambda_2 > 0$, we have:

$$(1/\mu_1 - a_{11}) > a_{21}, \text{ and } (1/\mu_2 - a_{22}) > a_{12}, \quad \text{where } a_{21}, a_{12} > 0.$$

It follows, $$(1/\mu_1 - a_{11})(1/\mu_2 - a_{22}) - a_{12}a_{21} > 0 \quad \text{... (11)}$$

The set of conditions (11) are structurally akin to the Hawkins–Simon conditions. From (10),

$$\delta(p'_1/p'_2)/\delta\lambda_1 = \lambda_2 [(1/\mu_1 - a_{11})(1/\mu_2 - a_{22}) - a_{12}a_{21})] / [(\lambda_1 a_{12} + \lambda_2(1/\mu_1 - a_{11}))]^2 \quad \text{... (12)}$$

The expression within bracket in the numerator to the right-hand side of equation (12) is positive by virtue of condition (11). So, $\delta(p'_1/p'_2)/\delta\lambda_1 > 0$; and similarly, $\delta(p'_1/p'_2)/\delta\lambda_2 < 0$. This is the same result as we had in the case of average (variable) cost pricing. The additional point, from equation (10), is that p'_1/p'_2 *falls as* μ_1 *falls and rises as* μ_2 *falls.*

In vector-matrix notation: $P'^T = wL^T(MZ - x)^{-1} = w\lambda^T(M - A)^{-1}$, where M stands for the diagonal matrix with diagonal elements $1/\mu_1$ and $1/\mu_2$. So, price is not straight-out the value of total direct and indirect labour input in a commodity; the mark-up has a role. The exercise shows that when labour coefficient in the progressive sector (λ_1) declines, the extent of price decline will also depend on the movement of the mark-up reflecting the intensity of competition.[36]

Appendix 5A.3 Methodology

Aggregation of IOTTs

There are nine input–output transactions tables (IOTT) published by the Central Statistics Office (CSO) for the Indian economy, mostly at five-year intervals, starting in 1968–69. The latest such tables are supply and use tables (SUT) for 2012–13; the level of disaggregation gradually increased from 60 to 140 sectors. The matrices are given at factor cost and are basically based on the information collected for the National Accounts Statistics (NAS). We have aggregated all the nine matrices in an eleven-sector classification fully consistent with the NAS. Nevertheless, an explanation is needed for the residual category 'other services'.

Our category 'other services' includes ownership of dwellings, real estate and business services (including computers and related activities, and legal services) apart from the NAS category of services not elsewhere classified. We had to use this very broad grouping as all the IOTTs before that of 2003–04 do not give break-up of the composite 'other services'. Though we would be comfortable treating business-related services as a separate subsector in the broader Service-I category, for compatibility with earlier IOTTs we have included business services in the subsector 'other services' in 2003–04 and 2007–08 also, as they are grouped in earlier matrices.

Computation of Price Indices

For inter-temporal comparison the IOTTs must be deflated by relevant price indices. NAS publishes price and quantum indices that are implicit indices constructed by taking the ratio of current and constant NDP. Instead, we have constructed price indices by using current and constant GDPs (at factor cost) except for the sectors agriculture, mining, construction and EHPAD. For the first three sectors values of output are given by NAS; so, we get direct estimates of price index from current-constant ratio of outputs. The case for EHPAD needed separate consideration as discussed below.

Sectoral Shares in GDP

The estimates of constant price sectoral value added given by the CSO are difficult to interpret as the concept itself is vague (Chapter 2 gives a detailed discussion of the point). Value added is defined at current prices. But using the national accounts identity between aggregate value added and GDP at factor cost, we take the latter as identical with aggregate final expenditure which is the value of the vector of final uses of all commodities and services (remembering that IOTTs, though not the SUT, give factor cost accounting). Since this vector has an interpretation in real terms, we are entitled to use the concept of real GDP as aggregate final expenditure at constant prices; hence, we compute the GDP deflator, say, P_Y. We apply this deflator on value added. Clearly, real sectoral value added is the absolute share of the relevant sector in the real GDP obtained after deflation. Thus, the relative share of a sector becomes the same at current and constant prices; both the numerator and the denominator are deflated by the same P_Y as, unlike output, value added is the same, irrespective of its sectoral origin.

Justification of Price Index

The CSO estimates of constant-price value added are useful for the price information they contain, though not as shares of real GDP. The logic may be explained by using the case of the registered manufacturing sector. The CSO follows the single deflation method for subsectors of registered manufacturing using the price of the concerned commodity as the deflator and then aggregates the deflated values. The ratio of current to constant price estimates in this case is the harmonic mean of prices of concerned commodities.

Let us use the superscript to refer to the commodity and subscript to refer to the time period. A second subscript, separated by a dot, refers to the price-base. Value-added in the whole of the manufacturing sector in period '1' at prices of period '0' ($V_{1.0}$) is the sum of those of its subsectors:

$$V_{1.0} = \frac{V_1^1}{p_1} + \frac{V_1^2}{p_2} + \ldots + \frac{V_1^n}{p_n}$$

or,

$$\frac{V_{1.0}}{V_{1.1}} = \frac{s_1^1}{p_1} + \frac{s_1^2}{p_2} + \ldots + \frac{s_1^n}{p_n}, \quad \sum_1^n s^i = 1$$

$$= \frac{1}{H} \text{ or, } H = \frac{V_{1.1}}{V_{1.0}}$$

[writing 's' for the share of the relevant sub-sector in GDP of the whole sector]

Thus, our method of computing price index has a firm basis for the registered manufacturing sector. Of course, harmonic mean is not our choice, but we do not have a better alternative.

Price Index for EHPAD

Constant price estimates for EHPAD needed special attention. NDP from public administrative services, which is a major part of EHPAD, comprises of compensation of employees only as operating surplus is taken to be zero. The CSO constant price estimates for the activities are worked out simply by deflating the current price estimates by the corresponding consumer price indices for industrial workers. The implication of the approach is that the growth in real remuneration paid to employees represents productivity improvement. But the general perception is that this sector is technologically relatively stagnant and remuneration in the sector is greatly influenced by that in the technologically progressive sectors. Keeping this point in view, we have adjusted the real remuneration by a catch-up factor: the ratio between real remuneration per employee in the public sector and real NDP per capita. Implicitly we take the productivity growth per employee in the whole of EHPAD to be at par with the national average. Rise of remuneration faster than that only adds to cost and price which is adjusted for using the catch-up factor. Determination of the catch-up factor, of course, involves some arbitrariness; but we considered that more acceptable than the arbitrary assumption underlying the CSO estimates. In fact, some arbitrariness is unavoidable because of the very nature of the case. Heston and Summers (1992) mention: 'The few studies that have been done on trends in the government sector for currently industrialized countries suggest some rise in productivity over time.' Keeping this finding in mind they have made an adjustment based on capital per worker.

Notes

1. In the context of IT services, Narayana Murthy (2017) writes:

   > The Rao government ... removed the restriction, allowing MNCs to hold 100 percent equity in their subsidiary. The result was the entry of leading-edge technology companies such IBM, Microsoft, Motorola, ... This was a godsend for the Indian software services companies for a very interesting reason: these companies were not competing with us for the market, since we were not focusing on the small-sized software-services market in India.... Our competition with these MNCs was for talent, which these companies were attracting away from us.... Since our revenue was low we could not give competitive salaries, we created one of the world's best Employee Stock Option Plans (ESOP).... We created the country's first and the world's second software campus with conferencing rooms, green lawns, libraries, shops, video conferencing rooms, modern computing and telecommunications technology, a cafeteria and comfortable commuting facilities.... Our rating, which was zero in 1992 – moved to 18 percent, a full 7 percent ahead of IBM and Unilever, by 1996. The rest, as they say, is history.

2. Credit Suisse stated in a 2011report that a full two-thirds of listed Indian companies are controlled by family businesses. But that does not make the positions of businesses secure. Almost three-fourths of the top-50 business families of pre-liberalization 1990 do not find a place in the top-50 of 2016, eighteen of them being first generation entrepreneurs while seventeen belong to the second generation (Piramal, 2017).
3. The observation is based on current price estimates. The CSO also provides constant price estimates giving the picture of stagnation from the mid-1990s. However, we ignore these estimates for reasons given in note 5.
4. It is defined as a ratio of two shares. The numerator is the share of the sector's exports in the country's total exports and the denominator is the share of the relevant exports by all countries in total world exports.
5. It is important to note here that we have deflated only output (not value added) by corresponding price indices. To obtain sectoral GDP shares it has to be kept in mind that value added is a 'balancing item' at current prices, without a quantity dimension (UN, 2009: 288); value added represents purchasing power independent of its sectoral of origin. So, its appropriate deflator is the GDP (aggregate value added) deflator, obtained from the ratio of aggregate final expenditure at current and constant prices. Thus all sectoral value added gets the same GDP deflator, which means constant price relative sectoral share is identical to the current price share. SNA recommends deflation of output, not value added. The CSO obtains constant price value added for

the manufacturing sector by deflating the sector's value added with product prices; the result defies sound interpretation (UN, 2009: 315), as it acknowledges (GOI, 2012: 127).

6. We should note here that personal travel and tourism is a final use service and supposedly highly income elastic. The same is true of personal uses of telecommunications and 'banking and finance'. These services are included in Service-I and separate estimates of these final uses are not available, just as is the case for 'business services' included in Service-II. But these are relatively minor parts that should not affect the general tenor of our argument.
7. In the mid-1970s value added in the registered and the unregistered segments were roughly equal, but then onwards the registered segment went ahead relatively. After nearly four decades, it generated two and a half times the value yielded by the unregistered segment.
8. There was a spike in the ratio in 1999–2000. A spike can occur in an individual year for several reasons. We are more interested in the trend here.
9. This observation is consistent with the tenor of argument of Rodrik and Subramanian (2005).
10. The growth of gross output seems to be better reconciled to the growth of GFCF(M).
11. The divergence would translate the constant capital to gross output ratio into a rising capital to value added ratio, which is very often portrayed as the capital-output ratio.
12. Obtained by deducting intra-sectoral intermediate input from the output of manufacturing, as given by the IOTTs (OECD, 2001: 31).
13. Remember our discussion in Chapter 2; sectoral value added shares in GDP are the same for constant and current price estimates when the deflation is right.
14. 'Manufacturing firms are ... more likely than other companies to introduce new and innovative products. Manufacturing makes up only about 11% of America's GDP, but it is responsible for 68% of domestic spending on research and development' (*Economist*, 2012a, 2012b).
15. This assumption is not strictly necessary; it simplifies the model.
16. The implication is that the skill levels are of the same order in the two sectors, only skill takes different forms in different sectors.
17. The expression gives a nice interpretation: price equals the value of total direct and indirect labour used in production of the relevant commodity.
18. This solution can be directly obtained after writing equations (3a) in intensive form and obtaining prices in wage units.
19. Nordhaus (2006) finds firm support for this hypothesis for the US economy.
20. One very comprehensive study on the American economy, spanning more than half a century from 1948, by Nordhaus (2006) finds a strong negative relationship between productivity growth and price growth, so much so that it concludes that consumers capture virtually all the gains from technological change (also see Fagerberg, 2000).
21. Triplett and Bosworth (2003) finds LP growth in services to be considerably greater after 1995 than before, which means that the services industries are consistent with the economy-wide scenario. They show that the post-1973 productivity slowdown was

greater in the non-goods producing parts of the economy than in manufacturing. But during 1995–2000 services industries on average have done about as well as the rest of the economy basically due to jump in multi-factor productivity (MFP). It has long been known that much of the IT investment has gone to services (Griliches, 1992). This IT capital contributed as it did earlier, but MFP growth is a major contributor to post-1995 service industry labour productivity growth. They claimed 'Baumol's Disease has been cured'.

22. This is a tautology, given Baumol's Proposition-3 that states that, under the assumptions made, labour continuously moves from the progressive to the stagnant sector.
23. Tata Steel, *Annual Report 2015–16.*
24. This tendency may have been aided by the relative decline of the unregistered segment of manufacturing.
25. It shows an increase from 0.69 to 0.70, *vide* Table A5.5.
26. It has to be remembered that the period saw booming service exports with implications for productivity and we have left out four years causing, in all probability, underestimation of manufacturing's productivity.
27. There is anecdotal evidence to support this contention, as mentioned earlier in the paper. Direct evidence from productivity studies is messy (Goldar, 2015); the basic reason for this state is lack of quality data on inputs and output and that '...ingenuity cannot fully or effectively compensate for lack of basic information'. Probably there is no study based on the IOTTs to estimate the intermediate input variables after proper deflation. Moreover, very often value added has been taken as the proxy for output (Bosworth and Collins, 2007; Virmani, 2004), but as we have argued in this paper, the value added trend underestimates the output trend in manufacturing with obvious impact on productivity estimates. Datta and Neogi (2013) tried to overcome the problems to a great extent and found evidence of productivity improvement in public sector oil refining after the abolition of administered pricing mechanism.
28. In Chapter 6 we have attempted to obtain quantitative estimates of the degree of slippage of sectoral value added by analysing nine sector IOTTs of the Indian economy. The study finds manufacturing to be a heavy loser (consistent with decline in relative price) over both the stretches 1978–79 to 1993–94 and 1993–94 to 2003–04. For the service sector, Service-I gained (consistent with lack of technical progress) during the first stretch but lost heavily during the later period. But EHPAD was a consistent gainer over both the stretches.
29. Interestingly, this correction would make India's share in 1980 to be 21 per cent (see Table 2.2).
30. The findings tally with that of Kochar et al. (2006) with respect to manufacturing and services but not for industry which includes mining, construction and utilities apart from manufacturing.
31. First industries are ranked on the basis of skill intensity defined to be the share of remuneration to skilled labour in total value added based on input–output matrix for South Africa. Using this ranking the ratio of aggregate value added, in above

median to that in below median industries of a country is taken as the value of the regress and for the country. The regression results were qualitatively unchanged for some variants of the definition of relative skill intensity.

32. In fact, Bangladesh is just above the bottom decile among 128 countries in terms of both ECI and COI even though its manufacturing's share in GDP is more than India's (Table 2.2).
33. Wage differential among firm size-classes is also the maximum in India, reflecting the fact that the micro and small firms are predominantly the abode of uneducated workers.
34. The period of our study spans up to the early 2010s. Subsequently there has been a slowdown in the growth of the Indian economy and its exports. See Chinoy (2019) and Gopinath and Lahiri (2019).
35. In our model the variable cost is based on labour-coefficient and fixed intermediate input coefficients. With fixed coefficients, the average and marginal costs are identical. When mark-up is applied on the marginal cost, the profit maximizing price level is given by the relation: $P = MC + MC[(1/\eta)/(1 - 1/\eta)]$; or mark-up rate $(\mu - 1) = [(1/\eta)/(1 - 1/\eta)]$ (Mansfield and Yohe, 2004: 414).
36. Theoretically a counter movement of μ_I can appropriate a part of the benefit of technical progress causing a fall in λ_I. Nordhaus (2006) finds that 95 per cent of the benefit of productivity gain has been passed on to the consumer through lower prices in the American economy over the second half of the last century (2006: 30).

6

Growth and Sectoral GVA Adjustments*

I WILL add one Thing although it be a little out of Place; ... But my Caution is occasioned by a Lady of your Acquaintance, married to a very valuable Person, whom yet she is so unfortunate as to be always commanding for those Perfections, to which he can least pretend.

—Swift, 'A Letter to a Young Lady, On Her Marriage, 1723', in Rawson and Higgins (2010: 269)

Introduction

The manufacturing sector has traditionally been the main theatre of technological progress. This sector constantly upgrades the existing products and creates new ones that are, unlike agricultural products, demanded more and more, apparently without a limit, as income rises. That is the amazing ability of the capitalist civilization to enlarge the sphere of its needs indefinitely. Yet, as per national product data of a typical modern economy, the manufacturing sector gradually gets eclipsed by service production. This has stirred the interest of many an observer. A simple hypothesis of differential productivity growth across sectors with competitive factor rewards, elaborated in the previous chapter, leads to the conclusion that the relatively technologically non-progressive activities, which are typically to be found more in the service sector than in manufacturing, will experience above average cost and price increases paving the way for increase in value added faster than output. The reverse narrative holds for the more progressive sectors, particularly for manufacturing. This idea has being churned ever since it was propounded though much has changed on the technological front with revolution in information technology that has kept the service sector on the boil in recent times (Triplett and Bosworth, 2003).

---

* The chapter draws heavily on Datta (2019b).

We have indicated in the last chapter that the Indian economy shows strong evidence of changes consistent with the above observations. It is of natural interest to ask, precisely how relevant the cost (and value added) adjustment have been in the context of stagnant relative GDP share of the manufacturing sector and rapidly rising share of services since the turn of the 1970s. The present discussion takes lead from the last chapter to obtain more specific answers to the question of GVA adjustments. Here the focus is roughly on the three decades since 1978–79, the choice of the specific year being based on the consideration that it lies close to the cusp of a change in the growth regime for the Indian economy and also the practical advantage of having an input–output transactions table (IOTT) for the year. In passing, we cast a glance at the preceding decade also for the natural curiosity about the state of things earlier.

We make extensive use of the nine (commodity x commodity) IOTTs published by the CSO. Inadequacies of measurement accuracy and that too in the meticulous format of IOTTs, are well known as we have discussed in Chapter 2. In our study, data inadequacies have been compounded by the requirement of conversion to constant prices for intertemporal comparisons. It is generally agreed that quality changes over time pose a challenge that price indices are unable to cope with. But we must use them, though with care, accepting the inadequacy. Looking at the positive side, our analysis yields fairly plausible and expected patterns that show the usefulness of data compiled systematically, in spite of limitations. Nevertheless, due to all sorts of doubts regarding the accuracy of data and compounding of error due to deflation, our estimates may be viewed as indicative rather than absolute. The next section discusses how the input–output format should be viewed and tackled for the analysis of changes in the sectoral shares in GDP. For a quick reading of the chapter's findings, this section may be omitted. The following section decomposes sectoral shares and defines the *final demand*, the *technical structure* and the *adjustment* effects, the last one being related to the trends in relative prices. Next, we take up an empirical appraisal of the effects, which show substantial erosion of value added from the manufacturing sector. This finding leads to the next section to highlight that the measures of productivity in Indian manufacturing based on value added are systematic underestimates. The final section summarises and concludes the chapter.

The Input–Output Structure and Sectoral Shares

In the course of economic growth the structure of final demand changes for all sorts of reasons. As per-capita income increases over time, the consumption pattern changes as more goods and services become affordable and new products appear generating new demands. Technological changes bring entirely new demands for both consumption and investment; the most obvious examples being mobile phones and their infrastructure. New processes lead to new demand for inputs and changes in the entire production environment. Changes in both the demand and supply sides lead to new relative prices and substitution in production and consumption. The IOTTs seek to present snapshots of the dynamic situation in the frame of input uses, final demands and sectoral GVAs. In the context of central planning one may think in physical terms; for a given set of real technology matrix (A matrix), the vector of real final demand (F) determines the vector of real gross output (X) (or simply, output). In a market setup prices evolve to bind the three sets of variables in the same vector-matrix relation of monetary flows and, thereby, the vector of sectoral GVAs (V) is obtained corresponding to a set of prices. The official IOTTs give recorded transactions as monetary flows of intermediate uses across sectors and final uses in a year. There exists an underlying set of average prices (indices) for commodities over the year concerned, which can translate the monetary flows into real flows[1] with reference to the base year. These flows yield the input coefficients or technology matrix, $A = [a_{ij}]$, where $a_{ij} = x_{ij}/x_{j,}$ that is, output of the ith sector used as intermediate input per unit of output of the jth sector. But, GVA in a year is the difference between the values of output and intermediate inputs at current prices.[2] Aggregate of GVAs over all the sectors is the GDP,[3] which has a real connotation in the form of the basket of real final uses. For comparison over time final uses can be deflated by the corresponding price indices and following the usual index number procedure a composite price deflator for aggregate final use (GDP) can be obtained, which is the GDP deflator.[4] Sectoral GVAs come from sectoral production but they cannot be deflated by the price of the sectoral produce. They are given the interpretation of being a part of the GDP-pie and so, the appropriate deflator is the GDP deflator.

For two IOTTs, say, at a decadal interval, the difference relates to changes in both quantities and in prices, causing changes in the value added coefficients of sectors. A little thought would convince that even for unchanged real A and F, changes in relative prices over time would change the current distribution of GVA[5] across sectors or, what we may call, the GVA structure. We can try to segregate, accepting limitations of index numbers, the two aspects of changes – one caused by relative price changes and the other caused by real changes. This requires translating the IOTTs to constant prices, which yields the vector of real aggregate final expenditure (F) and, thereby, GDP at constant prices. We know that the sectoral GVA in real terms cannot be obtained as the difference between the values of output and intermediate inputs at constant prices (remember the pitfalls of double deflation discussed in Chapter 2); for the purpose, the current price GVA needs to be deflated by the GDP deflator. Because of this common GVA-deflator for all sectoral GVAs, the constant price-conversion does not change the structure of sectoral GVA shares as determined at current prices. Thus while the sectoral GVA shares change over time, at any point of time the current and constant price GVA shares are the same (discussed in detail in Chapter 2).

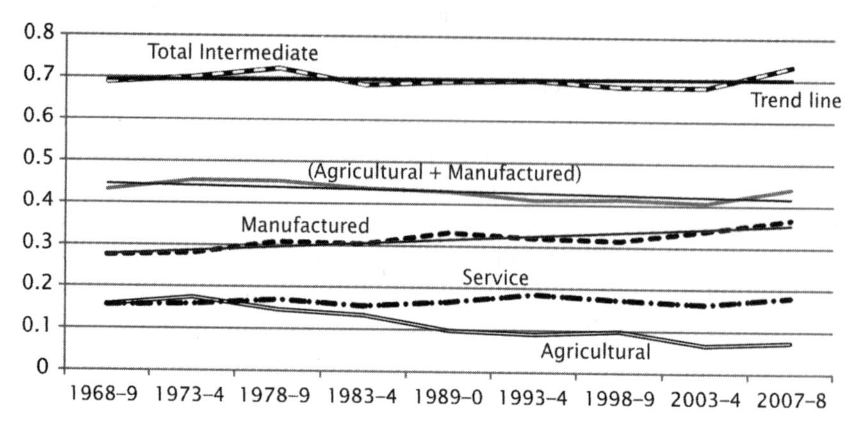

Figure 6.1 Intermediate Input Use in Manufacturing

Source: Table 5A.2.

A common assumption in input–output models is that the intermediate input coefficients are constant over short periods of time. But here we undertake comparisons over one and a half decades or a longer interval. How did the coefficients behave in India? Our focus in on the manufacturing sector, so let us look at that sector. Interestingly, in spite of all the changes in scale and technology over roughly the four decades since 1968–69, at the aggregate level and at constant prices there seems to be a clearly perceptible order relating to intermediate input use and value added per unit of output of the manufacturing sector. Intermediate input drawn from agriculture has declined but intra-sectoral input use has intensified to compensate to a great extent (Figure 6.1). As for service input intensity, with all the hesitations caused by conceptual difficulties regarding price indices,[6] it seems there may have been a marginal increase though the signal is neither very strong nor unambiguous. Remarkably, taking all intermediate inputs together, the trend of intensity of total intermediate input-use is absolutely flat. The intensity is almost the same in 2003–04 as in 1968–69, and in 2007–08 as in 1978–79. This means that for a hundred-rupees' worth of manufactured produce at base-year prices, the total value of intermediate input use has remained constant over the decades (at about 70 rupees), in spite of some changes in their sectoral origins. But the important point to note, as argued in Chapter 2, is that value added is not the difference between the two above quantities, as value added is a current price phenomenon; when converted to constant prices it only shows the purchasing power of current value added with reference to the base year.[7] We will see, below, that the value added coefficient for manufacturing has steadily declined consistent with relative price changes (discussed in the previous chapter).

We have noted in previous chapters that India started correcting towards a pro-industry policy regime in the early 1980s, reform gathered pace later and reached a crescendo after about a decade. However, the share of the manufacturing sector in GDP stayed stagnant around 15–16 per cent, apart from a couple of short spurts, over the three decades since 1978–79. Kochhar et al. (2006: 24) have noted: 'Instead of India's fast growing states reverting to a more traditional pattern of specialization in labour intensive industries, commensurate with India's income levels, they appear to have skipped directly to specialization in skill-intensive industries (within manufacturing)....' This development[8] indicates labour saving technical progress for the overall manufacturing sector and we have already noted that relative price of manufactures has declined over the period concerned. It should be interesting to check to what extent it had impacted the value added adjustment in the sector.

The Value Added Adjustment and Other Effects

IOTTs give us a compact view of the balance between the production and the expenditure sides of an economy. On the production side (columns, Table 3.1 in Chapter 3) we have intermediate input use and value added in each sector, while on the expenditure side (rows) we have sectoral outputs and their uses, both intermediate and final.[9] Total output may be taken as the sum of its intermediate and final uses:

$$X = AX + F = (I - A)^{-1}F \quad \dots (1)$$

Where, as we have already introduced the symbols briefly, X is the column vector of output; F is the column vector of final uses and A is the intermediate-input coefficients or the technology matrix. If we write V as the diagonal matrix of value added coefficients (that is, value added per unit of output) then the vector of sectoral value added may be written as:

$$\chi = VX = V(I - A)^{-1}F \quad \dots (2)$$

Thus, we view the sectoral structure of value added as the result of three broad influences:

(i) The composition of final demand (F),
(ii) The technology reflected in the intermediate input structure (A),
(iii) The structure of value added coefficients (V) determined by the price structure.

Using subscripts *1* and *0* to distinguish the two points of time (say, years) under comparison, we can write the vector of changes in sectoral value added ($\Delta\ \chi$) as:

$$\Delta\chi = \chi_1 - \chi_0 = V_1\,(I - A_1)^{-1}\,F_1 - V_0\,(I - A_0)^{-1}\,F_0$$

$$= V_0(I - A_0)^{-1}\,[\Delta F] + V_0\,[\Delta(I - A)^{-1}]\,F_1 + [\,\Delta V](I - A_1)^{-1}F_1 \qquad \ldots (3)$$

The explanation is that in the course of development the structure of final demand (F) changes and that drives change in the production structure (X). But sectoral structure of GVA (χ) may change in a different way from what would be indicated by changes in final demand only. The output of a sector meets the intermediate demand generated across the sectors depending on the inter-industry structure (the technology matrix, A) as well as the final demand. Changes in technology cause A to change and this would influence the new structure of intermediate input use and output, given the final demand vector. Further, the structure of sectoral product (GVA) is obtained after another transformation from output to value added, which is represented here by the sectoral value-added coefficients (that is, value added per unit of output)[10] which changes for reasons already discussed.

The first term on the left-hand side of (3), $V_0(I - A_0)^{-1}\,[\Delta F]$, gives the impact of a change in final demand on the sectoral composition of value added for unchanged structure of technical and value-added coefficients (A and V); this is what changes in sectoral GVA values would result had the current final demand been produced in period '0'. This takes into account the direct additional quantities demanded and the chain of additional indirect demands that would be created by the intermediate input needs under the inter-industry and price structure of period '0'. We call this component of overall change in the structure of value added between periods '0' and '1' the *final demand effect* based on period '0'.[11]

Similarly, the second term, $V_0\,[\Delta(I - A)^{-1}]\,F_1$ is the *technical structure effect.*[12] It represents additional (positive or negative) sectoral real output requirement due to changes in the technology matrix (A) in the current period converted to sectoral value added after using the value-added coefficients (V) of period '0'.' The matrix A changes for all sorts of reasons, which include technical substitution among intermediate-inputs caused by changes in relative prices, changes in organization (like splintering) and nature of the products causing process changes. In particular, an influence that would systematically impact the intermediate-input coefficients is increasing depth of the manufacturing process as it gets increasingly sophisticated with the introduction of new products. Figure 6.1 indicates[13] that this coefficient has steadily increased in India from 0.308 to 0.367 over the last three decades,[14] though there was a corresponding decline in agricultural inputs to manufacturing. On the whole, the sector's intermediate input intensity has not increased. Changes occur in non-manufacturing sectors as well. This suggests a significant sectoral pattern of technical structure effect.

Technical changes may also affect saving in intermediate-inputs (say, fuel) and, therefore, in costs of production. This should, contrary to splintering of services,[15] lead to the value added coefficient of the particular sector to rise if prices were held constant. But, it is the market structure that determines how the benefits are distributed to the final users through changes in prices and, hence, the value added coefficients of different sectors. Changes in technology in broad sense, affecting the A matrix, are a fact of life though it is not clear how systematic its impact is and how it causes value added coefficients to change.[16] On the whole, we have noted a flat trend of the intensity of intermediate input use (in real terms) in manufacturing, making V largely reflect price changes, which may be viewed as being caused by labour saving technical progress or decline in the degree of monopoly.[17] From the flat trend of intermediate input intensity mentioned earlier, one may surmise that the value added structure would not change very much in the absence of price change. The reality is that price trends show a considerable and systematic pattern of change with inevitable influences on the structure of sectoral value added as discussed earlier. Herein lies the importance of the last term in equation (3).

$[\Delta V](I\text{-}A_1)^{-1}F_1$ is the effect due to change in value added coefficients in the current year. The basic hypothesis underpinning our analysis is that some sectors of the economy are under the influence of systematic decline in prices while some others are relatively immune from that. Under a competitive setup relative prices go against the progressive sector causing the sector's value-added coefficient to decline while that for some typically non-progressive sectors increase. Based on this idea we call the above expression the (value added) *adjustment effect* which, under our hypothesis of cost disease, should depress the manufacturing sector the most and boost the part of services – EHPAD.

The three components of changes in the structure of sectoral GDP shares are bound by the fundamental national accounting identity between aggregate final demand and aggregate value added. This identity is maintained by the final demand effect in itself because we have used in its definition the base year production structure along with the corresponding value added structure.[18] The implication is that the sum of the technical structure and the adjustment effects must be zero.

Formally, writing u as the row vector of appropriate dimension having '1' as each of its elements (the summation vector), it is clear that

$$u\, V_1\, [(I - A_1)^{-1}]F_1 = u\, F_1,$$

because of the accounting identity between the production and expenditure sides. Similarly,

$$uV_0\, (I - A_0)^{-1}\, F_0 = u\, F_0.$$

Moreover,

$$u\, V_0 (I - A_0)^{-1} F_1 = u\, F_1,$$

since any final demand vector that could have been produced in period '0' would maintain the accounting identity for mutually consistent V_0 and A_0, which in the present case we have taken from the base year.

By subtraction, $u\, v_0 (I - A_0)^{-1} \Delta F = u\, F_1 - u\, F_0 = u\, \Delta\, \chi$ *[by equation (1)]*,

which is the difference between GDPs of the two periods. Then, from (3) we have:

$$uV_0[\Delta(I - A)^{-1}]\, F_1 + u\, [\Delta V](I - A_1)^{-1} F_1 = 0 \qquad \dots (4)$$

The first term is the aggregate technical structure effect while the second term gives the aggregate adjustment effect. Equation (4) shows, aggregate technical structure effect must be accompanied by an off-setting aggregate adjustment effect. However, this complementarity is valid only at the aggregate level, not at sectoral levels. Consider the hypothetical case when intermediate input coefficients do not change significantly; how and exactly in which sectors the adjustments happen, and by how much, depends on saving made on the use of primary factors of production. Theoretically,

when $\Delta(I - A)^{-1} = \mathbf{0}$ (the zero matrix),

we have zero technical structure effect $(u\, V_0 [\Delta(I - A)^{-1}]F_1 = \mathbf{0})$,

and also zero overall adjustment effect $(u\, [\Delta V](I - A_1)^{-1} F_1 = \mathbf{0})$.

Even this scenario does not preclude adjustment among sectors through changes in use of primary factors and, consequently, in relative prices. There seems to be a distinct pattern in sectoral value added adjustment in the Indian economy, following a consistent pattern of price changes. This pattern sheds some light on the stagnation of the manufacturing sector's share in GDP in India.

Estimates of the Three Effects for the Indian Economy

The First Phase: 1978–79 to 1993–94

We focus on the period 1978–79 to 2007–08; the choice is determined by the availability of comparable IOTTs and also the fact that the period roughly corresponds to acceleration of GDP growth.[19] Subsequent IOTTs are Use tables not fully comparable with the previous matrices. We will, however, cast a glance at the decade preceding 1978–79 using the IOTT 1968–69; the relevant computations are presented in the appendix. A look at Table 6A.1 (see appendix) reveals that relative price (vis-à-vis GDP) of manufacturing steadily declined since 1978–79 through 2003–04, levelling off thereafter before falling further. Such steady trend is shown, among other sectors, only by EHPAD but in the reverse direction. Reflections of these trends are clearly found in the value added-coefficients, as shown by Table 6.1. We divide the period of roughly three decades to 2007–08 into two phases: the first is from 1978–79 to 1993–94, and the other is from 1993–94 to 2007–08. In the first phase the average GDP growth rate was significantly higher compared to the previous decade, while the relative price of manufactures slid steadily[20] by almost 20 per cent and that of EHPAD increased by more than 30 per cent. Relative price movements in other sectors were neither as strong nor as consistent albeit, with some exception for 'Other Services', which includes 'Real Estate and Business Services' belonging to Service-II. The price movements are reflected in the value added per unit of output[21] and, hence, in the adjustment effect.

Table 6.1 Sectoral Value Added per Unit Output at 1993–94 Prices

Year	Agr	Ming	Manf	Cnstr	EGW	Trnsp	Comn	THR	B I F	O. Srv	EHPAD
1968–69	0.90	0.52	**0.43**	0.29	0.51	0.62	0.69	0.66	0.92	1.52	**0.47**
1973–74	0.92	0.46	**0.42**	0.30	0.40	0.50	0.61	0.64	1.03	1.39	**0.49**
1978–79	0.76	0.66	**0.43**	0.34	0.54	0.55	0.78	0.57	1.03	1.36	**0.58**
1983–84	0.72	1.00	**0.39**	0.37	0.42	0.45	0.60	0.66	1.03	0.94	**0.64**
1989–90	0.68	0.80	**0.34**	0.44	0.36	0.52	0.76	0.67	0.81	0.69	**0.80**
1993–94	0.72	0.74	**0.30**	0.41	0.37	0.49	0.84	0.72	0.85	0.73	**0.86**
1998–99	0.77	0.73	**0.27**	0.47	0.41	0.49	0.67	0.69	0.71	0.63	**0.98**
2003–04	0.65	0.77	**0.24**	0.42	0.26	0.49	0.30	0.70	0.69	0.85	**1.31**
2007–08	0.54	0.97	**0.21**	0.49	0.34	0.49	0.20	0.68	0.53	1.01	**1.60**

Source: Author's computation.

Note: GDP deflator has been used to obtain real VA and output from the IOTTs (details of methodology is given in Appendix 5A.3).

Abbreviations: Agr = agriculture, Ming = mining, Manf = manufacturing, Cnstr = construction, EGW = electricity, gas and water supply, Trnsp = transport, Comn = communication, THR = trade, hotels and restaurants, BIF = banking, insurance and finance, O.Srv = other services, EHPAD = education, health, public administration and defence.

Table 6.2 shows the three effects for 1993–94 with 1978–79 as the base year[22] (the first phase). Column 5 shows that the manufacturing sector gained handsomely (1.9 per cent) due to the technical structure effect, with augmented production of intermediate inputs basically for its own use, but also for use in other sectors.

Gains on this account by the 'other industry' (the non-manufacturing part of industry) as well as Service-I are even higher.[23] But, at the same time, there was an even stronger negative adjustment effect (4.8 per cent, column 6) affecting the manufacturing sector; it was as strong in magnitude as the positive adjustment effects for 'other industry' and Service-I taken together. Adjustment effect itself caused the gap between manufacturing and Service-I to widen by almost 8.5 per cent. Comparing column 2 with column 4 we find that manufacturing's share would have increased by about 3 percentage points had the structure (coefficients in *A* and *V*) of the base year prevailed during the reference year, that is, if production for the final demand of 1993–94 had actually been carried out in 1978–79; and in that case the share of Service-I would have remained roughly the same as in the base year (lower by 6 percentage points).

Table 6.2 Change in Sectoral Structure: 1978–79 to 1993–94 (1978–79 Prices)

	Col. 1	Col. 2	Col. 3	Col. 4	Col. 5	Col. 6
	VA:78–9	VA:93–4	$V_0(I - A_0)^{-1}\Delta F$	Col.1 + Col. 3	$V_0\Delta(I - A)^{-1}F_1$	$\Delta V(I - A_1)^{-1}F_1$
Agriculture	34,612	61,121	29,848	64,461	–5,894	2,555
Manufactures	18,548	36,616	24,410	42,957	4,090	–10,432
Manufactures' share*	*0.194*	*0.167*	*0.198*	*0.196*	*0.019*	*–0.048*
Other. industry	8,342	22,434	7,084	15,426	4,590	2,418
Service-I	20,811	59,111	25,960	46,770	4,275	8,067
Service-I.share*	*0.218*	*0.270*	*0.211*	*0.214*	*0.020*	*0.037*
EHPAD	7,030	20,363	11,420	18,451	410	1,503
Other Services	6,300	19,263	24,543	30,843	3,620	–15,200
Service-II	13,331	39,626	35,963	49,294	4,030	–13,697
Service-II.share*	*0.139*	*0.181*	*0.292*	*0.225*	*0.018*	*–0.063*
Total	95,643	218,909	123,265	218,908	11,090	–11,089

Source: Author's calculation (see Appendix 5A.3).

Notes: Other industry = industry other than manufacturing. Other services is residual services. Service-I refers to transport, trade, communications, banking and insurance. Service-II refers to the sum of EHPAD and Other Services.

*Percentages of respective column totals, except for columns 5 and 6, where reference is to the column 4 total.

The subsector 'other services', which includes 'real estate and business services',[24] also gained handsomely due to the technical structure effect; but the adjustment effect on this subsector was found to be negative and strong. EHPAD gained moderately, mostly due to the adjustment effect. The finding of loss of manufacturing and gain of EHPAD due to adjustment effect is fully consistent with the insight developed earlier in our restatement of Baumol's hypothesis (or the cost disease). Also, the finding highlights gain of Service-I due to adjustment effect to the extent of 3.7 per cent.[25] The technical structure effect (column 5) has been strong and positive for all sectors other than agriculture (where it is negative and strong) and EHPAD (where it is weak, though positive).

The Second Phase: 1993–94 to 2007–08

Table 6.3 Change in Sectoral Structure: 1993–94 to 2007–08 (at 1993–94 Prices)

	Col. 1	Col. 2	Col. 3	Col. 4	Col. 5	Col. 6
	VA:93–4	VA:07–8	$V_0(I-A_0)^{-1}\Delta F$	Col.1 + Col. 3	$V_0\Delta(I-A)^{-1}F_1$	$\Delta V(I-A_1)^{-1}F_1$
Agriculture	231,898	355,198	204,289	436,187	38,944	–119,933
Manufactures	138,923	363,123	291,093	430,016	91,446	**–158,339**
M-share*	*0.167*	*0.174*	*0.232*	*0.206*	*0.044*	***–0.076***
Other. Industry	85,118	277,312	142,041	227,159	9,812	40,341
Service-I	224,273	641,995	471,145	695,418	125,776	–179,200
Servc-I.share*	*0.270*	*0.308*	*0.376*	*0.334*	*0.060*	*–0.086*
EHPAD	77,258	207,530	35,666	112,924	–1,217	**95,823**
Other.Service	73,087	238,652	109,025	182,112	–10,881	67,420
Service-II	150,345	446,181	144,691	295,036	–12,098	163,243
Servc-II.share*	*0.181*	*0.214*	*0.115*	*0.142*	*–0.006*	*0.078*
Total	830,557	2,083,810	1,253,260	2,083,817	253,879	–253,886

Source: Author's calculation.

Notes: *Percentages of respective column totals, except for columns 5 and 6, where reference is to the column 4 total.

Sectors are the same as in Table 6.2.

The second phase experienced a further increase in the average growth rate of GDP compared to the first phase. Yet stagnation of manufacturing's share accompanied by a steady decline in the sector's relative price continued. While the IOTTs show the sector's relative share improving marginally from 16.7 per cent to 17.4 per cent over the period (Table 6.3, columns 1 and 2)[26], it would actually have been much higher – 20.6 per cent (column 4) – had the final demand vector for 2007–08 been produced in 1993–94 (column 4). Like in the first phase, the technical structure effect is positive and strong for both manufacturing and Service-I. But the drag from the adjustment effect (column 6) was much stronger;[27] the striking difference with the first phase is that the adjustment effect is strongly negative for Service-I in this phase too; so much so that gap between manufacturing's share and that of Service-I, apparently shrank by a percentage point due to adjustment effect as such. This finding is consistent with the widespread perception that productivity in services improved because of advances in information technology; the maximum contribution being from 'Banking, Insurance and Finance' (BIF) and communications. However, we should be cautious in interpretation. The effects on sectoral shares shown in the tables are based on observations at two points only; they should not be taken as trend over the interval concerned. This point in highlighted in the next table.

Table 6.4 Change in Sectoral Structure: 1983–84 to 2003–04 (1983–84 Prices)

	Col. 1	Col. 2	Col. 3	Col. 4	Col. 5	Col. 6
	VA:83–4	VA:03–4	$V_0(I - A_0)^{-1}\Delta F$	Col.1 + Col. 3	$V_0\Delta(I - A)^{-1}F_1$	$\Delta V(I - A_1)^{-1}F_1$
Agriculture	66,202	111,383	72,375	138,577	–16,707	–10,487
Manufactures	38,750	106,985	102,663	141,413	30,018	**–64,447**
M-share*	*0.195*	*0.181*	*0.261*	*0.239*	*0.051*	***–0.109***
Other Industry	19,985	64,653	30,254	50,239	18,694	–4,281
Service-I	40,314	178,449	117,185	157,498	36,369	–15,417
Servc-I.share*	*0.203*	*0.302*	*0.298*	*0.266*	*0.061*	*–0.026*
EHPAD	16,381	67,475	16,121	32,502	–8	**34,980**
Other Service	16,790	62,634	54,560	71,350	–2,834	–5,882
Service-II	33,171	130,109	70,681	103,852	–2,842	29,098
Servc-II.share*	*0.167*	*0.220*	*0.180*	*0.176*	*0.005*	*0.049*
Total	198,422	591,579	393,158	591,580	65,532	–65,533

Source: Author's calculation (see Appendix 5A.3).

Notes: Other industry = industry other than manufacturing. Other services is residual services. Service-I refers to transport, trade, communications, banking and insurance. Service-II refers to the sum of EHPAD and Other Services.

*Percentages of respective column totals, except for columns 5 and 6, where reference is to the column 4 total.

The story for 'other services' is the opposite in the second phase compared to the earlier one. As for EHPAD, which is the focus of our attention from the point of view of the hypothesis of the 'cost disease', adjustment effect is very strong giving full support to the hypothesis. The net result is that Service-II almost cancels out the negative adjustment effect on Service-I. From our point of view, the big story in the second phase, continuing from the first, is that of a big loss for the manufacturing sector and gain for EHPAD due to the adjustment of relative prices consistent with the 'cost disease' hypothesis. The additional point, as already noted, is that Service-I apparently did not suffer from this phenomenon. In drawing conclusions uneasiness arises from the fact that our observations in the two phases are based on just three years spread at intervals of roughly one and a half decades. Does the picture change qualitatively if we change the points of our observation? Toward this query, we take an overlapping phase.

The Overlapping Phase: 1983–84 to 2003–04

In this phase both the end points are different from the other two phases. Changes over the two decades are presented in Table 6.4. The changes in relative prices can be read from Table 6A.1, in the appendix. The results are more or less similar to those for the second phase. Quantitatively, the adjustment effect for the manufacturing sector is even stronger and of the same sign. In fact, as columns 1 and 4 (Table 6.4) show, share of manufacturing in aggregate GVA would have increased from 19.7 to 23.9 per cent over the two decades under the 1983–84 production structure. Adjustment effect alone dragged it down by almost 11 per cent while the technical structure effect pushed it by more than 5 per cent. EHPAD helped Service-II similarly. For Service-I the adjustment effect is negative as in manufacturing, though much weaker in the overlapping interval than the observation for the second phase. The technical structure effect is positive and substantial for manufacturing, 'other industry' as well as Service-I, as in other phases.

The robust takeaway from the above exercise is the absolute consistency of findings in manufacturing and EHPAD in line with our hypothesis of adjustment of value added. It is very significant and positive for manufacturing, and just the opposite for EHPAD in all the three time segments, as one would expect based on the assumption of differential technical progress. As for Service-I, we found its share increasing substantially in the first phase due to a push by both the technical structure and adjustment effects; but the situation changed in the second phase as well as in the overlapping phase when adjustment effects exerted a downward pull on the sectoral shares, suggesting productivity improvement[28]. Interestingly, to take a curious glance at the decade prior to 1978–79, when the economy trundled along at a slower rate of growth of GDP, manufacturing did not lose at all on account of the adjustment effect (Table 6A.2, in the appendix). The hypothesis of 'cost disease' does not apply to this phase, so far as we can glean from the IOTTs for 1968–69 and 1978–79.

Since manufacturing's share in GDP was roughly stagnant in spite of the persistent and substantial drag on the sector's value added due to decline in relative price, one would expect that after correcting for price change, the share of the sector in gross output and aggregate final expenditure should give us a truer picture of the trend of the level of activity in the sector. We observed in the previous chapter that these two shares increased consistently over the period concerned, in tandem with Service-I and faster than Service-II. All the above findings militate against the stagnancy of manufacturing; the flat trend of the sector's share in GDP conceals the adjustment of value added due to changes in relative prices.

A Caveat

Questions are often raised regarding the quality of data. Our task involves use of price indices for each of the subsectors, half of which are service subsectors with virtually intractable problems of estimation of quantities as discussed earlier. While we cannot but use the available data, we have tried to be careful in choosing deflators, as explained in Appendix 5A.3 of Chapter 5. Data being what it is, we do not emphasize on the precise absolute magnitudes of different effects estimated, but we note the signs and the order of magnitude of the effects and their consistency over different phases.

A related point – regarding estimates of multifactor productivity (MFP) for Indian manufacturing– deserves some discussion here. There are several estimates with mutually inconsistent results (one good collection of papers is Kathuria, Rajesh Raj and Sen, 2014). Basically, we know, MFP is defined as the difference between the growth rate of output and that of total inputs, which is generally decomposed into capital, labour and material (sometimes even further) inputs. In algebraic notations:

$$\Delta lnY = \nu_K \Delta lnK + \nu_L \Delta lnL + \nu_N \Delta lnN + MFP \qquad \dots (17)$$

Where ν stands for a suitable weight for the relevant variables shown as the subscript; other notations have obvious connotations. There are several questions regarding the theoretical propriety of this growth accounting technique – like the separability of intermediate inputs from the production function or even the very existence of sectoral production functions apart from a host of empirical questions (OECD, 2001; Cobbold, 2003).[29] To be practical, these questions are generally bypassed in empirical applications. Measurement of variables is no less nagging. Two alternative measures of output are used for the estimation of MFP. Equation (17) implies gross output measure of Y. Here, apart from issues regarding K and L, a knotty problem arises with respect to the measure of Y and N. Such measures are almost impossible to obtain without resort to Supply and Use tables (or IOTTs), which are available for only a few years at normally quinquennial intervals.

Such difficulties have led researchers to look for the softer option: use of value added as a measure of Y (most studies on the Indian economy take this approach, for example, Hulten and Srinivasan, 1999; Virmani, 2004; A. Datta, 2014). Value added at current prices is directly and easily available, but what is needed are the constant price estimates. In obtaining these estimates the unrealistic assumption of identical price index for output and intermediate inputs is made. The term involving N in (17) is dropped as that is supposed to be accounted for in the value added. *To compound difficulties, what we want to highlight is that our present study raises the specter of trend of value added deviating systematically downward from that of gross output for the manufacturing sector. Remembering that value added is the proxy for output, this divergence implies that these measures of multi factor productivity are, apart from other limitations, systematic underestimates for the Indian manufacturing sector over the period of our study.*

Summary and Conclusion

Sectoral shares in a modern economy are influenced by the relentless technological progress that characterizes our time. Manufacturing activities have traditionally been the most prominent vehicle for new technology that has increased labour productivity enormously. Competition has led to the distribution of most of the benefits from productivity gains across sectors through adjustment of relative prices. As a consequence value added per unit of output falls in the progressive sectors, and rises in the relatively stagnant sectors. The present chapter examines the maintainability of the above hypothesis using the IOTTs.

The growth trajectory of the Indian economy experienced shifts over the three decades since the turn of the 1970s. This had implications for the technical (intermediate input) structure of production as well as adjustment (erosion or build-up) of value added across sectors over the period. The manufacturing sector failed to raise its relative share in the GDP while the service sector raised its own, steadily. In this context we have observed in Chapter 5 that the relative price for the manufacturing sector (vis-à-vis the GDP deflator) declined steadily while that for the service subsector EHPAD (education, health, public administration and defence) increased fast over the period concerned. We have defined the value added adjustment effect to take into account the impact of these changes on sectoral shares.

The study decomposes changes in sectoral shares into three components. The final demand effect considers changes in sectoral shares due to change in the structure of final demand only, keeping technical structure and prices (and the resulting value added coefficients) unchanged. The technical structure effect accounts for changes in production, and the sectoral shares concerned, caused by altered requirement for intermediate inputs while the adjustment effect accounts for changes in sectoral shares caused by changes in the value added coefficients.

We have considered a period of almost three decades in two phases. The first phase covers one and a half decades from 1978–79 and the second phase covers the rest of the period up to 2007–08. We also consider an overlapping phase of two decades to 2003–04. The most interesting finding is the drag on the share of the manufacturing sector caused by the adjustment of value added, invariably, over all the three phases over the three decades. It is found by analysing the IOTTs that the technical structure effect has tended consistently and substantially to raise the share of the manufacturing sector. Use of manufactured inputs, not only in the manufacturing sector, increased in intensity. This required additional production of manufactured goods. But this substantial and positive effect was wiped out and the sector's GVA was, further, drained systematically by the strong adverse adjustment effect. The result is qualitatively robust to changes in the reference period.

A major part of the service sector – Service-I – includes services that are mostly used as intermediate inputs in industry and especially, manufacturing. Service-II accounts for mainly final product services – EHPAD and 'other services' including 'business services'. EHPAD, has been a clear standout for being a consistent and significant beneficiary of adjustment gains, in all the phases. The very consistent and opposite effects on the manufacturing and the EHPAD sectors over all the three phases of our study support the basic hypothesis of Baumol's disease for the Indian economy.

Specific consideration must be reserved for Service-I. This category of services increased its share in GDP in the first phase, being greatly supported by the adjustment effect. While the finding is by no means against the hypothesis of cost disease, it explains the widening of the difference between sectoral shares of manufacturing and Service-I over the phase to the extent of a huge 8.5 percentage points. Technical structure effect pushed both the sectors roughly to the same extent. But the second phase tells us a different story – the adjustment effect was strong and negative in Service-I as it was for manufacturing. The observation is consistent with strong gain in productivity in both the sectors. The picture projected by the overlapping segment (1983–84 to 2003–04) is qualitatively the same as that of the second phase but quantitatively more emphatic about the loss of manufacturing, particularly considering its relative size. Here, adjustment effect explains manufacturing's loss in terms of percentage of GDP to the extent of 10.9 points against Service-I's loss of only 2.6 points. EHPAD gained to the extent of 6 points.

Even admitting that the precise measures of gains or losses are inevitably subject to questions regarding data quality, the evidence strongly indicates cost disease as an important explanation of the stagnation of manufacturing's GVA share. One implication of the above development is that when total factor productivity is sought to be measured by taking value added as a proxy for output the result will be unreliable, being an underestimate for the progressive sectors and an overestimate for the relatively stagnant sectors.

Appendix 6A Tables

TABLE 6A.1 Price Index of Sectoral Final Uses

	1968–69	1973–74	1978–79	1983–84	1989–90	1993–94	1998–99	2003–04	2007–08
Agr	1.19	1.20	1.05	1.02	0.97	1.00	1.02	1.00	0.82
Manf	**1.15**	**1.15**	**1.21**	**1.14**	**1.05**	**1.00**	**0.91**	**0.87**	**0.88**
Transp	1.00	0.84	0.96	0.89	0.96	1.00	1.02	1.11	1.07
Comn	0.82	0.70	0.88	0.70	0.94	1.00	0.78	0.40	0.26
THR	0.85	0.86	0.90	1.01	0.99	1.00	0.94	0.96	0.96
B I F	1.10	1.20	1.26	1.26	0.99	1.00	0.91	0.90	0.64
EHPAD	**0.66**	**0.67**	**0.75**	**0.78**	**0.92**	**1.00**	**1.25**	**1.47**	**1.81**
O. Serv	1.70	1.50	1.55	1.25	1.13	1.00	0.96	1.07	1.27

Source: Author's calculations.

Note: Obtained from the IOTTs as the ratio between sectoral shares in aggregate expenditures at current and constant prices.

TABLE 6A.2 Change in Sectoral Structure: 1968–69 to 1978–79 (1968–69 Prices)

	Col. 1	Col. 2	Col. 3	Col. 4	Col. 5	Col. 6
	VA:68-9	VA:78-9	$V_0(I - A_0)^{-1}\Delta F$	Col.1 + Col. 3	$V_0\Delta(I - A)^{-1}F_1$	$\Delta V(I - A_1)^{-1}F_1$
Agriculture	14,975	17,914	6,037	21,012	125	-3,204
Manufactures	4,854	9,600	3,697	8,552	889	160
M-share*	**15.10**	**19.39**	**21.32**	**17.28**	**1.79**	**0.32**
Other Industry	2,454	4,318	1,020	3475	252	574
Service-I	5,654	10,772	4,247	9,901	1,843	-974
Servc-I.share*	**17.58**	**21.76**	**24.48**	**20**	**3.72**	**-1.97**
EHPAD	2,092	3,261	983	3,075	9	521
Other Service	2,125	3,639	1,361	3,486	268	-463
Service-II	4,217	6,900	2,345	6,561	277	58
Servc-II.share*	**13.11**	**13.94**	**13.52**	**13.25**	**0.56**	**0.12**
Total	32,157	49,503	17,346	49,503	3,386	-3,386

Source: Author's calculation (see Appendix 5A.3 for methodology).

Notes: * Percentages of respective column totals, except for columns 5 and 6, where reference is to column 4 total (GDP).

Theoretically, the sum of entries in columns 4, 5 and 6 should match column 2 for each row. Here there is a small discrepancy (about 0.15 percent) due to mismatch between row and column sums for agriculture in the original IOTT for 1968–69.

Table 6A.3 Change in Sectoral Structure: 1978–79 to 1993–94 (1978–79 Prices)

	Col. 1	Col. 2	Col. 3	Col. 4	Col. 5	Col. 6
	VA:78–9	VA:93–4	$V_0(I - A_0)^{-1}\Delta F$	Col.1 + Col. 3	$V_0\Delta(I - A)^{-1}F_1$	$\Delta V(I - A_1)^{-1}F_1$
1. Agr	34,612	61,121	29,848	64,461	–5,894	2,555
2. Min	1,303	5,519	1,123	2,427	2,107	986
3. Manf	**18,548**	**36,616**	**24,410**	**42,957**	**4,090**	**-10,432**
M-share*	*19.39*	*16.73*	*19.80*	*19.62*	*1.87*	*-4.77*
4. Const	5,399	11,652	3,744	9,143	–657	3,166
5. Elec	1,640	5,263	2,217	3,856	3,140	-1,734
6.Transp.	5,523	15,228	8,060	13,583	1,528	118
7.Comm.	712	2,499	918	1,630	574	295
8. THR	12,034	30,367	13,097	25,131	–2,446	7,682
9. B & F	2,541	11,018	3,885	6,426	4,620	-27
Srvc-I	**20,811**	**59,111**	**25,960**	**46,770**	**4,275**	**8,067**
Srvc-I.shr*	*21.76*	*27.00*	*21.06*	*21.37*	*1.95*	*3.68*
10.EHPAD	**7,030**	**20,363**	**11,420**	**18451**	**410**	**1,503**
11.O.Srvc	6,300	19,263	24,543	30,843	3,620	-15,200
Srvc-II	**13,331**	**39,626**	**35,963**	**49,294**	**4,030**	**-13,697**
Srvc-II.shr*	*13.94*	*18.10*	*29.18*	*22.52*	*1.84*	*-6.26*
Total	95,643	218,909	123,265	218,908	11,090	-11089

Source: Author's calculation.

Note: *Percentages of respective column totals, except for columns 5 and 6, where reference is to the column 4 total.

Table 6A.4 Change in Sectoral Structure: 1978–79 to 1993–94 (1978–79 Prices)

	Col. 1	Col. 2	Col. 3	Col. 4	Col. 5	Col. 6
	VA:93–4	VA:07–8	$V_0(I - A_0)^{-1}F$	Col.1 + Col.3	$V_0\Delta(I - A)^{-1}F_1$	$\Delta V(I - A_1)^{-1}F_1$
1. Agr	231,898	355,198	204,289	436,187	38,944	–119,933
2. Min	20,941	55,778	7,079	28,020	14,486	13,272
3. Manf	*138,923*	*363,123*	*291,093*	*430,016*	*91,446*	*–158,339*
Manf.shr*	***0.167***	***0.174***	***0.232***	***0.206***	***0.044***	***–0.076***
4. Const	44,208	186,692	97,024	141,232	15,174	30,287
5. Elec	19,969	34,843	37,938	57,907	–19,848	–3,217
6.Transp.	57,776	152,401	107,176	164,952	–13,505	954
7.Comm.	9,480	29,429	62,553	72,033	54,330	–96,934
8. THR	115,213	349,659	195,201	310,414	55,831	–16,586
9. B & F	41,804	110,506	106,216	148,020	29,119	–66,633
Srvc-I	*224,273*	*641,995*	*471,145*	*695,418*	*125,776*	*–179,200*
Srvc-I.shr*	**0.270**	**0.308**	**0.376**	**0.334**	**0.060**	**–0.0860**
10.O.Srvc	73,087	238,652	109,025	182,112	–10,881	67,420
11.EHPAD	77,258	207,530	35,666	112,924	–1,217	95,823
Srvc-II	*150,345*	*446,181*	*144,691*	*295,036*	*–12,098*	*163,243*
Srvc-II.shr*	**0.181**	**0.214**	**0.115**	**0.142**	**–0.006**	**0.078**
Total	830,557	2,083,810	1,253,260	2,083,817	253,879	-253,886

Source: Author's calculation.

Note: *Percentages of respective column totals, except for columns 5 and 6, where reference is to the column 4 total.

Table A6.5 Change in Sectoral Structure: 1983–84 to 2003–04 (1983–84 Prices)

	Col. 1	Col. 2	Col. 3	Col. 4	Col. 5	Col. 6
	VA:83-4	VA:03-4	$V_0(I-A_0)^{-1}\Delta F$	Col.1 + Col. 3	$V_0\Delta(I-A)^{-1}F_1$	$\Delta V(I-A_1)^{-1}F_1$
1. Agr	66,202	111,383	72,375	138,577	–16,707	–10,487
2. Min	5,402	14,737	–2,831	2,571	16,183	–4,017
3. Manf	38,750	106,985	102,663	141,413	30,018	–64,447
Manf.shr*	**0.20**	**0.18**	**0.26**	**0.24**	**0.05**	**–0.11**
4. Const	10,949	40,270	24,384	35,333	–591	5,528
5. Elec	3,634	9,645	8,701	12,336	3,102	–5,792
6.Transp.	10,083	41,101	29,084	39,166	–1,267	3,201
7.Comm.	1,329	9,817	6,822	8,151	10,853	–9,186
8. THR	23,029	91,079	57,505	80,534	3,445	7,099
9. B & F	5,873	36,452	23,774	29,647	23,337	–16,532
Srvc-I	40,314	178,449	117,185	157,498	36,369	–15,417
Srvc-I.shr*	**0.20**	**0.30**	**0.30**	**0.27**	**0.06**	**–0.03**
10. EHPAD	16,381	67,475	16,121	32,502	–8	34,980
11.O.Srvc	16,790	62,634	54,560	71,350	–2,834	–5,882
Srvc-II	33,171	130,109	70,681	103,852	–2,842	29,099
Srvc-II.shr*	0.17	0.22	0.18	0.18	0.00	0.05
	198,422	591,579	393,158	591,580	65,532	–65,533

Source: Author's calculation.

Note: *Percentages of respective column totals, except for columns 5 and 6, where reference is to the column 4 total.

Notes

1. Each sector has a number of products and their prices vary in the course of a year; so, no single price or quantity exists. Our unique sectoral price and quantity are abstractions.
2. Obtaining that from the deflated IOTT is meaningless.
3. This is true for computations at basic prices. Product taxes make a difference for GDP at market prices. Exact definitions are given in Chapter 3.
4. The GDP deflator is obtained as the ratio of current and constant price estimates of GDP, or aggregate final expenditure.
5. Which is the difference between the values of output and intermediate inputs.
6. We have discussed the methodology used for conversion to real terms in Appendix 5A.3 of Chapter 5.

7. The point has been discussed in detail in Chapter 2.
8. We have discussed the point in more detail in the previous chapter.
9. The IOTTs show total sectoral imports only on the expenditure side, but not its uses separately as intermediate inputs on the production side.
10. As we want to compare changes over time, all the variables expressed in money terms have to be adjusted for price changes. We have discussed the methodology used for conversion to real terms in Appendix 5A.3.
11. For evaluation, the current period's data must be converted at base year prices and base year value added structure used.
12. $(I - A)^{-1}$ is the total direct and indirect requirements matrix where A represents the technical coefficients structure.
13. The corresponding data is shown in Table 5A.2, in the appendix to Chapter 5.
14. Table 6A.1 indicates a mild increase in service input intensity of manufacturing production. In the view of the challenges of measurement it is hazardous to comment on the basis of such small observed changes. Nevertheless, it is interesting to look at how the multi-national companies strive to reduce their costs by de-verticalizing their activities – outsourcing certain functions and sub-contracting the production of numerous components forming a chain (for example in automobiles and electronics goods) world-wide (Yusuf, 2004: 2; Kraemer, Linden and Jason, 2011). Shift from single stage to multi-stage production process adds to the 'depth' of the process. Such processes may even take place within the limited confines of domestic boundaries. The Indian economy, one presumes, is not free from comparable effects adding stages to production while diversifying the production base. These changes may affect the intermediate (both manufactured and services) input coefficients of the relevant sectors.
15. A topical example of how V is dependent on A is the splintering of production. It causes a part of the production process and value added of some sector to be transferred to another sector. Thus when janitorial service that used to be generated, say, within a commercial bank, is outsourced from a specialized service provider, the change would be reflected in an increase of service input to the bank reducing its value added, but not the output; and equivalently, output as well as value added of the service provider ('other services') should increase as a result. There is enough casual evidence of such reorganization of production taking place and it may happen in the manufacturing sector as well.
16. Using V_0 for the technical structure effect may not be very appropriate because change in A would conceptually change V. The change may be significant in specific lines of production, but for the broad sectors that we are concerned with here, it may not be very significant, by our evidence given in Figure 6.1. Using V_1 instead is inappropriate as well, since in the presence of systematic changes in relative prices, as our analysis in Chapter 5 suggests to be the case, this change, rather than marginal changes in overall input use, is the more proximate cause of change in V. This change in V has been captured in the adjustment effect.
17. We have noted in Chapter 5 that capital–output ratio in manufacturing has remained stable while labour productivity has increased substantially.

18. The identity is independent of the final demand vector.
19. This can be checked from the 5-year moving average growth trend of GDP shown in Figure 4.1 in Chapter 4.
20. Though the reading is based on observations of only four years, the years are roughly equally spaced and the observations show a steady pattern.
21. In IOTTs, output is sum of direct and indirect requirements for production of the final demand. Hence it includes intra-sectoral intermediate use.
22. It should be noted that the sectoral shares obtained from the IOTTs, as shown in the table, are a bit different from the corresponding NAS estimates. In the estimates presented in the table, taxes on intermediate inputs are shown in the value added by the using sector. This was required to ensure equality between aggregate value added and aggregate final expenditure. See Chapter 3 for detailed discussion.
23. This is quite understandable as manufacturing's intra-sectoral intermediate input use as well as some other sectors' use of manufactured inputs increased. Manufacturing's use of agricultural inputs decreased and that is reflected in agriculture's technical structure effect (see more detailed table in the appendix).
24. We could not separate 'real estate and business services' from 'other services' as IOTTs clubbed them together in seven of the nine matrices available.
25. But the gain of the service sector as a whole was contained by a fall in prices for 'other services'.
26. Relative shares given by the IOTTs include indirect taxes on intermediate inputs and are, therefore, somewhat higher than the shares at factor cost given by the National Accounts Statistics.
27. It seems that the economy experienced substantial productivity gains during both the phases while evidence from productivity studies is generally not so emphatic. Many studies use value added at constant prices as the measure of output. Since value added per unit of output has declined steadily, such measures will underestimate productivity gains.
28. The inference is corroborated by the study of Dehejia and Panagariya (2013).
29. A collection of excellent papers on the theoretical and empirical issues is Hulten, Dean and Harper (2001).

7

Demand for Intermediate Services

Observation and description, definition and classification are the preparatory activities. But what we desire to reach thereby is a knowledge of the interdependence of economic phenomena.... Induction and deduction are both needed for scientific thought as the left and right foot are both needed for walking.

—Quoted from *Economic Generalizations Or Laws* (Marshall, 1961: 24)

Introduction

Input–output transactions tables (IOTTs) provide a very convenient tool to understand an economy's sectoral interconnections. It provides both the production and the expenditure sides of the economy in a compact form and is a very practical way of presenting national accounts that must show a balance between the two sides for conceptual accuracy. We had a glimpse of the importance of this balance for economic analysis in the previous chapters and we will continue to exploit the inter-industry relations in the rest of the book. However, since our experience concerns a multidimensional reality, capturing it in single or in two dimensions inevitably means a constrained view; but that serves to show how constrained we are.

What readily comes to mind is adding a time dimension to the two dimensional picture presented by the IOTTs. Just as a three dimensional object is sought to be understood by taking multiple slices – what can be thought of as two dimensional – of the object, we seek to understand an economy over time using multiple IOTTs at, more or less, regular intervals of time.[1] While an IOTT may be viewed as a snapshot of the economy, it really represents an interval – a year, collapsed to a single point. In computing the input (or technical) coefficients we divide the specific input required to obtain a quantity of output over a year, by the output quantity. Thus we compute the average, and in this sense, representative coefficient for the year.[2] One seeks to visualize a rule that explains movement from one observation to the next. Since reality is extremely complex, specification of a simple rule seems silly but its utility lies in generating an insight. In a simple dynamic analysis one may add a time dimension with a rule in the form of a fixed parameter, say, a uniform rate of growth of a variable per year to see its impact on some other variable under focus. What we aim to do in the rest of this chapter is to define a set of elementary rules (a model) that, in our view, represents the reality in some important aspects. The resulting model then projects the behavior of some variables under focus. The next task is to check the inferred behaviour against broad observations: how far the inferences from the model match the reality.

We have noted in Chapter 4 that in terms of GVA, Service-I has been the fastest growing sector of the Indian economy over several decades. The sector is constituted of three groups of activities: 'transport and communications', 'trade, hotels and restaurants' and 'banking, insurance and finance'. For convenience, henceforth, we refer to them simply as transport, trade and finance, respectively. Transport and trade are required mainly for the distribution of goods, though a part of transport services has direct final use for travel and other purposes. In IOTTs, the part of the services used for distribution of goods to, or used directly by, final users is taken as final service; and the rest, used for distribution of intermediate inputs, is taken as intermediate service. For finance, too, the same norm is applied for classification. But this norm should not distract us from the fact that demands for the relevant services are derived from the demand for commodities.[3]

Figure 7.1 shows that the rapid rise in overall services' share in GDP is largely a story of rapid growth in trade and transport services. As we have seen in earlier chapters, Service-I is the more dynamic part of the overall services sector while trade and transport explain roughly four-fifths of the GVA in Service-I. How do we understand this phenomenon of rapid growth of trade and transport services?[4]

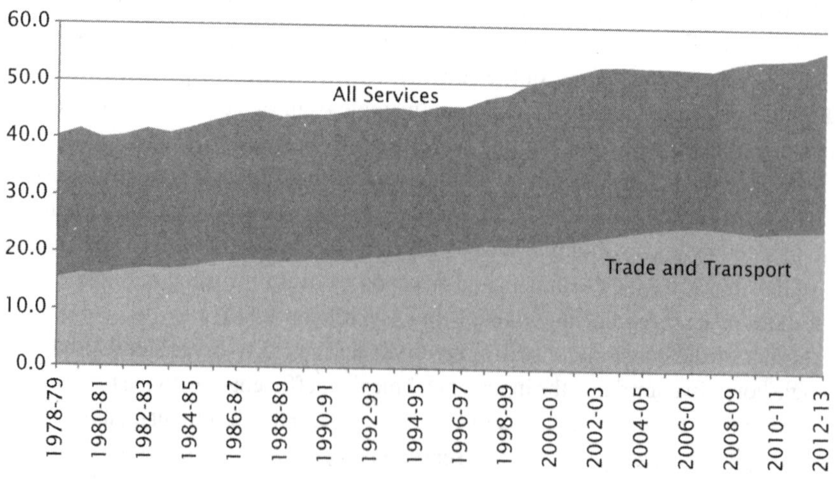

Figure 7.1 GDP Share – All Services and 'Trade and Transport' Service

Source: GOI, www.mospi.nic.in/data, GDP by Economic Activity at 2004–05 prices, accessed in October 2018.

An important point regarding the growth of an activity, as we have already discussed in the previous chapters, is the distinction between the two aspects of production – gross value added (GVA) and output. Conceptually, output has price and quantity dimensions, though for services these are often amorphous (discussed in Chapter 4). For practical purposes, there is a volume of service expressed in value terms and we have a quantity index. Technical coefficients in IOTTs refer to such quantities. We have discussed in Chapters 5 and 6 how systematic movement of relative price can, and did, generate systematic divergence between sectoral growth rates of GVA and output in India. In the present discussion we abstract from changes in price and input coefficients; we will discuss changes in the coefficients towards the end of the chapter. So, we are not concerned with the erosion of value added. Here we seek to focus on the demand for distributive services, constituted of trade and transport services.

In the next section we develop a simple model of industrialization with growing spread and depth of manufacturing as explained later, generating demand for distributive services. In this setup the growth of distributive service related to intermediate inputs surpasses that related to final demand. The following section takes a broader look to see how the conclusion of the model stands against the complexity of reality, and then the discussion proceed to check from the IOTTs how far the growth of Service-I can be understood from technical interrelations. The final section summarizes and concludes the chapter.

Derived Demand for Distributive Services

Demand for distributive trade is wholly a derived demand arising from demand for goods.[5] Also, transport is intimately related to trade (Martinez-Zarzoso and Maria, 2008), so a very large part of the demand for transport services is derived demand too. A similar point can be made regarding the demand for financial services. This means that the growth of the above services is linked to the growth of other activities; most prominently, manufacturing. The three services together, referred to as Service-I, as we know, account for more than half of the value-added in the service sector of the Indian economy in recent times. Here we proceed with our arguments in terms of trade and transport services; these services are unavoidable for the distribution of goods, be it for intermediate or final use. But, to the extent that productive activities are self-financed, the implicit financial service may not get separately reflected in the GDP. So, this demand is not inevitable though important and when it occurs, it is derived.

Keeping the intimate functional link between trade and transport services in mind, in the following discussion we will consider the two services as integrated in their distributive function and call this integrated service the TT service. In order to highlight the link of this integrated service with the structure of production of goods, we do not consider here the part of transport service that is dissociated from distributive trade and demanded for its own sake, like transport for travel. So, we consider only integrated TT service, demand for which is derived from the demand for goods. We can view it as final service (T_F) to the extent it is used to distribute goods to final users; and, as intermediate service (T_I) when it is used to distribute intermediate inputs.[6] The value of intermediate TT-service gets incorporated into the producer's price of relevant goods; but the final TT-service is paid for by final users only, the charge getting reflected in the purchaser's price.

The structural change in an economy is the manifestation of uneven growth of different sectors. We know while agriculture declines relatively due to the Engel effect, industry along with services expands.[7] An important part of manufacturing's growth is caused by expansion in scale and scope to meet consumer's choices. We may call it the spread effect. A very obvious example is carbonated soft drinks companies diversifying to 'new age' soft drinks like bottled water, tea-based ones etc. Similarly, milk dairies diversified from packaged milk to several milk products (Ghemawat, 1998: ch. 4). But there is a simultaneous process of achieving depth in the sense that in the course of economic development, gradually more and more sophisticated parts of a basically round-about production process become integrated with domestic production as links in a chain constituting a complete process; lengthening of these links adds to the depth.[8] The idea here is that the different sub-processes are often not vertically integrated; in fact, de-verticalization is often a conscious strategy for achieving efficiency in modern times (Yousuf, 2004). With the sophistication of technology, in general, the finished goods are increasingly the cumulative outcome of operations of a lengthening chain of sub-processes[9]. This may well have implications for TT intensities of production. The point may be explained in terms of the following structured argument.

A Model of Industrialization with Induced TT Services

Case-I: Rudimentary Manufacturing and Derived Demand

We first consider an economy under autarky, where final products come from agriculture and rudimentary manufacturing.[10] We will abstract from price changes; so we can take all the prices to be unity with suitable definition of units of quantity. Let us denote the output of agriculture by A and that of rudimentary manufacturing, which only processes minerals and does not take manufactured intermediate input, by M; we will introduce advanced manufacturing at a later stage. Let us assume that A is produced without any intermediate input while M takes intermediate inputs from mining and TT services but not agriculture. Let B be the output of mining used wholly as intermediate input in manufacturing.[11] The only service produced in the economy is TT service; it does not take any intermediate input, so that its output, T, is its value added. The input–output structure is represented by Table 7.1. Its different columns show inputs used by producing sectors and intermediate or final uses of outputs; the final column shows total uses or outputs. The rows corresponding to sectors show use of a sector's produce, while the last row shows factor payments, which is value added. Note that output of TT service – T – represented by a margin (τ) on goods handled, is:

$$T = \text{Sum of intermediate and final uses} = B\tau + (A + M)\tau. \quad \dots (1)$$

It can be seen from the 'TT service' row in Table 7.1. Output is also the value added, as already pointed out, of the sector as the service does not use any intermediate input, by assumption.[12]

Gross Domestic Product (Y) = Aggregate value added = Aggregate final uses.[13] From the column of final uses, which is identical with the last row sum in Table 7.1 we can write:

$$Y = (A + M)(1 + \tau) \quad \dots (2)$$

From (1) and (2), the share of TT-service in GDP $= (A + M + B)\tau / (A + M)(1 + \tau)$

Or, $$T/Y = [1 + B/(A + M)]\,\tau / (1 + \tau) \quad \dots (3)$$

Table 7.1 Inter-industry Flows with Rudimentary Manufacturing

	Agri-culture	Mining	Manu-facturing	TT-service	Intermediate Use (total)	Final Use	Output
Agriculture	0	0	0	0	0	A	A
Mining	0	0	B	0	B	0	B
Manufacturing	0	0	0	0	0	M	M
TT-service	0	0	Bτ	0	Bτ	(A + M)τ	T
Column total	0	0	B(1 + τ)	0	B(1+τ)		
Factor payments = Value added	A	B	M – B(1 + τ)	T = (A + M + B)τ		(A + M)(1 + τ) = **GDP** (Y)	

Clearly, *for case-I*, final trade share, $T_F/Y = \tau/(1 + \tau) \quad \dots (3a)$

And intermediate trade share, $T_I/Y = [B/(A + M)]\,\tau/(1 + \tau) \quad \dots (3b)$

So, for the rudimentary economy, $T_I/T_F = [B/(A + M)] \quad \dots (4)$

One may now introduce dynamics into the model in a simple way. One stylized fact about economic development is that manufacturing production grows much faster than agriculture in a developing economy (LDC). Accordingly, let us suppose, A and M grow smoothly at rates α and μ respectively $(\mu > \alpha)$.

Then, at time 't', $$A_t = a.e^{\alpha t} \quad \ldots (5)$$

and $$M_t = m.e^{\mu t} = V.B_{t.}\ (1 + \tau),\ \ V > 1. \quad \ldots (6)$$

Where, τ (> 0) is the TT-margin as before; V is the constant factor by which the value of intermediate input $B_t(1 + \tau)$ is multiplied in transformation into output M_t. So, $(V - 1)$ is the factor for value-added in the rudimentary manufacturing process. We do not need to specify the production functions beyond the maintained assumption of a constant intermediate input coefficient in manufacturing, as we presume industrialization and focus on the basic idea of induced demand for TT service. Clearly, from (5) and (6),

$a = A_0$ and $m = M_0 = V.B_{0.}\ (1 + \tau)$. Or, $B_0 = m / V(1 + \tau) = b$ (say) [clearly, $b < m$].

It follows immediately from (6),

$$B_{t.} = [m / V.(1 + \tau)].e^{\mu t} = b.e^{\mu t}, \quad \ldots (6.1)$$

Now, value-added (same as output, T) in TT services is the sum of value-added in intermediate TT (T_I) and final TT (T_F) services. So, T may be written in terms of a uniform TT-margin as:

$$T_t = [T_F + T_I] = (A_t + M_t)\ \tau + B_t \tau = (a.e^{\alpha t} + m.e^{\mu t})\ \tau + be^{\mu t}\tau \quad \ldots (7)$$

At this stage, A_t and M_t are the final uses of A and M respectively at producer's prices, while B_t is the intermediate use of minerals; we must add the TT service charge on final use to get GDP, which is the aggregate final demand at purchaser's prices (from the final use column of Table 7.1):

$$Y_t = (ae^{\alpha t} + me^{\mu t})(1 + \tau) \quad \ldots (8)$$

So, TT share in GDP,

$$\begin{aligned}[T_t / Y_t] &= \chi_t \text{ (say)} \\ &= \{(ae^{\alpha t} + me^{\mu t})\tau + be^{\mu t}\tau\}/(ae^{\alpha t} + me^{\mu t})(1 + \tau) \\ &= \{\tau / (1 + \tau)\} + [b / (a.e^{(\alpha - \mu) t} + m)].\{\tau / (1 + \tau)\} \quad \ldots (9)\end{aligned}$$

(9) may be compared with (3).

The first and the second terms in (9) stand for final and intermediate TT ratios in GDP respectively. It is clear that the final TT service is a constant proportion of the GDP (it can also be verified from Table 7.1). Further, the trade components ratio (or simply the trade ratio; the components are shown in equation [7]) is given by:

$$T_I / T_F = b / (a.e^{(\alpha - \mu)t} + m), \text{ where } (\alpha - \mu) < 0 \qquad \ldots (10)$$

Clearly, the ratio rises over time. The limiting value for a rudimentary economy is $b/m < 1$. So, χ_t rises over time due to intermediate trade. *This growth of the trade share is entirely explained by the spread effect caused by faster growth (spread) of manufacturing production vis-à-vis agricultural production, as manufacturing only involves intermediate trade in the model.* (This simplifying assumption can be justified from observations from all the IOTTs for the Indian economy, which confirm that trade and transport coefficients [that is, use per unit of output] for agriculture are much smaller than those for manufacturing.)

Case-II: Advanced Manufacturing and TT Services

In the course of development, as we have mentioned above, much of manufacturing evolves into multi-link chains; in that sense the depth of manufacturing increases. Let us introduce one higher stage of manufacturing; at this stage manufacturing uses a proportion, λ $(0 < \lambda < 1)$, of the output of rudimentary manufacturing (M) as input; the output of this higher stage being denoted by N. Thus, when two stages operate, total final use of manufacturing is $[(1 - \lambda)M + N]$. The input–output structure now is as follows:

Table 7.2 Inter-industry Flows with Advanced Manufacturing

	Agri-culture	Mining	Manufac-turing-I	Manufac-turing-II	TT-service	Intermediate Use	Final Use	Output
Agriculture	0	0	0		0	0	A	A
Mining	0	0	B		0	B	0	B
Manufac-turing-I	0	0	0	λM	0	λM	$(1 - \lambda)M$	M
Manufac-turing-II	0	0	0	0	0	0	N	N
TT-service	0	0	$B\tau$	$\lambda M\tau$	0	$(B + \lambda M)\tau$	$[A + (1 - \lambda)M + N]\tau$	T = row sum
Column total	0	0	$B(1 + \tau)$	$\lambda M(1 + \tau)$	0	$(B + \lambda M)(1 + \tau)$	$[A + (1 - \lambda)M + N](1 + \tau)$ = **GDP** (Y)	
Factor payments = Value added	A	B	$M - B(1 + \tau)$	$N - \lambda M(1 + \tau)$	T			

Now, T (row sum) $= (A + B + M + N)\tau$.

gross domestic product (Y) = aggregate final use (check the relevant column of Table 7.2) $= (A + (1 - \lambda)M + N)\,(1 + \tau)$

Share of TT-service in GDP (T/Y)

$$= (A + B + M + N)\,\tau \,/\, (A + (1 - \lambda)M + N)\,(1 + \tau)$$

$$= [1 + (B + \lambda M) \,/\, (A + (1 - \lambda)M + N)]\tau \,/\, (1 + \tau) \qquad \dots (11)$$

From the final use column of Table 7.2:

$$T_F / Y = \tau / (1 + \tau) \qquad \dots (11.1)$$

and

$$T_I / Y = [(B + \lambda M) \,/\, (A + (1 - \lambda)M + N)]\, \tau \,/\, (1 + \tau) \qquad \dots (11.2)$$

Or

$$T_I / T_F = [(B + \lambda M) \,/\, (A + (1 - \lambda)M + N)] \qquad \dots (12)$$

This advanced manufacturing uses λM and associated TT service as input for further processing resulting in output N. Let W (> 1) be the factor by which intermediate input is multiplied at this stage. So, output is:

$$N = W \lambda\, M (1 + \tau) \qquad \dots (13)$$

Substituting in (12),

$$T_I / T_F = (B + \lambda M) \,/\, [(A + M) + \lambda M\, \{W(1 + \tau) - 1\}] \qquad \dots (12.1)$$

Equation (12.1) may compare with (4). The final-TT ratio to GDP being the same in the two cases, the difference is purely for intermediate-TT share. Equation (12.1) adds λM to the numerator and $\{W(1 + \tau) - 1\}$ times λM to the denominator of (4).

Introducing growth over time, we can write:

$$N_t = W \lambda\, M_t (1 + \tau) = W \lambda\, m e^{\mu t} (1 + \tau) = n e^{\mu t} \qquad \dots (13.1)$$

Clearly, $n = W\lambda m (1 + \tau)$

The growth of manufacturing production now is caused not only by expansion in scale and scope, as in Case-I, but also by processing of manufactured products in the higher stage, adding depth to manufacturing. This also enhances intermediate TT to the extent of $\lambda M\tau$. So, total intermediate TT services now is: $T_{I.t} = (\lambda M_t + B_t)\tau$, and aggregate value-added in TT service is:

$$T_t = (A_t + B_t + M_t + N_t)\tau = (ae^{\alpha t}{}_{+}\, ne^{\mu t})\tau + (b + m)e^{\mu t}.\tau \dots (14)$$

Now GDP is: $Y_t = (ae^{\alpha s} + (1 - \lambda)me^{\mu s} + ne^{\mu t})(1 + \tau)$ ... (15)

Taking the ratio of (14) and (15), TT service as a ratio to GDP is:

$$\chi_t = \{\tau / (1 + \tau)\} + [(b + \lambda m)e^{\mu t} / (ae^{\alpha t} + (1 - \lambda)me^{\mu t} + ne^{\mu t})]\, \{\tau / (1 + \tau)\},$$

which further reduces to:

$$\chi_t = \tau / (1 + \tau) \, [1 + (b + \lambda m) / (ae^{(\alpha - \mu)t} + m + \lambda m\{W(1 + \tau) - 1\})] \quad \ldots (16)$$

So, the trade ratio,

$$T_I / T_F = (b + \lambda m) / (ae^{(\alpha - \mu)t} + m + \lambda m\{W(1 + \tau) - 1\}) \quad \ldots (17)$$

[This ratio may be checked against (12.1)]

We intend to compare (10) with (17), that is, trade ratios in stage-I and stage-II, to check how the ratio has changed. In (17) the numerator is that of (10) plus λm, while the denominator is higher by $\{W(1 + \tau) - 1\}$ times λm. What should be the value of the expression within the braces? We can do better than making conjectures by looking at information given by the IOTTs for the Indian economy. [We can try to be objective by looking at information given by the IOTTS. Table 6A.1in Chapter 6 (and Figure 6.1) shows that aggregate intermediate input coefficient of the manufacturing sector has remained fairly stable at 0.7 over the last four decades.[14] This observation may be a basis for a guestimate of W, which is the transformation factor on aggregate input. On the above basis we take the ratio of aggregate output to intermediate input for manufacturing to be 1.5. Similarly, the ratio between aggregate TT-input to aggregate material inputs in all the sectors turns out to be less than one-third; this indicates an upper-side estimate of $(1 + \tau)$ to be 4/3.] Based on the information it seems fair to take the estimate of $\{W(1 + \tau) - 1\}$, generally, not to exceed unity; which means (17) adds roughly the same quantity to the numerator and the denominator of (10).

As for the expression for trade ratio (T_I / T_F) in stage-I, $b / (a.e^{(\alpha - \mu)t} + m)$, given by (10), we may note that value (at factor cost) of agricultural output was almost at par with that of manufactures in 1978–79.[15] So, taking $t = 0$ at that point, we have $a = m$. Further, going by equation (6.1), $b = m/V(1 + \tau)$. Taking $V = 3/2$ (the same as W) and $(1 + \tau) = 4/3$, as determined above, b is half of m, that is, one-fourth the denominator in (10). Based on this consideration, T_I/Y, at $t = 0$, is around 1/4 in the present construct.[16]

Clearly, by adding the same positive quantity, roughly λm, to the numerator and the denominator, (17) takes a jump over (10) due to addition of depth to manufacturing; and magnitude of this jump is positively related to λ. In fact, even in the limiting case, as t tends to infinity, with $m = 2b$, addition of a new stage of manufacturing enhances the intermediate trade ratio. So, even though our analysis in only indicative, we conclude; *rising depth of manufacturing causes the trade ratio to continually shift up over time.*[17] An immediate implication is that the relative share (or proportion) of TT services in GDP is boosted as $\chi_t = (T_I + T_F) / Y = T_F / Y(1 + T_I / T_F)$. (Note that *$T_F / Y$ is constant.*) *The intuition is simple: since intermediate demand for TT services come basically from manufacturing, as the* *sector grows fast the services also grow fast and this service growth gets a boost as manufacturing achieves depth leading to rise in intermediate input intensity.* Are there any offsets or fillips to this trend? We need further considerations.

Further Considerations on the Trade Components Ratio

The abstraction from reality in the above arguments is obvious. The trade components ratio (T_I / T_F) given by equation (10) considers only the spread effect while expression (17) brings into focus our basic idea of growing depth of manufacturing. Abstraction from agricultural inputs to manufacturing does not seem to affect the trend of the trade ratio very much because from the point of view of our model it does not matter if input comes from agriculture or mining. Similarly, our abstraction from final-product services also does not seem to seriously affect the dynamics of trade share, as the services are not much related to either intermediate or final trade.

Probably the most glaring omission from the model is the sector – construction. This activity takes intermediate input more intensively than the manufacturing sector itself though the produce of the sector is not distributed through trade (see sectoral interrelations matrix, Table 7A.1 through Table 7A.3); so the relevant demand for the TT service is wholly for handling intermediate inputs. Another impropriety is in assuming away intermediate inputs of the transport sector. The above sectors may be viewed as raising the relative share of TT services in GDP through the spread effect, but it is the manufacturing sector that boosts the relative share through both spread and depth effects.

There may be several other causes acting to qualify the conclusion of the model. Thus, intermediate TT may be restrained by vertical integration and boosted by de-verticalization. Variation of TT margins across activities and over time[18] may bring complications into the straightforward account given above. Thus, how the relative shares of intermediate and final TT services will behave in the course of economic growth will inevitably depend on a host of developments apart from the growing spread and depth of manufacturing; but that does not detract from the importance of two effects – the spread effect and, specifically, the depth effect of manufacturing – for the trade ratio.[19]

The above discussion makes it abundantly clear that trade and transport and, by the same logic, finance and business services, should not be discussed in the same strain as other services like public administration, education, health and personal services grouped together in national accounts as 'community, social and personal services' (CSP). CSP is demanded mainly for direct gratification of personal and community needs while the former category of services that we call Service-I, is predominantly linked to goods production. With enough justification, one may say that the growth of Service-I is derived from the growth of goods production. *It is from this vantage point that the phenomenal growth of value added in Service-I of the Indian economy, leaving the goods sector (primary and secondary) way behind (discussed earlier), needs to be viewed with caution.*

The Trade Ratio, Sectoral Interrelations and the Demand Structure

We have seen in Chapter 4 (Table 4.1) that trade and transport subsectors taken together (roughly, what we have called TT-service plus direct use of transport) have increased rapidly relative to other sectors in terms of sectoral GDP. At current prices, the relative share of the group in GDP has increased from 16 per cent in 1980–81 to almost 25 per cent in 2012–13. Over the same period the relative share of the subsector 'banking, insurance and finance' has almost doubled from 3 per cent. This, of course, does not project a true picture of real growth, which is distorted by relative price movements as we have discussed in Chapters 5 and 6. A better picture of real growth is given by that of sectoral gross output at constant prices (the trickiness of measurement of volume of services notwithstanding), which is a little bit slower, shown in Table 4.2. It emerges that the growth of Service-I has been of the same order of magnitude as that of manufacturing over the three decades since the turn of the 1970s, as one would expect from the logic of the model presented here.

We obtained estimates of the trade components ratio (T_I / T_F) from the IOTTs. The trend of the ratio shows a definite sign of increase. The ratio increased from 0.713 in 1968–69 to 1.041 in 2007–08. Taking the average of observations from two consecutive IOTTs, the ratio increases from 0.725 (average from 1968–69 and 1973–74 IOTTs) to 0.943 (from 2003–04 and 2007–08 IOTTs). If we take only distributive trade, then the corresponding increase is found to be of the same order of magnitude, from 0.760 to 0.975. This is, again, in perfect tune with our analysis of the dynamics of the TT service. While this finding seems to be in perfect tune with our analysis of the dynamics of the TT service, our analysis based on equation (10) suggested a much smaller ratio (around one-fourth) as we abstracted from intermediate trade in several activities. Further, the assumptions of a uniform trade margin, along with a closed economy and all that, militate against reality. Nevertheless, as an academic curiosity, we computed the ratio of the part of TT service having intermediate use in manufacturing and the remaining part from the IOTTs. Following the logic of treating all intermediate TT services in activities that we have abstracted from as final service, this ratio should be of interest in the context of equations (10) and (17). The average of the ratios for 1973–74 and 1978–79 is 0.239. It increases to 0.254 in 1993–94 and, again, the average of the ratios in 2003–04 and 2007–08 is higher still, 0.281. These observations are in perfect tune with our analysis.

Readings from the IOTTs, after conversion to constant prices, show that the manufacturing sector's self intermediate input coefficient almost steadily increased from 0.275 in 1968–69 to 0.367 in 2007–08 (Table 5A.2 in Chapter 5). The observation is consistent with the hypothesis of increasing depth of manufacturing production. A more comprehensive index of this self intermediate input intensity is the total (direct plus indirect) requirement shown by the relevant column of the Leontief inverse matrix (given in the appendix, Tables 7A.1 to 7A.3). The total requirement of output of manufactures to obtain one unit of manufactured goods for final use has steadily increased – from 1.437 in 1973–74 to 1.580 and 1.741 in 1993–94 and 2007–08 respectively.

Table 7.3 Sectoral Shares in Aggregate Final Use (at 1993–94 Prices)

	1968–69	1978–79	1989–90	1993–94	2003–04	2007–08	2012–13*
Agriculture	0.356	0.315	0.270	0.265	0.169	0.133	0.077
Mining@	–0.004	–0.015	–0.020	–0.021	–0.041	–0.043	
Manufacturing	0.163	0.209	0.278	0.244	0.304	0.311	0.355
Construction	0.161	0.148	0.117	0.112	0.140	0.144	
EGW	0.003	0.005	0.009	0.007	0.008	0.010	
Transport, etc.	0.056	0.048	0.052	0.066	0.077	0.095	
Trade, etc.	0.084	0.119	0.106	0.113	0.120	0.117	
Banking, etc.	0.006	0.008	0.007	0.012	0.022	0.022	
Service-I	0.150	0.180	0.170	0.196	0.235	0.264	0.236*
EHPAD	0.140	0.126	0.115	0.105	0.086	0.075	
O. Serv.	0.031	0.032	0.059	0.091	0.099	0.106	
Service-II	0.170	0.158	0.174	0.197	0.185	0.181	0.224*

Source: IOTTs for the Indian economy published by the CSO (GOI, various years), New Delhi.

Notes: *2012–13 figures are not comparable with those from previous (commodity x commodity) IOTTs, because those are based on Use table and include product taxes. Also, due to reclassification, Service-I and Service-II are somewhat different in the Use table compared to the earlier IOTTs.

@Negative figures indicate large imports of mainly petroleum crude, used as intermediate input.

The above observations highlight the key role of manufactures in generating demand for TT-service (and more broadly, Service-I) in the increasingly roundabout production processes. Of natural interest (though not directly related) here – how did the weight of manufactures and, more broadly, products of different sectors, in final demand (not output, which is the sum of intermediate and final demands) evolve over time? Table 7.3 presents the information taken from the IOTTs after conversion to the price base of 1993–94.[20] It shows that manufacturing's weight has almost doubled in four decades since the turn of the 1960s. Service-I also has raised its weight, somewhat to a lesser extent, as one might expect due to the predominant intermediate input use of the sector's output. Weight increments have been possible due to the decline in the weight of agriculture.

Summary and Conclusion

The chapter analyses the dynamics of the most prominent intermediate service – distributive trade and related transport, put together as TT-service. The growth experience of the Indian economy shows a relentless rise in the relative share of TT service in GDP. Demand for the service is derived from the demand for goods – to study the implication of this interdependence, we develop a simple model of industrialization to highlight the growing spread and depth of manufacturing. With growing complexity of techniques the finished goods are increasingly the cumulative outcome of operations of a lengthening chain of sub-processes. We have focused on the deepening of links in the interconnected manufacturing process, what we have called the depth effect. This has implications for TT intensity of production. Our simple model shows that rising depth of manufacturing causes the relative share of TT services in GDP to rise over time. This process should work to enhance the relative importance of intermediate TT service and raise the trade components ratio (T_I / T_F). The whole gamut of influences determining the GDP-share of the broader sector – Service-I, which includes, apart from TT services, direct use of transport as well as financial services – is a complex and dynamic process, and we have not ventured into any quantitative exercise other than what can be read directly from the IOTTs. Our inquiry is centred on the key role of the manufacturing sector in creating demand for intermediate and final TT service. This demand is boosted by other activities to which it is the key supplier of intermediate inputs, most prominently constructions. Evidence from the sectoral interrelations given by the Leontief inverse matrices, substantiates the point.

Our model highlights that the share of TT service in GDP is driven by its two components – the intermediate trade ratio (T_I / Y), which is the more dynamic part and the final trade ratio (T_F / Y), which is expected to be rather stable. Intermediate trade is influenced by the growing spread of industry and rising depth of manufacturing. This derived nature of TT services, and more generally demand for Service-I, makes it imperative that the phenomenal growth of value added in Service-I of the Indian economy, leaving the goods sector (primary and secondary) way behind as discussed earlier, needs to be viewed with caution. As a related curiosity, we have examined the movement of relative weights of different sectors in aggregate final use (and also aggregate consumption). The finding is that manufacturing is the most dominant sector that has increased its weight in final use more than the sectors trade or transport, or even Service-I.

Appendix 7A

Table 7A.1 Leontief Inverse Matrix, 1973–74, Converted to 1993–94 Prices

Sector	1	2	3	4	5	6	7	8	9
1. Agriculture	1.220	0.015	0.318	0.141	0.040	0.088	0.015	0.109	0.012
2. Mining	0.007	1.009	0.101	0.039	0.140	0.029	0.005	0.011	0.005
3. Manufcture	0.076	0.059	1.437	0.257	0.135	0.236	0.053	0.056	0.042
4. Cnstruction	0.013	0.013	0.015	1.006	0.048	0.045	0.022	0.016	0.008
5. Elctricity&c.	0.011	0.027	0.043	0.010	1.268	0.020	0.009	0.004	0.017
6. Trnsport&c.	0.014	0.009	0.069	0.042	0.093	1.100	0.048	0.071	0.029
7. Communicn	0.001	0.000	0.002	0.001	0.006	0.011	1.001	0.006	0.037
8. Trade&C.	0.027	0.013	0.156	0.099	0.064	0.069	0.015	1.046	0.017
9. Banking&c.	0.005	0.003	0.025	0.008	0.007	0.016	0.002	0.018	1.054
10. O. Service	0.001	0.010	0.020	0.004	0.005	0.007	0.005	0.003	0.012
11. EHPAD	0.000	0.000	0.000	0.000	0.000	0.001	0.000	0.000	0.003

Table 7A.2 Leontief Inverse Matrix, 1993–94

Sector	1	2	3	4	5	6	7	8	9
1. Agriculture	1.188	0.033	0.180	0.096	0.036	0.079	0.013	0.059	0.006
2. Mining	0.015	1.043	0.120	0.097	0.255	0.053	0.017	0.020	0.007
3. Manufcture	0.129	0.219	1.580	0.523	0.218	0.391	0.098	0.133	0.042
4. Cnstruction	0.010	0.015	0.014	1.018	0.023	0.031	0.027	0.021	0.011
5. Elctricity&c.	0.031	0.072	0.097	0.067	1.320	0.115	0.052	0.038	0.018
6. Trnsport&c.	0.046	0.049	0.126	0.130	0.134	1.080	0.023	0.053	0.011
7. Communicn	0.003	0.005	0.013	0.014	0.012	0.017	1.014	0.012	0.016
8. Trade&C.	0.047	0.041	0.136	0.145	0.109	0.098	0.023	1.039	0.014
9. Banking&c.	0.018	0.035	0.068	0.062	0.051	0.088	0.033	0.069	1.087
10. O. Service	0.008	0.024	0.045	0.033	0.029	0.044	0.010	0.056	0.023
11. EHPAD	0.001	0.001	0.001	0.001	0.001	0.011	0.005	0.001	0.000

Table 7A.3 Leontief Inverse Matrix, 2007–08, Converted to 1993–94 Prices

Sector	1	2	3	4	5	6	7	8	9
1. Agriculture	1.258	0.032	0.144	0.130	0.034	0.069	0.008	0.086	0.010
2. Mining	0.016	1.038	0.142	0.090	0.091	0.044	0.007	0.019	0.008
3. Manufcture	0.185	0.341	1.741	0.906	0.326	0.529	0.087	0.216	0.084
4. Cnstruction	0.011	0.029	0.020	1.148	0.024	0.019	0.003	0.011	0.010
5. Elctricity&c.	0.028	0.057	0.060	0.063	1.200	0.041	0.010	0.023	0.021
6. Trnsport&c.	0.050	0.083	0.127	0.161	0.079	1.081	0.011	0.074	0.033
7. Communicn	0.011	0.024	0.053	0.044	0.043	0.063	1.011	0.026	0.093
8. Trade&C.	0.098	0.069	0.164	0.225	0.098	0.178	0.012	1.080	0.037
9. Banking&c.	0.027	0.043	0.072	0.090	0.071	0.045	0.005	0.054	1.048
10. O. Service	0.008	0.034	0.039	0.046	0.016	0.037	0.004	0.015	0.009
11. EHPAD	0.000	0.008	0.002	0.001	0.001	0.002	0.002	0.000	0.001

Notes

1. Along a column we have the inputs of production of a particular sector while the distribution of the output is shown along the corresponding row of a commodity x commodity matrix. Thus, rows and columns constitute the two dimensions giving a picture of the whole economy.
2. The point here is not that the technical coefficient in a particular line of production fluctuates randomly. What is important to remember is that a sector in an IOTT represents a group of activities or lines of production and the relative weights of activities in a group vary over the years; this makes the technical coefficient variable, even within a year.
3. Detailed break-up of GDP shares is given in Table 4.1 in Chapter 4.
4. Detailed break-up of GDP shares is given in Table 4.1 in Chapter 4.
5. That, of course, does not mean that the service is wholly an intermediate service; IOTTs show part of the service, which is related to the distribution of final goods, as final use of the service.
6. This is how it is done in IOTTs. Packaged milk is an interesting example of the spread of rudimentary manufacturing. In the absence of processing, milk would be considered a final product of animal husbandry (grouped with agriculture) and it would be distributed largely without the intermediation of traders. The new stage of processing has led to enormous value addition in trade and transport of milk. It is a case of spread of manufacturing generating mostly final trade.
7. We have seen in earlier chapters that value added may not always give the right reflection of the movement; one may have to look at expenditure and output in real terms.
8. The classic example given by Bohm Bawerk (1923) is worthy of note.

> I am short-sighted, and wish to have a pair of spectacles. For this I require ground and polished glasses, and a steel framework. But all that nature offers towards that end is silicious iron ore.... I must take the silicious earth and fuel, and build furnaces for smelting and glass from the silicious earth; the glass thus obtained has to be carefully purified worked, and cooled by a series of processes; finally, the glass thus prepared – again by means of ingenious instruments carefully constructed beforehand – is ground and polished into the lens fit for short-sighted eyes. Similarly, I must smelt the ore in the blast furnace, change the raw iron into steel, and make the frame therefrom.... Thus, by an exceedingly roundabout way, the end is attained.

9. An example may not be very far to seek. A country may gradually make more and more sophisticated parts of an automobile or aircraft, to run an assembly plant taking inputs largely from domestic manufactures, thus adding to the depth of production at home. India, in fact, has been going through such a process.
10. Our objective is limited to highlighting the interrelations relevant to derived demand for TT service only. So, we do not raise complex questions of agricultural productivity and openness of the economy in the context of overall macroeconomic balance. For enlightened discussion of these questions the reader is referred to Murphy, Shleifer and Vishny (1989) and Matsuyama (1992).
11. There are other activities in the economy, like mining and the TT service. For simplicity, we abstract from final services like education, health, and so on, that do not practically use TT service, as our objective is to highlight the key role of manufacturing in creating demand for directly related services. For simplicity, we also abstract from mineral export and agricultural intermediate input in manufacturing.
12. In the present model agriculture and mining also do not use intermediate inputs, so their outputs are the respective sector's value added too.
13. We ignore taxes on products, for simplicity. So the only distinction between prices is between producers' and purchasers' prices accounted for fully by the distributive (TT) margin.
14. It means 70 per cent of the value of output is accounted for by intermediate inputs and the ratio did not change much in the course of growing sophistication in manufacturing.
15. Based on the IOTT for the year.
16. In reality, it should be much less as we have excluded several activities from our hypothetical economy, restricting the GDP.
17. Some authors have talked of a reverse causality, which in our view is putting the cart before the horse (see Balakrishnan and Parameswaran, 2007).
18. Emergence of e-commerce must be affecting the organization and margins of TT services.
19. Datta (2001) studies the trend of distributive trade services (separately from transport) over 1950–51 to 1996–97. The study concludes that the final trade ratio over the period has been roughly constant while the intermediate trade ratio increased very significantly and steadily over the period, both, because of what we have called in the present study spread and depth effects (2001: 86). This is perfectly in tune with our model's conclusion.

20. We may note here that the weights are significantly different from those obtained at current prices because, as we have seen in Chapter 5, relative prices have changed quite significantly against manufactures and in favour of Service-II.

8

Linkages and Key Sectors in the Indian Economy

Do you anticipate sentiment, and poetry, and reverie? … Calm your expectations; … Something real, cool, and solid, lies before you; something unromantic as Monday morning, when all who work wake with a consciousness that they must rise and betake themselves thereto.

—*Shirley: A Tale*, Charlotte Brontë (1888: ch. 1)

Introduction

The literature on the strategy of economic development initiated by Hirschman (1958) can be viewed as the primary inspiration for attempts to measure the pattern of industrial interlinkage. Hirschman advocated unbalanced growth to incentivize investment into areas served by strong demand or supply linkages, in the absence of serious structural rigidities like shortages, bottlenecks, low elasticities of demand and supply, and so on. The underlying assumptions were encouragement to private enterprise and responsiveness to market signals. Interindustry linkages have been studied with the objective of identifying pivotal industries in the sense of those having strong interrelations with other industries by way of being a key source of either demand for their products or supply of crucial intermediate inputs for production. Such industries, with maximum potential for being a spur to the system, are central for industrial development through their demand and supply interrelations. The present chapter is an exercise in the applicability of input–output based linkage measures in an analysis of interdependence in the Indian economic structure. Though the chapter follows linkage specifications within the Hirschman-Rasmussen tradition, it ventures into the supply-side model proposed by Ghosh (1958) for what is supposed to be a better measure of forward linkage.

In the next section, we discuss the intricacies of the relations between output on the one hand and final demand or value added on the other. The discussion helps explain interrelations that do not show up on the surface to final users, paving the way for classification of backward and forward linkages. The next section defines the concepts of linkages based on Leontief and Ghosh inverse matrices while the estimates of the linkage indices are presented in the appendix to the chapter. The subsequent section concludes the chapter by arranging the different sectors of the Indian economy according to the linkage intensities, by identifying the key sectors. The conclusion brings to sharp focus the justification of our division of services into two separate parts – Service-I and Service-II in the entire discourse.

Production Network, Final Demand and Value Added

Interconnectedness of productive activities is the hallmark of a modern economy. The links in the network of activities are multidimensional. Some activities are more densely connected to the network and are identified as key sectors while others, less so. The interconnections are captured in an input–output transactions table (IOTT) that is a two dimensional representation of the reality. It shows, along the rows, flows of output of each sector (represented by a row) to intermediate (that is, inter-industry) as well as final uses. Each column, on the other hand, shows uses of intermediate inputs for the production of a specific sector (identified with a composite commodity in a commodity x commodity matrix) and also the value of primary inputs used in the production of the sector. The value of primary inputs is the value added in the sector. The row at the bottom of Table 8.1below shows the value-added in different sectors. While each column sum is the value of output, it must be identical with the corresponding row sum showing total uses of the output; it follows logically that the row sum of value added must strike a balance with the column sum of final uses. The final uses column shows the aggregate sector-wise final expenditures, also referred to as final demands. If we can abstract from indirect taxes, the sum of the elements of this column is the aggregate final demand or the GDP, which is identical to the row sum of value added.

Looking at a particular sector, its total output (corresponding column sum) is used up in meeting intermediate and final demands shown along the corresponding row. So, it is possible for a sector to have a large output with a negligible intermediate (as in the case of SRVC-II in Table 8.1) or final demand (as in the case of MNG). Contribution of a sector to the GDP is its value added, which is the difference between the value of output and that of intermediate inputs. Thus, value added (or gross product) in a production process need not be related particularly to either the intermediate demand or the final demand for the commodity concerned. The demand for intermediate use of a commodity is related to the final demand for several commodities through the interrelated structure of production sought to be portrayed by the IOTTs, just as the production of the commodity itself generates demand for several commodities. Therefore, a commodity may basically be an input in the production of other commodities while it may be, at the same time, using several commodities as its own intermediate input. It is here that the concept of linkage in production comes up.

Table 8.1 Input–Output Transactions Table: Indian Economy, 2003–04 (INR Billions)

	AGL	MNG	MNF	CNST	UTL	SRVC-I	SRVC-II	II Use ($\Sigma_j x_{ij}$)	F.USE (F_i)	Total (X_i)
AGL	1,505	0	1,334	55	4	352	6	3,255	4,470	7,725
MNG	0	6	1,608	181	183	4	0	1,983	−1,108	875
MNF	545	103	5,881	1,380	233	1,874	318	10,334	6,963	17,297
CNST	42	20	152	107	27	138	114	600	3,815	4,415
UTL	86	25	510	100	401	213	18	1,352	205	1,558
SRVC-I	548	52	2,765	789	274	1,839	212	6,478	7,386	13,864
SRVC-II	12	10	259	1	3	174	311	769	4,752	5,522
($\Sigma_i x_{ij}$)	2,739	215	12,508	2,613	1,126	4,593	979	24,773	26,483	51,256
GVA (U_j)	4,986	660	4,790	1,803	431	9,313	4,500			
Output (X_j)	7,725	875	17,297	4,415	1,558	13,864	5,522	51,256		

Source: Aggregated and adapted from the original IOTT published by CSO (GOI, various years).

Abbreviations: AGL = agriculture; MNG = Mining; MNF = Manufacturing; CNST = construction; UTL = Utilities. SRVC-I = transport, communication, trade and financial services. SRVC-II = rest of services; IIUse = intermediate input use, FUse = final use.

A Technical Note

Here, a brief note on some technical issues regarding the IOTT is in order. A practical problem arises in relating the value added to the demand for commodities. The problem is that a commodity may be the main product of one process and, at the same time, a byproduct of another process; thus more than one production processes may yield the same commodity. This means the relation between production processes and commodities need not be one-to-one. This reality is captured by what is referred to as the make-matrix. IO statisticians use the information from a make-matrix (which is in industry x commodity format) to convert use-matrix (which is in commodity x industry format) into commodity x commodity IOTTs using several assumptions to make things manageable. From a practical point of view, studies have shown that differences between results of impact analysis under possible alternative assumptions are often not very serious (Miller and Blair, 2009: 223). In the present study we use an aggregated commodity x commodity table, which effectively obliterates the distinction between commodity and industry. In this case the concept of production process gets modified as several processes are aggregated to form a sector, which we also refer to as a broad industry representing a broad commodity group. Thus, we use the terms – sector, industry and commodity – interchangeably.

The intermediate input intensity – which means the proportion of the value of output accounted for by intermediate inputs going into its production – of different sectors varies just as some commodity (for example, minerals) may be used basically as an intermediate input, its final use being relatively unimportant (see Table 8.1). A sector that has high intermediate input intensity and, at the same time, is geared to meeting demand for intermediate inputs by other sectors is viewed as central to the production network and is considered a key sector. This dependence means that a sector's share in aggregate final use is not a good guide for its share in aggregate value added; because: (*a*) the proportion of the value of output accruing as value added depends on intermediate input intensity and (*b*) the proportion of output going to final use depends on the intensity of its use as intermediate use by other sectors. Thus, only a small proportion of an industry's output may find an outlet to final use. We now turn out attention to the measurement of these backward and forward linkages.

Backward and Forward Linkages

Our model in Chapter 7 highlights that manufacturing activities essentially use intermediate inputs from other sectors intensively whereas Service-I basically lends itself for the servicing of other sectors' activities. In this simple model, the former is connecting upstream, as the flows come from other sectors to it and the latter, downstream as flows start from there. The two types of linkages have been called the backward and the forward linkages respectively. Thus backward linkage helps the viability of upstream industries through expanding their market. Similarly forward linkage allows an industry to supply intermediate inputs downstream, thus smoothening the supply line for inputs and possibly reducing the cost of the linked industries. The application of linkages in the strategy for development and planning was highlighted by Hirschman (1958). But even before that, IOTTs have been used to obtain measures for the physical inter-industry flows, upstream and downstream, by Rasmussen, in his doctoral thesis (1957). The idea was to identify the sectors that play a key role in economic development by creating, on the one hand, demand for other sectors' products and on the other hand, the source of supply of crucial intermediate inputs. Of course, it has to be, and has been, realized that the linkages being measured are mechanical and apparent, not abstract and potential. Thus there are sectors not well connected by physical flows, for example, education and health, but their influence goes to the root. Before we attempt to measure the physical linkages in the Indian economy we briefly discuss, below, the concepts underlying the suggested indices for forward and backward linkages. We will confine ourselves only to the most commonly used measures.

Backward Linkage

For obtaining this measure, the inter-industry transactions are transformed into intensive forms as input-coefficients. Let us write the inter-industry transactions matrix as $x = \{x_{ij}\}$, $i, j = 1, 2, \ldots, n$. We can write the input coefficients matrix as $A = \{a_{ij}\}$, with $a_{ij} = x_{ij}/X_j$; where X_j = output of the jth sector; Thus a_{ij} = intensity of use of the ith commodity in the jth sector.

An absolute measure of backward linkage for the jth sector is given by $\Sigma_i a_{ij}$, the jth column sum in A matrix. In order to convey a sense of the jth sector's standing relative to the average of all sectors, an index of direct backward linkage has been defined as:[1]

$$BL(d)_j = n\,(\Sigma_i\, a_{ij})/(\Sigma_{ij}\, a_{ij}) \qquad \ldots (1)$$

A parallel but more comprehensive measure is total backward linkage based on the total (direct and indirect) requirements matrix, which is the well known Leontief inverse denoted by $L = (I - A)^{-1} = \{l_{ij}\}$. This more sophisticated but intuitive measure replaces a_{ij} by l_{ij}, the total (direct and indirect) requirement of the ith commodity per unit of final demand for the jth commodity. Thus we write the comprehensive relative measure of total backward linkage in terms of L matrix, which corresponds to (1), as:

$$BL(t)_j = n\,(\Sigma_i\, l_{ij}) \,/\, (\Sigma_{ij}\, l_{ij}) \qquad \ldots (2)$$

This is, clearly, the appropriate column sum, standing for the total value of direct plus indirect requirements of all commodities required as intermediate input in the production of one unit of final demand for the concerned (jth) commodity, divided by the unweighted average of all column sums of the total requirements matrix. A value greater than one for the index simply means that the intensity of the concerned sector's backward linkage is greater than the average of total requirements of all the sectors by a multiple given by the index.

Forward Linkage

Row sums of A and L matrices have been used to obtain measures of direct and total forward linkages respectively (Rasmussen, 1957; Guo and Planting, 2000) though their interpretations are rather strained. Jones (1976) questioned these measures of forward linkage, arguing that there is not much economic sense in exploring, as the row sums of A and L matrices do, what happens to an industry if all industries are to experience a simultaneous unit increase in their output or final demand. In order to make the row sums more relevant, weighted sums have been used by several researchers including Rasmussen. One problem with this weighted measure is that when comparing the structures over two points considerably removed in time, the weights (that is, for total linkage, the proportion commanded by a sector in aggregate final demand) would vary considerably even if the input-coefficients-structure (A matrix) remains unchanged. Instead, Jones (1976) proposed to utilise the output inverse matrix, G, of the supply-side I-O model in the calculation of the index. This measure is generally preferred (Miller and Blair, 2009: 556) and, possibly, gives a more sensible interpretation though on the basis of questionable assumptions.

G is calculated from output coefficients (x_{ij} / X_i). Let, $B = \{b_{ij}\}$, where $b_{ij} = x_{ij} / X_i$ = proportion of the output of the ith commodity used as intermediate input in the jth sector. Writing X and V as column vectors of output and value added respectively, $X^T - X^T B = X^T(I - B) = V^T$; where superscript ^{T} is used to denote the transpose operation.

$$\text{Clearly, } X^T = V^T(I - B)^{-1} \qquad \ldots (3)$$

Writing $G = (I - B)^{-1} = \{g_{ij}\}$, the ith a row of the G matrix[2] is interpreted as the additional production of all the different sectors attained by utilizing an additional unit of value added (or primary input) in the ith sector. More specifically, g_{ij} is the additional production of the jth commodity attained by direct and indirect utilization of the given allocation (to all sectors) of the ith sector's increased output brought about by an additional unit of primary input into the sector. So, $\Sigma_j g_{ij}$ is the total direct and indirect additional production of all the sectors, that is, the total additional output of the system, obtained from an additional unit of value added (or, equivalently, primary input) in the ith sector. The interpretation comes from the fact that in supply-side models the output-coefficients (b_{ij}) are held constant as V and X change. So, any additional use of primary input (or generation of value added) in the ith industry, leading to its additional output in the first instance, will be supplied in the given proportions to the consuming industries as inputs leading to additional production in such industries which will, in turn, be allocated in fixed proportions; so that after the first level (direct) and a series of subsequent (indirect) impacts the equilibrium is given by (3).[3]

Thus, $\Sigma_j g_{ij}$ is taken as the absolute measure of total direct and indirect forward linkage. So, the relative measures of direct and total forward linkages are given by row sums:

$$FL(d)_j = n\,(\Sigma_j b_{ij}) / (\Sigma_{ij} b_{ij}) \qquad \ldots (4)$$

and

$$FL(t)_j = n\,(\Sigma_j g_{ij}) / (\Sigma_{ij} g_{ij}) \qquad \ldots (5)$$

We have studied these linkages for the Indian economy at three points over the period of roughly three decades from 1978–79 to 2007–08.

Linkages in the Indian Economy and Identification of the Key Sectors

We have taken up an eleven sector classification of the Indian economy in which the whole of the manufacturing sector is taken as one sector while mining, construction and electricity are shown as separate sectors. Trade and transport too have been shown as separate sectors. Classifications are known to affect the values of linkage indices. So, a bit of caution is needed in interpreting results. For example, merging of consumer goods manufacturing with other manufacturing sectors blurs the differences in forward linkages of the two parts. Similarly, even though the demand for distributive services is wholly derived demand, the IOTTs treat the part of distributive services going with the delivery of final goods as final services. This practice undermines their derived nature and, thereby, their forward linkage index. Another point to note is that, for mining, intermediate use is far greater than output. It reflects the huge import of petroleum crude. This fact makes the intermediate use coefficients (b_{ij}) very high, which indicates that imports bias the strength of linkages upward. Keeping this consideration in view we have, somewhat arbitrarily, relaxed the criterion for high and low linkages. The normal practice is to take unity as the cut-off point; but we have lowered the bar to the value 0.9. On the basis of this cut-off criterion for total (direct and indirect) forward and backward linkages, we have made a four-way classification of the sectors. Those with both the total forward and total backward linkages greater than 0.9 are the key sectors while those with both the indices below the mark are the least linked. Forward and backward linkage indices for the eleven-sector classification of the Indian economy are presented in the appendix to this chapter in Tables 8A.1 and 8A.2. Tables 8.2a, 8.2b and 8.2c present sector classifications based on the values of total forward and backward linkages for the Indian economy presented in tables 8A.1 and 8A.2, panels A and B.

Table 8.2a Linkage Classification: 2007–08

Backward Linkage	Forward Linkage: FL(t) →	
BL(t) ↓	Value of Index < 0.9	Value of Index > 0.9
Value of Index < 0.9	Agriculture, Trade Other Services; EHPAD	Communication; Banking
Value of Index > 0.9	Construction Transport	Mining, Manufacturing Electricity, etc.

Table 8.2b Linkage Classification: 1993–94

Backward Linkage	Forward Linkage: FL(t) →	
BL(t) ↓	Value of Index < 0.9	Value of Index > 0.9
Value of Index < 0.9	Agriculture; Trade	Communication, Banking
Value of Index > 0.9	Construction Other Services	Mining, Manufacturing Electricity, etc., Transport

Table 8.2c Linkage Classification: 1978–79

Backward Linkage	Forward Linkage: FL(t) →	
BL(t) ↓	Value of Index < 0.9	Value of Index > 0.9
Value of Index < 0.9	Other Services; EHPAD	Mining, Communication Banking
Value of Index > 0.9	Agriculture, Construction Trade	Manufacturing Electricity, etc. Transport

Source: Author's calculations.

Conclusion

Results show that the sectors – manufacturing and electricity – are the key sectors in all the three years of our observation, 1978–79, 1993–94 and 2007–08. Mining and transport also emerge as key sectors in two out of the three reference years. On the other hand, EHPAD alone emerges as the least linked sector consistently; agriculture, trade and 'other services' fall in the same (that is, least linked) category in two out of three years. Banking as well as communication shows strong forward linkage consistently while construction shows strong backward linkage equally consistently.

Going back to our simple model of Chapter 7, the emergence of manufacturing and electricity as key sectors fully supports the intuitions developed there. The idea is that a large part of output of these sectors serves as input in further production (strong forward linkage) and hence may be viewed as intermediate input to further manufacturing and other production. Similarly, they draw substantial inputs from mining and manufacturing, as postulated, and also from other sectors (strong backward linkage, see for example, Table 7A.1 in Chapter 7). Mining shows strong forward linkage as postulated in the model but what our model in Chapter 7 does not show is that the sector has a strong backward linkage by virtue of drawing large inputs from manufacturing, construction, transport and utilities.

The distributive services (trade and transport) were treated in our model as having derived demand only, implying that they provide the whole of their output to be used as intermediate input. From this point of view, trade services being classified as least linked is rather counter intuitive. The catch here is that in the IOTTs (a large chunk, around half of) these services are treated as final services since they distribute goods for final use, undermining their true forward linkage. Moreover, transport has stronger linkages than trade because transport uses a lot of fuel (backward linkage) and provides transportation service not linked to trade also. Keeping this point in mind and considering the strong forward linkage for banking and communications services, there is clearly a strong case for grouping all these services (trade, transport and banking) together to show them separately from 'other services' and EHPAD so far as production linkages are concerned. Herein lies the logic of our division of services into two groups – Service-I and Service-II.

Appendix 8A Forward and Backward Linkages in the Indian Economy

Table 8A.1 Forward Linkages in the Indian Economy: 1978–79 to 2007–08

	Panel A Direct Forward Linkage [FL(d)]				Panel B Total Forward Linkage [FL(t)]		
	1978–79	1993–94	2007–08		1978–79	1993–94	2007–08
AGLR	0.613	0.563	0.695	AGLR	0.774	0.730	0.798
MNG	3.113	2.870	4.091	MNG	2.158	2.101	2.952
MNFG	0.966	0.991	0.901	MNFG	0.950	0.962	0.923
CSTN	0.215	0.235	0.292	CSTN	0.591	0.578	0.538
UTL	1.493	1.579	1.203	UTL	1.352	1.395	1.170
TPS	0.979	0.948	0.721	TPS	0.971	0.943	0.823
CMN	0.929	1.163	0.859	CMN	0.945	1.072	0.909
THR	0.816	0.743	0.782	THR	0.876	0.834	0.842
BKIN	1.259	1.431	1.068	BKIN	1.107	1.212	1.021
OSR	0.612	0.433	0.345	OSR	0.789	0.688	0.594
PAD	0.005	0.043	0.043	PAD	0.487	0.485	0.429

Source: Author's calculation after aggregating the relevant IOTTs provided by CSO (GOI, various years).

Abbreviations: AGLR = agriculture, forestry & fishing; MNG = mining & quarrying; MNFG = manufacturing; CSTN = construction; UTL = electricity, gas & water supply; TPS = transport and storage; CMN = communication; THR = trade, hotels & restaurants; BKIN = banking and insurance, OSR = other services including real estate & business services; PAD = public administration and defence.

Table 8A.2 Backward Linkages in the Indian Economy: 1978–79 to 2007–08

	Panel A Direct Backward Linkage [BL(d)]				Panel B Total Backward Linkage [BL(t)]		
	1978–79	1993–94	2007–08		1978–79	1993–94	2007–08
AGLR	0.898	0.779	0.814	AGLR	0.931	0.881	0.866
MNG	0.469	0.720	0.756	MNG	0.824	0.905	0.912
MNFG	2.338	1.929	1.799	MNFG	1.495	1.402	1.387
CSTN	1.242	1.628	2.045	CSTN	1.132	1.288	1.588
UTL	1.728	1.740	1.281	UTL	1.247	1.289	1.110
TPS	1.241	1.414	1.627	TPS	1.119	1.183	1.307
CMN	0.326	0.447	0.175	CMN	0.762	0.775	0.628
THR	1.009	0.788	0.808	THR	0.974	0.885	0.887
BKIN	0.630	0.423	0.431	BKIN	0.823	0.727	0.693
OSR	0.643	0.753	0.671	OSR	0.871	0.912	0.811
PAD	0.476	0.380	0.594	PAD	0.822	0.753	0.812

Source: Author's calculation after aggregating the IOTTs provided by the CSO (GOI, various years).

Abbreviations: AGLR = agriculture, forestry & fishing; MNG = mining & quarrying; MNFG = manufacturing; CSTN = construction; UTL = electricity, gas & water supply; TPS = transport and storage; CMN = communication; THR = trade, hotels & restaurants; BKIN = banking and insurance, OSR = other services including real estate & business services; PAD = public administration and defence.

Notes

1 For a detailed discussion, see Miller and Blair (2009).

2 The notation *G* follows the name of the pioneer of the output-coefficient based I-O model (Ghose, 1958).

3 An important point to note here is that the above mechanism implies that in the course of unfolding of the impact, the technical coefficients (a_{ij}) inevitably change. This is contrary to the more sensible demand-side approach that assumes stability of the *A* matrix. However, studies have shown that for small changes the implied instability of *A* matrix is not a major issue (Miller and Blair 2009: 551).

9

Conclusion

A Perspective of Indian Economic Growth

What's past is prologue.

—Inscription on the National Archives Building, Washington, DC, from *The Tempest*, Shakespeare

Past may be prologue, but which past?

—Henry Hu, quoted from Lowenstein (2000: ix)

A Macroscopic View

India transitioned from a slow-growing to a decently growing (about 5 per cent per annum) economy in the second half of the 1970s but was temporarily pulled down by the devastating drought of 1979–80, an event that pushed the annual growth rate of the GDP 5.2 percentage points below zero. This severe external shock has influenced the break-point analysis of growth regimes. The 5-year moving average growth rate picked up in the next three years to reach the level achieved before the shock, and over the following three decades the average fell only narrowly below 5 per cent level in just two short stretches of three and two years respectively in the mid-1980s and early 1990s (Figure 2.1 in Chapter 2). But there were prolonged phases when the average remained above 6 or even 8 per cent; these phases were located in time after the big comprehensive reform of 1991. Naturally, much of the attention of observers is focused on this phase. The present study, however, concentrates on roughly three decades since 1978–79. The study exploits the rich information contained in the input–output transactions tables (IOTTs) of the Indian economy, apart from data available from other official sources; the IOTTs are available roughly at quinquennial intervals and our reference dates are often based on their availability. In 1980 sectoral relative shares were in conformity with the stylized facts of economic growth (as discussed in Chapter 3). The relative share of the manufacturing sector reached a peak in 1979–80, which, frustrating expectations, has not been surpassed in the subsequent decades. Also, from about that time onwards the country was on the lookout for new policy directions. So, from the point of view of analysis of structural change, the turn of the 1970s provide a vantage point in time.

Some observers maintain reservations regarding the reliability of the IOTTs of the Indian economy as these are produced after adjustments for statistical discrepancy between production and expenditure sides, though sources of data are the same for the IOTTs and the National Accounts Statistics (NAS). Our initial hesitations regarding the messy nature of the data were assuaged as we discovered their positive side — these are broad consistency with NAS,[1] the great wealth of information contained in the IOTTs, and broadly regular and understandable patterns revealed by the data, as presented in different chapters of the book.

Our study goes into the details of the nature of macroeconomic aggregates; in particular, the association between gross output and gross value added (GVA), and points to the pitfalls of the common practice of taking the sectoral GVA as a measure of the level of sectoral activity. In this context, conceptual issues regarding deflation of value added for intertemporal comparisons receive our attention. Sectoral real GVA does not have separate price and quantity dimensions; the real GVA is to be interpreted as a share of the real GDP-pie. The deflator of current price sectoral GVA[2] must not distort the fundamental national accounts identity between aggregate GVA and aggregate final expenditure that holds at current prices and, by implication, should be valid in real terms too. An implication of this approach is that sectoral relative GDP shares at constant prices (using implicit GDP deflator for both the numerator and the denominator) are the same as those at current prices (discussed in detail in Chapter 2). From this consideration we work with the current price data for relative shares in aggregate GVA unless special contexts arise. The scope of the book is limited to the analysis of the broad sectoral structure of output, expenditure and GVA, leaving aside analysis of the employment structure unless contextual imperatives demand it. Intra-sectoral developments also remain largely outside the ambit of the study.

The Aberrant Nature of India's Growth Story

There is a broad consensus that the pattern of growth in India in recent years has been an unconventional one. It is unusual not only with reference to the recent experience of countries in East Asia and China, but also with reference to the historical stylized facts brought to prominence by Colin Clark, Simon Kuznets and several other authors – what we have referred to as the K-CT norm. The norm tells the typical story about the economic development of a country – in the initial phases as the relative share of agriculture in GDP declines rather rapidly, manufacturing's (and industry's) share rises generally faster than that of service activities. In India the share of manufacturing remained stagnant since the early 1980s and showed no sign of picking up, even as the process of liberalization and globalization progressed since the early 1990s. On the contrary, the service sector showed dynamism to largely fill up the space vacated by agriculture. Interestingly, it is acknowledged that in several areas – like automobiles and auto-parts, oil-refining, pharmaceuticals, and some other high-tech and capital intensive manufacturing – activities have expanded reasonably, but that cannot be said of many low-tech and labour intensive manufacturing segments.

Similarly, in the service sector high-tech activities in communications and information technology related activities have charted phenomenal growth thereby giving a fillip to the sector's growth; but the service sector also witnessed a rapid growth of major activities like distributive trade, transport and finance that we have grouped together as Service-I. This is what the sectoral GDP data reads. These latter services are mainly non-traded (internationally) and demand for them is basically derived demand. So, growth of these services should be related to the growth of the activities utilizing them, that is, those mostly in manufacturing or, more generally, the industry sector. A stagnant industrial sector is not supposed to support thriving Service-I activities. How could this still happen? Service exports have risen rapidly particularly since the mid 1990s, though from a small base. In our study, the relevant services, basically based on information technology, are classified with Service-II, hence service exports do not help explain the gap between the growth rates of manufacturing and Service-I. Further, the apparent stagnation of manufacturing is a phenomenon extending back to the 1980s when, incidentally, service export was not important and, yet, the service sector grew rapidly.

The centrality of the manufacturing sector in people's perception of vitality of an economy and, in this context, relative stagnation of the sector in India's growth experience has caused general concern. The centrality comes not only from the pivotal role of many manufactured products – like plants, machinery and all sorts of equipment – in modern life, but also from the role of the sector as the laboratory of scientific research and the fountainhead of innovations responsible for long term economic growth in advanced countries. An underdeveloped country like India tries to keep pace with the world's technological progress by acquiring advanced machinery, learning to use it, adapt it through research and learning by doing. If manufacturing stagnates, the growth of knowledge stock is impacted too. This role of manufacturing as the theatre of technological progress, even in less developed countries where scientific research is not too strong, is the basic theme underlying the present study. A telling indicator of India's move along the path of accumulation of productive knowledge is its position right on top in 2010, as discussed in Chapter 5, with respect to the 'complexity outlook index', which puts a value to the adeptness of a country in progressing to the production of more and more complex products, given its position in the product space. Understanding the stagnant share of manufacturing in GDP is particularly important in this context. The findings of the study are summarized below.

The Aberrant Growth Story

Trends and Major Questions

1. The couple of years after the severe drought of 1979 were choppy due to external shocks in the form of surging oil prices and domestic socio-political disturbances. India brought attitudinal changes to jettison long-held inhibitions about private capital, first incrementally and then, gradually, more substantially. The private sector responded and it was reflected in increases in private as well as aggregate saving and investment. Inevitably these changes had a bearing on the performance of the economy.
2. A careful study leads one to three alternative sets of estimates of sectoral relative shares obtained from official sources. The constant price estimates are often preferred by researchers for comparison over time. But constant price GVA can have meaning only when deflated uniformly by the same GDP deflator, which may be obtained from the ratio of aggregate final expenditure at current and constant prices. In that case, sectoral shares become identical at current and constant prices. So, constant price value added, as prepared by the CSO of India, is inappropriate and these are unnecessary for the study of the trend of sectoral relative share in GDP. Thus we are left with two sets of estimates – current price NAS estimates, which is our default series, and the IOTT-based estimates. The two sets give us roughly the same trend except in the case of Service-II, more specifically in respect of income from dwellings, which is not of major interest for the present study.
3. The primary sector's relative share in GDP has declined over the six decades from 1950–51 steadily from more than a half to about a fifth. The secondary sector (identified with industry here) captured one-third of this released share, while the tertiary sector (or services) captured the rest. But a closer look reveals that the secondary sector captured what it did practically in the first half of the whole period and very little since 1978–79, the period over which the present study focuses. Correspondingly, the tertiary sector moved relatively slowly during the first half, but faster in the later half when manufacturing's share (the predominant part of the secondary sector)

stagnated. This is paradoxical for two reasons – first, the steady increase of Service-I, which mostly derives its demand from the manufacturing sector, does not match the stagnation of manufacturing; and second, the K-CT stylized facts as well as the recent experience of major developing countries do not match the Indian experience. We need to explain these points for a proper understanding of structural changes in the Indian economy. Relative price changes come into consideration here.

Is India an Outlier?

4. IOTTs compiled at factor cost for the Indian economy give estimates of indirect taxes like excise duty, import tax, etc. paid on intermediate inputs by each sector. Since these taxes are collected almost wholly from industry, particularly from manufacturing, and the manufacturing sector itself pays a good part of these taxes in purchasing its own intermediate inputs, we have argued in Chapter 3 that a first approximation of the sector's value added at producer's price can be obtained by adding these payments with value added at factor cost.
5. In the presence of substantial excise duties, producer's price estimates of sectoral relative shares in GDP will be higher than those at factor cost for manufacturing and industry, and the reverse would be the case for other broad sectors. Some countries (including China) provide their estimates at producer's (or market) prices while others (including India) give factor cost estimates making international comparison tricky. We have observed that for the Indian economy, modified value added based on IOTTs suggest the difference between factor cost and market price estimates for the industry or manufacturing sector to be of the order of 3 percentage points.
6. For a proper international comparison, relative GDP shares of Indian industry or manufacturing sectors need to be adjusted as suggested above and this implies a corresponding correction for the service sector by two percentage points downward. Even after this correction there are wide differences between India and China. A part of the explanation must be aberrations in Chinese estimates by the yardstick of the SNA; China has been working for some time to bring their estimates in line with international standards. This suggests a case for studying the Indian performance after controlling for the Chinese influence. We have made an international comparison to judge India's standing under the K-CT norm after the above adjustments for comparability with producer's (or market) price estimates provided by many countries.
7. The conclusion from the above analysis is the following:

India's position as a manufacturer has never been inspiring but when we exclude China from comparison, India's experience seems to be less out of tune with international experience – India was an outlier on the lower side only in 2001, not in 1981 or in 2011. But, interestingly, for industry as a whole which includes manufacturing, India was an emphatic outlier on the higher side in 1981, lapsing into the status of a negative outlier in 2001 and maintaining that status in 2011. The case of services was a mirror image of that of industry. It is important to note that India's performance, judged by official data as it is, looks much more dismal than the picture projected above because of two factors – first, India's estimates for industry and manufacturing show a negative bias vis-à-vis its neighbours; second, aberrations in Chinese estimates put Indian performance in poor light.

GVA and Output and Expenditure

8. As we have pointed out, during the 1980s, manufacturing's GVA growth trend was below that of Service-I. During the early 1990s manufacturing picked up pace just like Service-I, but let off steam over the second half; the growth rate of Service-I hovered several notches higher. During the next decade (the 2000s) manufacturing shot up again but remained below Service-I all throughout. Considering that demand for Service-I is derived from the demand for goods, basically manufactured goods, how is it that Service-I consistently grew much faster than manufacturing? Is this phenomenon supported by other relevant aggregates?
9. Sectoral GVA has been used as a proxy for sectoral output in many of the economic analyses by scholars. The estimates of output based on IOTTs show faster growth for the manufacturing sector (than the GDP). It is found to be as much as that of the fastest growing subsector, that is, Service-I. However, GVA growth of the manufacturing sector is slower, as reflected in flat sectoral GDP shares. This paradox of the Indian economy, since the turn of the 1970s, raises a question about the suitability of the GVA measure for inquiry into the growth of the level of sectoral activity. Very significantly, even during the period of fastest growth of services (1993–94 to 2007–08), due to the 'Service Revolution' ushered in by communications and information technology-enabled services, the growth of output of manufacturing did not lag behind that of Service-I significantly; it was much ahead if the service sector was to be taken as a whole.
10. Findings from the expenditure side also contradict the widespread impression that the service sector of the Indian economy is a super performer while manufacturing is a laggard. Comparing in real terms, total final demand

for manufactures expressed as a proportion of the GDP at constant prices, increased no less than that for the more dynamic part of services – Service-I – over the whole period concerned; the lead of manufactures over Service-I did only marginally narrow down in the mid-2000s, when India's service revolution was in full swing and observers expected services to take the lead. How should we explain this phenomenon in the light of stagnation of manufacturing's GVA-share in GDP? Further, capital formation in the sector progressed at an accelerating pace over the three decades without reflection in the GVA share.

What Does the Trend in GVA Signify for Manufacturing?

11. Findings from the International Comparison Project (undertaken by Kravis, Heston and Summers [1978] and later by Summers and Heston [1984, 1991]) give strong evidence that in poor countries productivity is lower in both commodity and services production compared to rich countries, but it is lower by a larger margin in commodities. When it comes to cost reduction for existing products or services, technological change is more frequent and more powerful in its effects in the commodity sector. This conclusion from cross-section studies does not establish, but definitely indicates a bearing of the phenomenon on sectoral GVA shares as a country moves from poverty to affluence. That may cause a systematic pattern of rising relative price of services vis-à-vis commodities. The same insight is drawn from Baumol's rudimentary model (1967) of unbalanced growth.
12. We have made a restatement of Baumol's model which predicts declining relative price for manufacturing and the reverse for many important service activities, as a consequence of differential technical progress. The model underlines the implication of the trend of relative prices for the trend of sectoral value added. Analysis of expenditure data from the IOTTs verifies the predicted price trend for the manufacturing and EHPAD sectors over the three decades under study. More specifically, *the major story for the Indian economy is a systematic decline in relative price in the manufacturing sector and systematic rise in the EHPAD.* A sector experiencing a significant and sustained fall in relative price will lose in GDP share disproportionately to its output trend and that has happened to the manufacturing sector of India since the turn of the 1970s.
13. Thus the *apparent stagnancy of manufacturing (in terms of sectoral relative share in GDP) conceals the story of growth of output of the sector with slippage of value added, away from the sector through decline in relative price. By implication, value added is not a reliable indicator of the level of*

activity in the sector and inevitably, conventional measures of total factor productivity growth, using value added as a proxy for output, systematically underestimate productivity growth.

14. Nevertheless, the point still remains that the sector's low share in GDP marks India as a low outlier by international comparison. Was the relative price trend a unique Indian experience? We do not know of such studies for other developing countries. However, there are indeed some unique aspects of Indian industrialization. From the very beginning, a labour surplus and capital scarce newly independent India chose the path of skill based planned industrialization looking at the private entrepreneurs askance. The attitude towards private capital and stringent labour laws, that still survive, seems to have created a void in the middle firm-size segment of relatively low-skill enterprises, unlike in the countries of East Asia or China. The void reflects lost opportunity and should explain to some extent the low peak in manufacturing's relative share. However, that does not lead to *growth* of manufacturing (output) lagging overmuch behind that of Service-I, either quantitatively or qualitatively.

Relative Price and GVA Adjustments

15. Transition to higher growth trajectories with the liberalization and globalization of the economy had implications for the technical (intermediate input) structure of production as well as adjustment (erosion or build-up) of value added across sectors through changes in relative prices over the period. We have decomposed the changes in sectoral shares into three components. *The final demand effect* considers changes in sectoral shares due to change in the structure of final demand, keeping technical and value added coefficients unchanged. *The technical structure effect* accounts for changes in sectoral shares, evaluated at the base year value added coefficients, due to changed production requirements consequent to changes in intermediate input coefficients as well as the real output vector. The value added *adjustment effect* accounts for the impact on the sectoral shares attributable to changes in the sectoral value added coefficients with the new real output vector. Since, by definition, aggregate GVA (basic prices) is identical to the aggregate final demand, a positive technical structure effect must be accompanied by offsetting value added adjustment effect in the aggregate. However, this complementarity is not valid at the sectoral levels. In other words, changes in relative prices may lead to adjustments of sectoral value added even after accounting for changes in the sectoral technical structure. Herein lies a source of change in the sectoral structure of the GDP. Evidence strongly suggests

that the adjustment effect had significant impact in different broad sectors in India over the period concerned.

16. We have considered a period of almost three decades in two phases. The first phase covers one and a half decades from 1978–79 and the second phase covers the rest of the period up to 2007–08. Since every phase is judged by just two end points, the findings may not be taken as trends. To check the robustness of our conclusion, we have introduced an overlapping phase of two decades up to 2003–04, thus bringing into consideration two different observations. *The most interesting finding is the drag on the manufacturing sector due to value added adjustment invariably over all three phases of the three decades.* The technical structure effect too has been consistent, but in the opposite direction, as the use of manufactured inputs not only in the manufacturing sector itself, but also in other sectors increased in intensity. But this substantial and positive effect was wiped out and the sector's GVA was systematically drained by the strong adverse value added adjustment effect.
17. EHPAD has been a clear standout for being a consistent and significant beneficiary of adjustment gains in all the phases. The very consistent behaviour of the manufacturing and EHPAD sectors over all three phases of our study supports the basic hypothesis of Baumol's disease for the Indian economy. *The present analysis suggests the paring of manufacturing's value added by the adjustment effect to be an important explanation for the stagnation of relative share of manufacturing in the GDP of India.*
18. Specific consideration must be reserved for Service-I. This category of services increased its share in GDP in the first phase, being greatly supported by the adjustment effect. Our data explains a widening of the difference between sectoral shares of manufacturing and Service-I over the phase, to the extent of a huge 8.5 percentage points. Apparently the technical structure effect pushed both the sectors to the same extent. The observations are consistent with output trends of the two sectors. But the second phase projects a different picture – the adjustment effect was strong and negative as it was for manufacturing. The picture projected by the overlapping segment (1983–84 to 2003–04) is qualitatively the same as that of the second phase but quantitatively more emphatic about the loss of manufacturing. Here, leaving aside the technical structure effect, the adjustment effect explains manufacturing's loss in terms of percentage of GDP to the extent of 10.9 points against Service-I's loss of only 2.6 points. EHPAD gained to the extent of 6 points. *Even remembering that the findings of the study should be taken as only indicative rather than absolute due to data issues, the evidence clearly*

supports the hypothesis of relative price changes leading to value added adjustment as an important explanation of stagnation of manufacturing's GVA share.

Sectoral Interrelations

19. Distributive trade and related transport, grouped together as TT-service, represent the most prominent intermediate service. The basic idea is that this service is not demanded for its own sake, its demand is derived from that for traded goods. We have focused on the deepening of links in the interconnected manufacturing process, what we have called the depth effect. This process should work to enhance the relative importance of intermediate TT-service. The whole gamut of influences determining the GDP-share of the broader sector – Service-I, is a complex and dynamic process, and we have not ventured into any quantitative exercise other than what can be read from the IOTTs. Our objective has been limited to tracing the broad trends. Our explanations are centred on the key role of the manufacturing sector in creating demand for intermediate and final TT-service. This role is boosted by other sectors to which it is the key service provider, most prominently, constructions. Evidence from IOTTs, and particularly the sectoral interrelations given by the Leontief inverse matrices, substantiate the point.
20. The manufacturing sector's (and industry's) own-input intensity has risen over time, being subjected (at least partially) to the influence of rising depth of the production process. This is manifested in the sector's own technical coefficient – manufactured products used as intermediate input per unit of the sector's own production. This coefficient, calculated at constant prices, has gradually increased from 27.5 to 36.7 per cent over the four decades since 1968–69. At the same time the sectoral value added (deflated by the GDP deflator) per unit of own real output for manufacturing, which was almost constant at 0.43 during the first decade since 1968–69, was halved over the next three decades, declining sharply and steadily to 0.21 in 2007–08. As a result, even though manufactures' share in aggregate final uses almost doubled in 2007–08 from 16.3 per cent in 1968–69 after reaching 20.9 per cent in 1978–79, manufacturing's relative share in GDP was more or less stagnant since the turn of the seventies. The whole burden of explanation for the stagnant value added share falls on the declining value added coefficient mentioned above. We have already referred to this phenomenon as the value added adjustment effect.

Forward and Backward Linkages

21. Manufacturing activities use intermediate inputs from other sectors and also supply intermediate input to other sectors, whereas trade or financial services basically lends itself for the servicing of other sectors' activities. These are the ideas of backward and forward linkages. The former link (backward) refers to connecting upstream, as the flows come from other sectors to it; and the latter (forward linkage) downstream, as flows start from here, going down. The idea of linkages has been applied in the strategy for development and planning to identify the industries that came to be viewed as key industries for creating demand for other sectors' products while being a source of supply of crucial intermediate inputs, thus creating favourable growth conditions for other industries. Of course, it has to be realized that the linkages being measured are only mechanical and they encompass only intermediate inputs. There are all sorts of interrelations; specifically there are sectors which are not visibly well connected to the production process in terms of physical flows – for example education and health – but are extremely important, with their influence on human capital and knowledge stock, which are supposed to be instrumental for endogenous technical progress.
22. Our measures show that the sectors of manufacturing and electricity are the so called key sectors in all the three years of our observation – 1978–79, 1993–94 and 2007–08. Mining and transport also emerge as key sectors in two out of the three years. On the other hand, EHPAD alone emerges as the least linked sector consistently, its crucial importance notwithstanding. Agriculture, trade and 'other services' fall in the same category in two out of three years. Banking as well as communication show strong forward linkage consistently while construction shows strong backward linkage, as one might expect.
23. Referring to the simple model presented in Chapter 7, the emergence of manufacturing, electricity and also mining (the model does not account for the large input of transport service) as key sectors fully supports the intuitions developed there. The distributive services were treated in our model as only having derived demand but in the IOTTs a large chunk (almost half) of these services, catering goods to final users, are treated as final services undermining their 'derived' nature, or forward linkage. With this consideration and considering the strong forward linkage for banking and communications services, there is clearly a strong case for grouping the above services together, as we have done, insofar as production linkage is concerned and treat their demand as derived demand.

Notes

1. Reservations are expressed about data given in the NAS too (*vide* Chapter 3). Without undermining the need for improvement in estimates one may view the adjustments for statistical discrepancy as giving the estimates a desired mooring by tying up the production and expenditure sides. Moreover, in empirical studies like the present one, one does not vouchsafe the exactness of data; the basic interest is in the broad trends and patterns.
2. This assumes that the constant price estimate of GDP should be arrived at by deflating final uses; sectoral real value added can be estimated only at the next step after obtaining the GDP deflator.

References

Arrow, K. (1962). 'Economic Implications of Learning by Doing'. *Review of Economic Studies* 29(June): 155–73.

Bai, J. and P. Perron (1998). 'Estimating and Testing Linear Models with Multiple Structural Changes'. *Econometrica* 66(1): 47–78.

——— (2003). 'Computation and Analysis of Multiple Structural Change Models'. *Journal of Applied Econometrics* 18: 1–22.

Bajaj, R. (2010). 'I Knew Subaah Zaroor Ayegi'. *Economic Times*, 6 May.

Balakrishnan, P. and M. Parameswaran (2007a). 'Understanding Growth Regimes in India: A Prerequisite'. *Economic and Political Weekly* 42(27–28): 2915–22.

——— (2007b). 'Understanding Economic Growth in India: Further Observations'. *Economic and Political Weekly* 42(44).

Banerjee, A. V. and E. Duflo (2019). *Good Economics for Hard Times*. New Delhi: Juggernaut Books.

Banik, A. and P. K. Bhaumik (2010). 'Technology Transfer'. In *The Concise Oxford Companion to Economics in India*, ed. K. Basu and A. Maertens, 180–86. New Delhi: Oxford University Press.

Basant, R. (2008). 'Bangalore Cluster: Evolution, Growth and Challenges'. In *Growth Industrial Clusters in Asia: Serendipity and Science*, ed. S. Yusuf, K. Nabeshima and S. Yamashita, 147–93. Washington DC: The World Bank.

Baumol, W. J. (1959). 'Prerequisites of Economic Growth'. In *Employment, Growth and Price Levels*, 2792–96. Report, Hearings before the Joint Committee of the Congress of the US. Washington, DC: U. S. Government Printing Office.

——— (1967). 'Macroeconomics of Unbalanced Growth: The Anatomy of Urban Crisis'. *The American Economic Review* 57(3): 409–20.

Baumol, W. J. and W. G. Bowen (1965). 'On the Performing Arts: The Anatomy of Their Economic Problems'. *The American Economic Review* 55(1/2): 495–502.

Baumol, W. J., S. A. B. Blackman and E. N. Wolff (1985). 'Unbalanced Growth Revisited: Asymptotic Stagnancy and New Evidence'. *The American Economic Review* 75(4): 806–17.

Beckerman, W. (1991). 'National Income'. In *The World of Economics*, ed. J. Eatwell, M. Milgate and P. Newman, 483–88. London: The Macmillan Press Ltd, U.K.

Berndt, E. R. and C. R. Hulten (2007). 'Introduction'. In *Hard to Measure Goods and Services: Essays in Honour of Zvi Griliches*, ed. E. R. Berndt and C. R. Hulten, 4–14. Chicago: University of Chicago Press.

Bhagwati, J. N. (1984a). 'Why Are Services Cheaper in Poor Countries?' *Economic Journal* 94(374): 279–86.

——— (1984b). 'Splintering and Disembodiment of Services and Developing Nations'. *The World Economy* **7**(2): 133–43.

Bhattacharya, A. (2019). 'Labour Market Flexibility in Indian Industry: A Critical Survey of the Literature'. Working Paper No. 296, Centre for Development Economics, Delhi School of Economics, Delhi.

Bhattacharya, S. (2012). 'Indian Science Today: An Indigenously Crafted Crisis'. In *India's World*, ed. A. Appadurai and A. Mack, 246–64. New Delhi: Rain Tree.

Bohm Bawerk, E. von (1923). *The Nature of Roundabout Production: The Positive Theory of Capital*, trans. William Smart, quoted from R. Slesinger and A. Isaacs (eds), *Contemporary Economics* (Boston: Allyn and Bacon, 1963).

Bosworth, B. and S. M. Collins (2007). 'Accounting for Growth: Comparing China and India'. Working Paper No. 12943, NBER, Cambridge, USA, February.

Caselli, G.P. and G. Pastrello (1992). 'The Service Sector in Planned Economies of Eastern Europe: Past Experiences and Future Perspectives'. *The Service Industries Journal* 12(2): 220–37.

Chenery, H. B. and L. J. Taylor (1968). 'Development Patterns: Among Countries and Over Time'. *Review of Economics and Statistics* 50(4): 391–416.

Chenery, H. B. and M. Syrquin (1975). *Patterns of Development: 1950–1970*. New York: World Bank, published by Oxford University Press.

Chenery, H. B., S. Robinson and M. Syrquin (1987). *Industrialization and Growth: A Comparative Study*. New York: Oxford University Press.

Chinoy, S. Z. (2019). 'De-Risking the External Sector'. In *What the Economy Needs Now*, ed. A. Banerjee, G. Gopinath, R. Rajan and M. S. Sharma. New Delhi: Juggernaut Books.

Clark, C. (1940). *Conditions of Economic Progress*, 3rd edn.. London: Macmillan.

Cobbold, T. (2003). 'A Comparison of Gross Output and Value Added Methods of Productivity Estimation'. Australian Government Productivity Commission, Research Memorandum Cat No: GA511, Melbourne.

Cohen, D. (2003). *Our Modern Times: The Nature of Capitalism in the Information Age*, Cambridge, MA: MIT Press.

Cuello, F. A., F. Mansouri and G. J. D. Hewings (1992). 'The Identification of Structure at the Sectoral Level: A Reformulation of the Hirschman-Rasmussen Key Sector Indices'. *Economic Systems Research* 4(4): 285–96.

Datta, A. (2014). 'A Study of Productivity Growth in the Registered Manufacturing Sector of India: 1980–81 to 2003–04'. In *Productivity in Indian Manufacturing*, ed. V. Kathuria, Rajesh Raj S. N. and Kunal Sen. London: Routledge.

Datta, M. (1989). 'Tertiary Sector and Net Material Product: Indian Economy during 1950–51 and 1983–84'. *Economic and Political Weekly* 24(38): 2149–54.

——— (2001). *The Significance and Growth of the Tertiary Sector: Indian Economy – 1950 to 1997*. New Delhi: NBC.

——— (2012). 'Service Boom in the Indian Economy: An Analysis of Causal Influences'. *Applied Economics* 44: 987–98.

——— (2019a). 'Manufacturing Sector of the Indian Economy: Output–Value Added Symbiosis'. *Journal of Asian Economics* 63: 75–87.

——— (2019b). 'Technological Progress and Sectoral Shares in GDP: An Analysis with Reference to the Indian Economy'. *Structural Change and Economic Dynamics* 51: 260–69.

Datta, M. and C. Neogi (2013). 'Reform Raises Efficiency of Oil Refining Public Sector Enterprises in India'. *Indian Economic Review* 18(2): 239–62.

Datta, M., C. Neogi and A. Sinha (2015). 'Sectoral Shares in Indian GDP: How to Regard It?' *Structural Change and Economic Dynamics* 35(C): 1–11.

Dehejia, R. and A. Panagariya (2013). 'Services Growth in India: A Look inside the Black Box'. In *Reforms and Economic Transformation in India*, ed. J. Bhagwati and A. Panagariya, 86–118. New York: Oxford University Press.

Denison, E. F. (1967). *Why Growth Rates Differ: Postwar Experience in Nine Western Countries*. Washington, DC: Brookings Institute.

Dertouzos, M. L., R. K. Lester and R. M. Solow (1990). *Made in America: Regaining the Productive Edge*, New York: Harper Perennial.

Desai, M. (2009). *The Rediscovery of India*. New Delhi: Penguin Books.

Dholakia, R. H. and A. A. Sapre (2011). 'Estimating Structural Breaks Endogenously in India's Post-Independence Growth Path: An Empirical Critique'. *Journal of Quantitative Economics* 9(2): 73–87.

Dongyou, Zhang (2009). 'Improvement in Real GDP Estimation by Production Approach'. Paper presented in OECD, Paris.

Drejer, I. (2002). 'Input–Output Based Measures of Interindustry Linkages Revisited: A Survey and Discussion'. Centre for Economic and Business Research, Ministry of Economic and Business Affairs, Copenhagen, Denmark.

Drèze, J. and A. Sen (2013). *An Uncertain Glory: India and Its Contradictions*. London: Penguin Books.

Echevarria, C. (1997). 'Changes in Sectoral Composition Associated with Economic Growth'. *International Economic Review* 38(2): 431–52.

Economist (2012a). 'Special Report: Manufacturing and Innovation'. 21–27 April, p. 5.

——— (2012b). 'The Industrial Revolution'. 21–27 April, p. 11.

Fagerberg, J. (2000). 'Technological Progress, Structural Change and Productivity Growth: A Comparative Study'. *Structural Change and Economic Dynamics* 11: 393–411.

Fisher, A. G. B. (1935). *The Clash of Progress and Security*. London: Macmillan.

Francois, J. F. and K. A. Reinert (1996). 'The Role of Services in the Structure of Production and Trade: Stylized Facts from a Cross-Country Analysis'. *Asia-Pacific Economic Review* 2(1): 1–9.

Frisch, R. (1955). 'Market Price versus Factor Cost in National Income Statistics'. *Sankhya: The Indian Journal of Statistics* 15(1 and 2): 1–14.

Ghemawat, P. (1998). *Strategy and the Business Landscape: Text and Cases*. Hong Kong: Pearson Education Asia.

Ghose, A. K. (2016). *India Employment Report 2016*. New Delhi: Institute for Human Development and Oxford University Press.

Ghosh, A. (1958). 'Input–Output Approach to an Allocation System'. *Economica* 25(1): 58–64.

Government of India (GOI) (1978). *National Accounts Statistics*. New Delhi: Central Statistical Organization (CSO).

——— (1981). *National Accounts Statistics*. New Delhi: Central Statistical Organization (CSO).

——— (1989). 'Input–Output Transactions Table, 1978–79'. New Delhi: Central Statistical Organization.

——— (1990). 'Input–Output Transactions Table, 1983–84'. New Delhi: Central Statistical Organization.

——— (1997). 'Input–Output Transactions Table, 1989–90'. New Delhi: Central Statistical Organization.

——— (2000). 'Input–Output Transactions Table, 1993–94'. New Delhi: Central Statistical Organization.

——— (2005). 'Input–Output Transactions Table, 1998–99'. New Delhi: Central Statistical Organization.

——— (2008). 'Input–Output Transactions Table, 2003–04'. New Delhi: Central Statistical Organization.

——— (2010). *National Accounts Statistics*. New Delhi: Central Statistics Office.

——— (2011). *National Accounts Statistics*: *Back Series*. New Delhi: Central Statistics Office.

——— (2012). *National Accounts Statistics: Sources and Methods*. New Delhi: Central Statistics Office.

——— (2014). *Economic Survey: 2013–14*. New Delhi: Ministry of Finance, Economic Division and Oxford University Press.

——— (2016). *Supply and Use Table, 2011–12 and 2012–13*. New Delhi: Central Statistics Office.

——— (2018). 'Seventh Central Pay Commission – Principles of Wage Determination for Central Government Employees', https://7thpaycommissionnews.in.

Goldar, B. (2015). 'Productivity in Indian Manufacturing in the Post-reform Period: A Review of Studies'. In *Productivity in Indian Manufacturing*, ed. V. Kathuria, Rajesh Raj S. N. and K. Sen, 75–105. London: Routledge.

Gopalakrishnan, R. (2017). 'Liberalization and a Tale of Two Companies: Open the Cage and Let the Birds Fly'. In *India Transformed*, ed. R. Mohan, 575–90. New Delhi: Penguin Random House India.

Gopinath, G. and A. Lahiri (2019). 'India's Exports'. In *What the Economy Needs Now*, ed. A. Banerjee, G. Gopinath, R. Rajan and M. S. Sharma. New Delhi: Juggernaut Books.

Gordon, J. and P. Gupta (2004). 'Understanding India's Service Revolution'. IMF Working Paper WP/04/171, September 2004.

Griliches, Z. (1992). 'Introduction'. In *Output Measurement in the Service Sectors*, Studies in Income and Wealth, Vol. 56, ed. Z. Griliches, 1–22. Chicago: University of Chicago Press.

Grootaert, C. and T. V. Bastelar (2002). *Understanding and Measuring Social Capital: A Multidisciplinary Tool for Practitioners*. Washington, DC: The World Bank.

Guo, J. and M. A. Planting (2000). 'Using Input–Output Analysis to Measure U.S. Economic Structural Change Over a 24 Year Period'. WP 2000-01, BEA, USA.

Gupta P., R. Hasan and U. Kumar (2009). 'Big Reforms but Small Payoffs: Explaining the Weak Record of Growth in Indian Manufacturing'. In *India Policy Forum 2008–09*, ed. S. Berry, B. Bosworth and A. Panagariya, 59–108. New Delhi: Sage Publications India Pvt. Ltd.

Hansen, A. H. (1941). 'The Dynamic versus the Circular Flow Economy'. In *Fiscal Policy and Business Cycles*, 301–09. New York: W.W. Norton and Company, Inc.

Hasan, R. and K. R. L. Jandoc (2013). 'Labour Regulations and Farm Size Distribution in Indian Manufacturing'. In *Reforms and Economic Transformation in India*, ed. J. Bhagwati and A. Panagariya, 15–48. New York: Oxford University Press.

Hausmann, R., C. A. Hidalgo, S. Bustos, M. Coscia, A. Simoes and M. A. Yildirim (2013). *The Atlas of Economic Complexity: Mapping Paths to Economic Prosperity*. Cambridge, MA: MIT Press.

Heston, A. and R. Summers (1992). 'Measuring Final Product Services for International Comparison'. In *Output Measurement in the Service Sectors*, Studies in Income and Wealth, Vol. 56, ed. Z. Griliches, 493–516. Chicago: University of Chicago Press.

Hicks, J. R. (1971). *The Social Framework: An Introduction to Economics*, 4th edn, Oxford: Clarendon Press.

Hill, T. P. (1977). 'On Goods and Services'. *Review of Income and Wealth* 23: 315–38.

Hirschman, A. O. (1958). 'Interdependence and Industrialization'. In *The Strategy of Economic Development*. New Haven, CT: Yale University Press.

Hoffman, P. G. (1960). 'Underdeveloped Countries'. Quoted from R. E. Slesinger and A. Isaac (eds), *Contemporary Economics*. (Boston: Allyn and Bacon, 1963).

Holland, S. Lady (1855). *A Memoir of the Reverend Sydney Smith*, New York: Harper.

Hulten, C. and S. Srinivasan (1999). 'Indian Manufacturing Industry: Elephant or Tiger? New Evidence on the Asian Miracle'. Working Paper 7441 1999. NBER, Cambridge, MA, USA.

Hulten, C. R., E. R. Dean and M. J. Harper (2001). *New Developments in Productivity Analysis*, Chicago: The University of Chicago Press.

Inman, R. P. (1985). 'Introduction and Overview'. In *Managing the Service Economy: Prospects and Problems*, ed. R. P. Imran, 1–26. New York: Cambridge University Press.

Jones, L. P. (1976). 'The Measurement of Hirschman Linkages'. *Quarterly Journal of Economics* 90(2): 323–33.

Kalyani, B. (2017). 'Indian Manufacturing Industry: On the Path to Global Leadership'. In *India Transformed*, ed. R. Mohan, 299–311. Gurgaon, India: Penguin Random House.

Kathuria, V., Rajesh Raj S. N. and K. Sen (eds). (2014). *Productivity in Indian Manufacturing*. New Delhi: Routledge.

Kochhar, K., U. Kumar, R. Rajan, A. Subramanian and I. Tokatlidis (2006). 'India's Pattern of Development: What Happened and What Follows'. Working Paper 12023, NBER, Cambridge, February.

Kohli, A. (2006). 'Politics of Economic Growth in India: 1980–2005, Part I–The 1980s'. *Economic and Political Weekly* 41(13): 1251–59.

Kongsamut, P., S. Rebelo and D. Xie (2001). 'Beyond Balanced Growth'. *The Review of Economic Studies* 68(4): 869–82.

Koopmans, T. C. (1947). 'Measurement without Theory'. *The Review of Economics and Statistics* 29(3): 161–72.

Kraemer, K. L., G. Linden and D. Jason (2011). *Capturing Value in Global Networks: Apples iPad and iPhone*. Research report, University of California, Irvine; University of California, Berkeley; and Syracuse University.

Kravis, I. B., A. W. Heston and R. Summers (1978). *International Comparisons of Real Product and Purchasing Power*. Baltimore: Johns Hopkins University Press.

Krugman, P. (1998). *Development, Geography and Economic Theory*. Cambridge, MA: MIT Press.

Kulshreshtha, A. C. and R. Kolli (1999). 'Deflation Procedure in National Income and Expenditure in the Context of 1993 SNA'. *Journal of Income and Wealth* 21(1).

Kuznets, S. (1941). *National Income with Composition: 1919–38*. New York: NBER.

——— (1954). 'Underdeveloped Countries and the Pre-industrial Phase in the Advanced Countries: An Attempt at Comparison'. Reprinted in *The Economics of Underdeveloped Countries*, ed. A. N. Agarwala and S. P. Singh, 135–53. New York: Oxford University Press, 1958.

——— (1965). *Economic Growth and Structure*. New York: W. W. Norton and Company Inc.

——— (1971). *Economic Growth of Nations: Total Output and Production Structure*. Cambridge, MA: The Belknap Press of Harvard University Press.

——— (1972). 'Problems in Comparing Recent Growth Rates in Developed and Less-Developed Countries'. *Economic Development and Cultural Change* 20(2): 185–209.

Lewis, W. A. (1954). 'Economic Development with Unlimited Supplies of Labour'. *The Manchester School* 22(2): 139–91.

Little, I. M. D. and V. Joshi (1994). *India: Macroeconomics and Political Economy – 1964–1991*. New Delhi: Oxford University Press.

Mahalanobis, P. C. (1955). 'The Approach of Operational Research to Planning in India'. *Sankhya* 107(2): 407–37.

Mankiw, N. G., D. Romer and D. N. Weil (1992). 'A Contribution to the Empirics of Economic Growth'. *The Quarterly Journal of Economics* 107: 407–37.

Mansfield, E. and G. Yohe (2004). *Microeconomics: Theory/Applications*. New York: W. W. Norton and Company.

Martinez-Zarzoso, I. and E. Maria (2008). 'Do Transport Costs Have a Differential Effect on Trade at the Sectoral Level?' *Applied Economics* 40(24): 3145–57

Marx, K. (1863). *Theories of Surplus Value*, Part I. Moscow: Progress Publishers, published 1963.

Mason, P. (1985). *The Men Who Ruled India*. New Delhi: Rupa and Co.

Matsuyama, K. (1992). 'Agricultural Productivity, Comparative Advantage and Economic Growth'. *Journal of Economic Theory* 58: 317–22.

Meier, G. M. and J. E. Rauch (2000). *Leading Issues in Economic Development*, 7th edn. New York: Oxford University Press.

Mill, J. S. (1948 [1944]). *Essays on Some Unsettled Questions of Political Economy*. London: London School of Economics, reprint.

Miller, R. E. and P. D. Blair (2009). *Input–Output Analysis: Foundations and Extensions*. Cambridge, UK: Cambridge University Press.

Mohan, R. (2017). 'The Road to the 1991 Policy Reforms and Beyond: A Personalized Narrative from the Trenches'. In *India Transformed: 25 Years of Economic Reforms*, ed. R. Mohan., 3–43. Gurgaon, India: Penguin Random House India.

Murphy, K. M., A. Shleifer, and R. W. Vishny (1989). 'Industrialization and the Big Push'. *Journal of Political Economy* 97(5): 1003–26.

Murthy, N. (2017). 'The Impact of the 1991 Economic Reforms on Indian Businesses'. In *India: Transformed*, ed. R. Mohan. New Delhi: Penguin Random House India.

Nicholson, J. L. (1955). 'National Income at Factor Cost or Market Prices?' *The Economic Journal* 65(258): 216–24.

Nordhaus, W. D. (2006). 'Baumol's Diseases: A Macroeconomic Perspective'. Working Paper 12218, NBER, Cambridge, USA.

Nurkse, R. (1953). *Problems of Capital Formation in Underdeveloped Countries*. New York: Oxford University Press.

OECD (2001). *Measuring Productivity: Measurement of Aggregate and Industry Level Productivity Growth*. OECD Manual.

Panagariya, A. (2004). 'Growth and Reforms during 1980s and 1990s'. *Economic and Political Weekly* 39(25): 2581–94.

Piramal, G. (2017). 'Animal Spirits: Stray Thoughts on the Nature of Entrepreneurship in India's Business Families after Liberalization'. In *India Transformed*, ed. R. Mohan, 485–507. Gurgaon, India: Penguin Random House India.

Rakshit, M. (2007). 'Services-led Growth: The Indian Experience'. *Money and Finance* 3(1): 91–216.

——— (2009). *Macroeconomics of Post-Reform India*. New Delhi: Oxford University Press.

Ramaswamy, K. V. (2015). 'Employment Protection Legislation and Threshold Effects'. In *Labour, Employment and Economic Growth in India*, ed. K. V. Ramaswamy, 239–64. New Delhi: Cambridge University Press.

Rangarajan, C., P. I. Kaul and Seema (2007). 'Revisiting Employment and Growth'. *Money and Finance: ICRA Bulletin* 3(2): 57–66.

——— (2009). 'Employment Performance of the States'. *Money and Finance: The ICRA Bulletin* 3(4): 45–60.

Ranis, G. and J. C. H. Fei (1961). 'A Theory of Economic Development'. *American Economic Review* 51(4): 533–65.

Rao, V. K. R. V. (1952). 'Investment, Income and the Multiplier in an Underdeveloped Economy'. *Indian Economic Review* 1(1): 55–67.
Rasmussen, P. N. (1957). *Studies in Inter-sectoral Relations*. Amsterdam: North-Holland.
Ray, D. (2010). 'Uneven Growth: A Framework for Research in Development Economics'. *Journal of Economic Perspective* 24(3): 45–60.
Reserve Bank of India (2018). *Handbook of Statistics on the Indian Economy – 2017–18*. https://dbie.rbi.org.in (accessed in November 2018).
Rodrik, D. and A. Subramanian (2005). 'From "Hindu Growth" to Productivity Surge: The Mystery of the Indian Growth Transition'. *IMF Staff Papers* 52(2): 193–228.
Romer, D. (1996). *Advanced Macroeconomics*. Singapore: McGraw-Hill International Editions.
Romer, P. M. (1990). 'Endogenous Technological Change'. *Journal of Political Economy* 98(5) Part 2 (October): S71–S102.
Rosenstein-Rodan, P. N. (1943). 'Problems of Industrialization of Eastern and South-Eastern Europe'. *The Economic Journal* 53(210/211): 202–11.
Rostow, W. W. (1960). 'The Five Stages of Growth: A Summary'. In *The Stages of Economic Growth*, 4–16. Cambridge: Cambridge University Press.
Roy, T. (2000). *The Economic History of India*, 3rd edn. New Delhi: Oxford University Press.
Saich, T. (2001). *Governance and Politics in China*. New York: Palgrave.
Samuelson, P. A. (1939). 'Interaction: the Acceleration Principle and the Multiplier'. *Review of Economic Studies* 21(2): 75–78.
Sastry, D. V. S., B. Singh, K. Bhattacharya and N. K. Unnikrishnan (2003). 'Sectoral Linkages and Growth Prospects: Reflections on the Indian Economy'. *Economic and Political Weekly* 38(24): 2390–97.
Schumpeter, J. (1947). *Capitalism, Socialism and Democracy*, 2nd edn. New York: Harper and Brothers.
——— (1954). *History of Economic Analysis*. New York: Oxford University Press.
Sen, A. (2010). *The Idea of Justice*. London: Penguin Books.
Shaw, B. (1928). *An Intelligent Woman's Guide to Socialism and Capitalism*. London: Constable and Company Ltd..
Siegel, D. and Z. Griliches (1992). 'Purchased Services, Outsourcing, Computers and Productivity in Manufacturing'. In *Output Measurement in the Service Sectors*, ed. Zvi Griliches, 429–60. Chicago: University of Chicago Press.
Singh, K. and M. R. Saluja (2017). 'Input–Output Table for India, 2013–14: Based on Supply and Use Tables'. *Journal of Income and Wealth* 39(2): 161–79.
Sinha, A. (2013). 'Goods versus Services Production in the Indian Economy: Projections for 2020'. Ph.D. thesis, University of Kalyani, India.
Smith, A. (1776). *An Inquiry into the Nature and Causes of Wealth of Nations*. London: W. Strahan and T. Cadell.
Solow, R. (1956). 'A Contribution to the Theory of Economic Growth'. *Quarterly Journal of Economics* 70(1): 65–94,
——— (2000). *Growth Theory: An Exposition*, 2nd edn. New York: Oxford University Press.
Srinivasan, T. N. (2003). 'India's Statistical System: Critiquing the Report of the National Statistical Commission'. *Economic and Political Weekly* 38(4): 303–06.

——— (2009). 'Comments on Gupta Poonam, Rana Hasan and Utsav Kumar (2009), *Big Reforms but Small Payoffs: Explaining the Weak Record of Growth in Indian Manufacturing*'. In *India Policy Forum 2008–09*, ed. Suman Berry, Barry Bosworth and Arvind Panagariya, 109–114. New Delhi: Sage Publications India Pvt. Ltd.

Srivastava, V. K., A. K. Shukla, V. Seth and B. Priyadarshi (2018). 'Statistical Discrepancies in GDP Data: Evidence from India'. *RBI Bulletin*, February, 31–48.

Stiglitz, J. E. (2013). *The Price of Inequality*. London: Penguin Books.

Stone, R. (1970). 'A Comparison of SNA and MPS'. In *Mathematical Models of the Economy and Other Essays*. London: Chapman and Hall.

Studentski, P. (1958). *The Income of Nations*. Washington Square: New York University Press.

Summers, R. and A. Heston (1984). 'Improved International Comparisons of Real Products and its Composition: 1950 to 1980'. *Review of Income and Wealth* 30(2): 207–62.

——— (1991). 'The Penn World Table (Mark 5): An Expanded Set of International Comparisons, 1950–1988'. *The Quarterly Journal of Economics* 106(2): 327–68.

Sundaram, A., R. N. Ahsan and D. Mitra (2013). 'Complementarity between Formal and Informal Manufacturing in India: The Role of Policies and Institutions'. In *Reforms and Economic Transformation in India*, ed. J. Bhagwati and A. Panagariya, 49–85. New York: Oxford University Press.

Syrquin, M. (2011). 'GDP as a Measure of Economic Welfare'. ICER Working Paper No. 3/2011, Torino.

Tata Steel (2016). *Tata Steel Integrated Reports and Annual Accounts 2015–16*. Mumbai: Tata Steel.

Tata, R. N. (2010). 'Tata, The House of'. In *The Concise Oxford Companion to Economics in India*, ed. K. Basu and A. Maertens, 175–77. New Delhi: Oxford University Press.

Triplett, J. E. and B. P. Bosworth (2003). 'Productivity Measurement Issues in Services Industries: "Baumol's Disease" Has Been Cured'. *FRBNY Economic Policy Review* 9(3): 23–33.

Trotsky, L. (2002). *Marx: In His Own Words*. New Delhi: Rupa and Co.

United Nations (UN) (1971). *Basic Principles of the System of Balances of the National Economy*. Studies in Methods, Series F, No. 17, New York.

——— (2013). 'National Accounts Statistics (2013)'. UNSD, New York. https://unstats.un.org/home/ (accessed in September 2013).

——— (2009). *System of National Accounts: 2008*. New York: Oxford University Press.

Vakil, C. N. and P. R. Brahmananda (1956). *Planning for an Expanding Economy*. Bombay: Vora and Company.

Virmani, A. (2004). 'Sources of India's Economic Growth: Trends in Total Factor Productivity'. Working Paper no. 131, ICRIER, New Delhi, India, May.

Wallack, J. C. (2003). 'Structural Breaks in Indian Macroeconomic Data'. *Economic and Political Weekly* 38(41): 4312–15.

World Bank (Various years). World Bank Development Indicators Data Files: Sectoral Shares as Percentage of GDP, www.data.worldbank.org (accessed in April 2014).

——— (2004). 'Sustaining India's Services Revolution: Access to Foreign Markets, Domestic Reform and International Negotiations'. Report on the South Asia Region, India. Washington, DC: World Bank.

Xu, Xianchun (2009). 'The Establishment, Reform and Development of China's System of National Accounts'. *Review of Income and Wealth*, Series 55 (Special issue, 1 July): 442–65.

Yueh, L. (2013). *China's Growth: The Making of an Economic Superpower*. Oxford: Oxford University Press.

Yusuf, S. (2004). 'Competitiveness through Technological Advances under Global Production Networking'. In *Global Production Networking and Technological Change in East Asia*, ed. S. Yusuf, M. A. Altaf and K. Nabeshima, 1–34. Washington, DC: World Ban.

Index